EDWIN H. SAUER

Harvard University Graduate School of Education

English
in the Secondary
School

HOLT, RINEHART AND WINSTON · NEW YORK

August, 1961

Acknowledgment of Selections

Baker, Russell, "Lexicon of Gobbledygookese," *The New York Times*, Jan. 26, 1958. Reprinted by permission.

Conant, James B., *The American High School Today*, published by McGraw-Hill Book Company, copyright 1959 by James B. Conant. Reprinted by permission.

Croce, Benedetto, *The Defence of Poetry*, 1933. Reprinted by permission of The Clarendon Press, Oxford.

The English Language Arts, prepared by The Commission on the English Curriculum of The National Council of Teachers of English. Copyright, 1952, The National Council of Teachers of English. By permission of Appleton-Century-Crofts, Inc.

Faulkner, William, "The Bear," copyright 1942 by Curtis Publishing Company; copyright 1942 by William Faulkner. Reprinted from *Go Down, Moses, and Other Stories*, by William Faulkner. Reprinted by permission of Random House.

Funk, Wilfred, "The Strange Magic of Words," *The Reader's Digest*, 1956. Reprinted by permission.

Hayakawa, S. I., *Language in Action*, 1941, published by Harcourt, Brace and Company, Inc. Reprinted by permission.

Jespersen, Otto, *Growth and Structure of the English Language*, copyright 1905, The Macmillan Company, and used with their permission.

Lafore, Laurence, "Jargon Control Program," *Harper's Magazine*, August, 1957. Reprinted by permission.

Millay, Edna St. Vincent, "Sonnet VI," from *Fatal Interview*, by Edna St. Vincent Millay, published by Harper & Bros., copyright 1931. Reprinted by permission of Norma Millay Ellis.

Orwell, George, *Nineteen Eighty-four*, copyright, 1949, by Harcourt, Brace and Company, Inc. Reprinted by permission.

Orwell, George, *Shooting an Elephant and Other Essays*, copyright, 1945, 1946, 1949, 1950, by Sonia Brownell Orwell. Reprinted by permission of Harcourt, Brace and Company, Inc.

Read, Herbert, *English Prose Style*, published by Pantheon Books. Reprinted by permission of G. Bell & Sons, Ltd.

Sapir, Edward, *Culture, Language, and Personality*, published by University of California Press and reprinted by permission.

Shapiro, Karl, "Why Out-Russia Russia?" *The New Republic*, June 9, 1958. Reprinted by permission.

Sledd, James, "Grammar or Gramarye," *The English Journal*, reprinted by permission.

Sledd, James, *A Short Introduction to English Grammar*, 1959, published by Scott, Foresman & Company. Reprinted by permission.

Stein, Gertrude, "Stanzas in Meditation," from *Poetry Magazine*, 1940.

Wilson, Edmund, *A Piece of My Mind*, published 1956 by Farrar, Straus, and Cudahy. Reprinted by permission.

Yeats, William Butler, "Sailing to Byzantium," from *Collected Poems*, by William Butler Yeats, copyright 1928 by The Macmillan Company. Reprinted by permission.

To
Howard Mumford Jones
with special thanks for Peacham
and with deep admiration for a number of
other things

Preface

Books like *English in the Secondary School* are often the result of the author's dissatisfaction with other similar books in the field. This one is not. There are already in existence excellent books on the teaching of English in the American high school, and they have proved instructive and practical both for prospective teachers and those already on the job. The writing of this book was not intended as criticism, either explicit or implicit, of the efforts of other educators to prepare young men and women for effective careers in the teaching of English. The high school English course being the great complex of activities which it is today, teachers of English must be as familiar as possible with a wide variety of writings on the subject; and though some pieces here will necessarily duplicate characteristics and even programs and suggestions of others, they will demonstrate different degrees of emphasis and persistency. Probably no one could write a book today on the teaching of English which large numbers of readers, professional or otherwise, would regard as final or ultimate. There have to be many books and many points of view—and repeated revisions—as we try to keep abreast of educational philosophy, language study, literary criticism, research, and community pressures for curriculum expansion and development.

If there is a significant difference between this book and others on the teaching of secondary school English, it is that I have made an effort to see the many activities in English as *one* subject—that is, I insist on the interrelatedness of its parts. In their understandable attempts to provide topics for discussion to instructors in curriculum and methods courses and to offer prospective teachers specific suggestions for classroom activities, the authors of books on the teaching of English sometimes become, in my judgment, overly pragmatic and analytic; as a result, chapters stand out in isolation from one another—punctuation seems not at all related to spelling or pronunciation or vocabulary; and literature and composition are polar opposites. The reader of such a book is not made constantly aware of how the various activities of the class ought to support one another—in short, of how *all* are activities in language study and develop a systematic and affirmative analysis of language success.

Obviously the teacher's knowledge of what constitutes language success must be sensible and secure, and this understanding is possible in a particular language, I believe, only when the teacher is aware of some of the shaping events in the history of that language. The approach to a positive and constructive program begins with attention to how English got to be what it is, as students learn the evolutionary character of all language. When they have learned this, they can begin to see that language success is not a matter of rigid adherence to a code of prescriptions no longer adequate to present-day practice. They will see that language is forever a matter of risk, adaptation, experiment, judgment, and common sense, and that its vigor and resourcefulness are in proportion to our willingness to take chances with it. This book invites its readers to question their notions of what proficiency in language really is—to ask themselves whether or not it may be something other than what we have rather too easily supposed it to be.

I have tried to take proper cognizance of the new emphases in the teaching of English, and, of course, the major of these is composition. Here, too, I have invited the reader to question the traditional objectives of the writing program, principally the assumption that writing is only for the superior student, an effort to give him stylistic elegance and charm. The objectives of the high school writing program go far beyond this, and their primary interest is the clarification and organization of thought. The writing man is, first of all, the thinking man; and this book insists on the reciprocal relation between thought and composition: the attempt to form the thought in good prose is often the most expeditious way of discovering what we want to say. Thus writing is for *all* of our students, and however different our expectations of them, the writing program can be uniform. But it must be sequential and systematic, coherent and carefully planned.

I would hope that this book has something to say to many outside the profession—to all with an interest in the problems of language and of language instruction. We live in a time when people of diverse interests and associations have been sharply vocal in their evaluations of what our schools do in English instruction. This is as it should be, and we profit to hear their judgments. But public views of what the schools do in English are often limited in the understanding of how particular practices are related to language theory and research, and, more importantly, to a fundamental philosophy of language. This book is not an attempt to hasten into public conflict, but, again, it invites reconsideration of what critics have perhaps too comfortably assumed proper instruction to be.

All of the faults of this book are mine. It grew out of a course in the Curriculum and Methods in English in Secondary Schools at the Harvard University Graduate School of Education. I am deeply grateful to students in that course who have contributed valuable suggestions and materials and especially to those who, in their apprentice teaching or later, have tested assertions and practices developed in class. Miss Dorcas M. Bishop, librarian at the Graduate School of Education, has given invaluable help, as has every colleague from whom I have sought assistance. Most of the writing was done in northern Vermont, and I acknowledge the kindness of Howard and Bessie Jones in allowing me to use their summer place in Peacham. Miss Carol Copeland and Mrs. Edith Gray transformed chaotic manuscript into clean and accurate copy in a very limited amount of time.

My debt to other studies of the teaching of English is everywhere apparent and, I hope, is duly acknowledged.

ACKNOWLEDGMENTS

Some of this material has appeared in *The English Journal*, the Bulletin of the College Conference on Composition and Communication, *The Harvard Educational Review*, the University of Chicago *School Review*, the Harvard University School of Education *Alumni Bulletin*, the Wellesley College *Alumnae Bulletin*, the Reports and Speeches of the Yale Conference on the Teaching of English, 1956, *The English Leaflet*, and *Ohio Schools*. Other chapters or sections of chapters were papers read before annual sessions of the National Council of Teachers of English, the School and College Conference on English at Barnard College, the Greater Cleveland, Ohio, Council of Teachers of English, the Florida State College Series of Lectures on English, Springfield, Lowell and Fitchburg Colleges in Massachusetts, and before evaluation sessions of the Advanced Placement Program at Kenyon and Haverford Colleges and at Ann Arbor High School.

E. H. S.

Cambridge, Mass.
October 31, 1960

Contents

The English Course of Study: A Definition

THE BEGINNING TEACHER OF ENGLISH, no matter how well he may feel that he knows his subject, may be in some doubt about what his subject *is*. Certainly, on a purely logical basis, knowledge of one's subject would seem to preclude such doubt, but so many activities, practices, and exercises have been crowded into the high school English program that sufficient consideration of first objectives is sometimes sacrificed to frenetic attempts merely to keep abreast of what's new. There is the New Criticism as well as the New Grammar; there are always the New Poetry, the New Drama, and the New Fiction; there will forever be the New Vocabulary, and we are perhaps not too far away from a New Spelling and a New Punctuation. For many of us, however, there has been not quite enough of the Old *Defining*: what is the sense of coherence, if any, behind the multiplication of activities in the English course? what is the relation of our projects to one another? what is the logic behind the arrangement of so many parts of literature, so many parts of composition, so many parts of sentence structure, usage, and diction?

Teachers of English are teachers of *language*. This is their first responsibility, and it is perhaps one quite heavy enough. Language has two chief functions, but these are so far-reaching that they cover all of man's experience: language is the instrument of social enterprise and of esthetic discovery. Language, that is, is both a science and an art, and the arrangement of the English course of study in the secondary school (and, for that matter, in the elementary school and college) is simply a matter of determining what skills and understandings in the science and art of language are appropriate to various age levels and abilities.

This means that we, along with our students, must start with the most fundamental understanding of all, namely, that language is the *invention* of man, not a discovery. Man *made* his language; it did not drop full-blown from the heavens. It grew slowly and awkwardly through dark years of prehistory as a means of serving man's needs—physical, social, intellectual, and esthetic, probably in that order of chronological emphasis.

Thus, as language grew out of man's needs, so we can approach the teaching of it most effectively if we show its continuing relation to man's needs, at every level of his experience. Specifically, this means getting the student to use language in composition, as a means of providing him with the instrument for expressing what he will want to say. Seeing his efforts in composition, we have a beginning for our English program: we make a course of study of the results.

The composition as the basis of the English course of study is not an easy arrangement, for, perhaps more than any other system, it makes knowledge of the child the major obligation. Jacques Barzun insists that all of us write only in order to be read, and diffident students will give no evidence of caring whether anyone listens to them or not. But all students really do care—the silent students probably care more desperately than the fluent ones—and our task is to discover what they want to talk about. This is not to suggest that the teacher encourage confessions, confidences, or intimate revelations; when and if these must be heard, they should be handled by the trained personnel of the guidance department. But it does mean that the teacher who believes that students truly want others to listen to them will not have forgotten that he and the simplest and most limited of his students have in common the basic conditions of life: family relationships, the desire to be well thought of, economic needs, birth, death, and song.

Language study starts properly with the sentence as a unit of thought. Let us forget for the moment that structural linguists may be able to demonstrate units which do not follow conventional syntactical patterns, and let us be definite in our insistence that thought must find and shape form. Junior high school youngsters need training in the structuring of sentences, so the teacher directs experimentation with a variety of sentence patterns. The sequential and systematic movement forward from this point is inevitable;

establishing the relationship of one sentence to another becomes the goal. Clarity and order are the earliest imperatives of the composition program, and it is easy to show how the conventions of grammar, sentence structure, spelling, and punctuation serve the needs of clear and orderly expression.

Obviously, just as language serves the expression of any one man's thought in social communication, it serves also the expression of the quite different thought of many others, and it is instinctive in us to be curious about the thoughts of our neighbors—the way *they* use language to express ideas and observations. We want to discover whether or not they and we have had the same ideas and observations, what experiences they may have had different from ours—in other words, we want to know what we can *share*. This is, of course, our reason for reading, on the most practical and immediate level, whether we read personal letters, the account of a scientific experiment, or a cook book.

When we enter the more sophisticated area of literature, we must help our students to see that with language, as with any of man's inventions, there is the constant urge within the inventor to toy with his creation, to bring it to higher levels of subtlety, precision, and form. The essence of literature is delight in language, whatever the subject. The documents that move us most are as notable for their rhetoric as for their content; literature is man's pleasure in his language. As man takes joy in knowing himself and the world around him, so he wants his music, his drawings, and especially his words to keep pace with the excitement of his discovery. Thus he puts words together in patterns which he hopes will be the equivalent of his living; his stories, poems, and plays are the record of his identity as man.

Observation indicates that courses of study in English are becoming more tightly organized in our secondary schools. Chiefly this is a matter of trying at last to avoid the repetition that has always been characteristic of the English program. Too often students have gone on doing the same things year after year, from grade three through grade twelve, writing the same business letters, diagnosing the same errors in usage, even in some unfortunate instances, reading the same stories. (One student read *The Red Badge of Courage* as part of his English course in grades ten, eleven, and twelve, and *at the same school*.) If this repetition is to be avoided, the teacher must never cease in the determination to know what skills and understandings in the science and art of language are appropriate to the classes he serves, as well as to grade levels above and below. Acquisition of such knowledge will regularly test his ingenuity, and he should be properly suspicious of easy and ready-made answers. The successful teacher knows only persistence here: to work, think, plan, try, test, and evaluate.

In the "truest" possible sense all lessons of the English course are language lessons, whether attention be given to spelling or to *Macbeth*. The division of the course of study into so many parts of grammar, so many parts of vocabulary work, so many parts of literature, so many parts of punctuation, is artificial and hazardous. Many students never see the relationship of the parts; to most of our high school youngsters grammar and literature are entirely separate subjects. The results, particularly for later literary study, are often painful, for college professors tend to assume that at least the syntax in a poem is clear. Too many students labor without profit through *Paradise Lost* for the simple reason that they are unable to see the subjects and predicates.

The study of any piece of literature must attend the whole composition, and this means analysis not only of its meaning and not only of its form but also of the shaping it receives from the simple fact that it is written in the English language. Obviously this means attention to syntax, to pronunciation (especially in the matter of stress and emphasis), to word meanings, and, if necessary—and it often is—to punctuation. Similarly any discussion of the conventions of syntax, grammar, usage, punctuation and vocabulary should be directed toward specific illustrations in the literature of the course. Every part of the English curriculum is seen to serve every other part, and the chapters of this book will attempt to show teachers of English how this interdependence can always be demonstrated and insisted upon. This, then, is a book about the teaching of English in the secondary school, but with the difference that, whatever activity of the curriculum is being discussed, English teaching is thought of as language teaching.

In addition, some of the chapters will deal with what might be regarded as curriculum reform in the teaching of English—new materials, new interpretations, new applications, new methods. The reader will find a chapter introducing him to the literature of the "New Grammar," or structural linguistics, and the longest chapters of all will consider thoroughly the new emphasis on composition, partly the result of the recommendations of Dr. James B. Conant in *The American High School Today*. Dr. Conant says that 50 percent of the high school English course should be given to composition; if this is to come about, teachers must re-examine many of their present composition practices, for it can be safely said that very few English teachers at present give half the class time to writing, nor, using their present methods, could they possibly do so.

The literature side of the English course is undergoing change, too. A later chapter asks for a reconsideration of the whole literary program in the high school, with marked curtailment recommended. It is time to question the genuine literary value of much that we go on teaching year after year, just as it is past time to ask for a clear and reasonable statement of the objectives of the literature program. Dreadful sins have been committed in the name of "appreciation," a term much beloved by those who have a very limited understanding of literary art. Some students have been frightened away from literature forever by the "gushers" and the whimsy hunters among us. A major reformation in the teaching of high school literature is the insistence on a reasonable amount of attention to literary *form*—to prosody and figurative language in poetry, to theme, structure, and texture in the novel, and to complication and denouement in the dramatic conflicts of a play. Literature is *something*, something demonstrable and teachable, or it is nothing. Many of our students fail to respect literature because they see *nothing*.

Three specific recommendations in the teaching of literature are made, (1) the introduction of more twentieth-century literature, (2) the introduction of some continental literature, and (3) the widespread use of paperback books. Reasons for each of the recommendations are given in the appropriate places.

Various reports and publications have been looked at in making these and other recommendations, chiefly *The English Language Arts in the Secondary School*, a publication of the Curriculum Committee of the National Council of Teachers of English, 1956; *The Basic Issues in the Teaching of English*, being Definitions and Clarifications presented by members of the American Studies Association, the College English Association, the Modern Language Association, and the National Council of the Teachers of English, 1958; and *Finding and Educating the Academically Talented Student in the Secondary School*, a publication of the National Education Association, 1958. It would be impossible for me to mention all the individual, or local, courses of study I have looked at; these would range from the programs at Exeter and Andover to those at excellent large high schools like Walnut Hills in Cincinnati, The Bronx High School of Science, New Trier High School in Illinois, and Newton High School in Massachusetts. I have found immensely valuable suggestions in all, and they go far toward convincing me that secondary school English is being taught better today than ever before in American educational history. This book is presented in the conviction that we can do even better.

PART I

The Science of Language

CHAPTER ONE

A Philosophy of Language for Today's Student

IN READING THE ESSAYS OF T. S. ELIOT *On Poetry and Poets*, one finds that many of the essays are fundamentally on the subject of language—or, more accurately, of the poet's influence on language. Read together, the two famous papers on Milton are seen as exercises in determining whether or not the special language *based on* English which, according to Eliot, is the special invention of Milton, had a harmful effect on writing and speaking after Milton's time. The essay on Samuel Johnson is chiefly a tribute to Johnson's sensitivity to the character, shape, and design of his native tongue. Eliot says at the end of the piece: "But amongst the varieties of chaos in which we find ourselves immersed today, one is a chaos of language, in which there are discoverable no standards of writing, and *an increasing indifference to etymology and the history of the use of words.** And of the responsibility of our poets and critics for the preservation of the language, we need to be repeatedly reminded." Interestingly, Mr. Eliot's newly acquired appreciation of the verse of Kipling derives principally from his recognition that "no writer has ever cared more for the craft of words than Kipling."

This concern for the forms and structure of language, in literary criticism or elsewhere, is a new development for recent times. Twenty-five years ago the following remark of Miss Mary McCarthy would not have been taken well; in that time of intense

* *Italics mine.*

9

ideological seriousness, it might have been thought flippant or redundant.

Eugene O'Neill's lack of verbal gift was a personal affliction that became a curse to the American stage. He belongs to that group of American authors, which includes Farrell and Dreiser, whose choice of vocation was a kind of triumphant catastrophe; none of these men possessed the slightest ear for the word, the sentence, the speech, the paragraphs. How is one to judge the great logical symphony of a tone-deaf musician?

All too frequently in recent decades, it has been our custom to evaluate literature only according to what it may seem to have contributed to democratic liberalism; our critics have had a limited social orientation, and we have tended to excuse in authors not only an almost total unresponsiveness to esthetics but a wholesale insensitivity to language as well. If the author was convinced of the supreme importance of his material, he felt that he was under no obligation to refine the way of presenting it. A concern for prose style came to seem frivolous and effete—the province only of writers like Pater, Oscar Wilde, George Moore, and possibly Lafcadio Hearn, men who, we were ready to assert, had really nothing to say. A mark of the great seriousness was casual syntax and the avoidance of rhetoric. Indeed, rhetoric became an offensive word, with connotations of deceit; its practice came to seem a form of word manipulation used by charlatans and predatory politicians. Documents that might and probably ought to have been impressive were sometimes a burden to readers who had retained a feeling for the reciprocal relationships between precision and readability. Here is Edmund Wilson writing about an editorial experience of his youth.

In my youthful days as an editor, I had once to prepare for publication a series of articles by the late John Dewey on a trip he had made to China. This ought really not to have involved him in obscurity, since he was merely telling what he had seen and the opinions to which it had led him; but when I came to edit the articles, I found that they both called for and resisted revision in a peculiarly exasperating way. It was not only a question here of clarifying the author's statements but of finding out what he meant; and when you did get the sense of his meaning, there was no way of straightening out the language: you would have had to try to give his meaning in a language of a different kind. But John Dewey, as I presently found out—though typical—was not by any means the worst American writer on education. Later on, the liberal weekly for which I worked ran a supplement on this subject, and the articles we received were incredible. How, I wondered, could a man set up as an authority on teaching the young when he was not himself sufficiently well-educated to have mastered the rudiments of writing? As for my experience with articles by experts in anthropology and sociology, it has led me to conclude that the requirement, in my ideal university, of having the papers in every department passed by a professor of English might result in revolutionizing these subjects—if indeed the second of them survived at all.

This is all very well, the teacher or prospective teacher may say; certainly educators ought to write well, at least well enough to be understood, and no one is likely to argue very heatedly over the advantage to an author in being steeped in an understanding of the instrument which he is to use, but the title of this chapter is "A Philosophy of Language for Today's Student," and the teacher of English surely does not consider that his major objective is to turn out poets, novelists, and dramatists, or even educators. Yet any consideration of prose style is only part of the larger study of the forms and structures of a given language through the various periods of its history, and some teachers of English have come more and more to believe that many of our conspicuous failures in the teaching of English on the secondary school level have resulted from our almost complete failure to give students any idea of the English language *as language*, any experience, that is, with the exact nature of how it functions when they use it daily. The instrument which they employ in all activities of communication, from buying a dozen eggs to writing a love letter, is never seen as we see an idea, a nation, or a great man—as an object with a history. Generally, secondary schools disregard altogether the record of the English language, the complexities of its origin, its evolution and development, the political, intellectual, and martial events which changed it and gave it its present vigor and magnitude. How many of our secondary school students are ever asked to consider that it is only language which makes possible all other accomplishments of man's civilization? How many have ever been asked to visualize the period before the history of language, when men must have groped in blindness and inarticulateness until they had codified the grunts which made them at least partly secure against the dangers of the forest, the climate, and their own desperate needs? To be sure, language scholars are highly cautious in their discussions of the origins of language, but whether we accept or reject any of the various theories of how language came into being, the story of its development is part of the illustrious record of the achievements of man and should be recognized as such by our students.

In our English classes students almost never discuss with their teachers the fundamental character of their native tongue and how that character was shaped through the experiences of the nations that have known and used English, a history at once so fascinating and lively that it can change altogether the quality of a child's thinking. For as the child sees the long account of language change and of man's constant need to alter and expand language, as he becomes aware of how large an element of chance has always operated in making language more manageable, he is likely to stand a little less in awe of it, a little less uncomfortable about the conventions of usage, a little less tongue-tied when he tries to make it work for him.

The teaching of English becomes then something other than a firm, unyielding, uncompromising discipline without relation to student interests or capacities, something other than a year-after-year cacophony of conjugating verbs, writing formal invitations, memorizing Whittier, Holmes, or Longfellow, and trying, as Professor Edward Gordon of Yale puts it, to find out just where Silas buried the money. The thrilling story of the record of their language is not lost to our students. No longer are they propelled into the study of grammar without first knowing why it seemed essential to language scholars in the eighteenth century that English have a formal grammar—some nine or ten centuries, so far as we can determine, after English had achieved a high degree of order. (How many of today's secondary school students know that ever since the eighteenth century there have been scholars of language who have doubted that the imposition of this grammar was genuinely salutary for English, that as these scholars see it, a *natural* English was made to conform to a grammar *unnatural* to it?)

With some understanding of the nature of his language, the student is no longer hurled into the study of literature without hearing what it is that, partly at least, makes a literature inevitable: that man becomes heady with the intoxication of what he can make language do and wants at once to use it to express the urgings, yearnings, and cravings which are the innermost part of his being. Suddenly there are excitement and fun in the classroom. How many of today's boys and girls know the fun of word study, not what is now called "vocabulary drill" (though if handled properly, that can be fun, too), but, rather, the practice of learning how words got into our language, and where they came from, and how their meanings have changed through the years, and why? This kind of language study, carefully conceived and planned, can greatly affect the teaching of English in the secondary school, bringing about not only a greater interest in and enjoyment of the subject, but, more importantly, a greater precision and ease of communication for the complexities of today's living. How do we begin?

First of all, we must put the student at ease. Most of our youngsters are ill at ease with their native language, and they use English ineffectively and badly because of discomfort rising out of fear. For them, studying English is, more than anything else, the memorization of a series of "don'ts," the majority of which have far more to do with the conventions of upper-middle-class gentility than with language sense and order. A case in point is our unequivocal resistance to the student's use of "ain't," a perfectly sensible and authoritatively sanctioned contraction when used with the first person pronoun, far preferable, especially in questions, to the barbarous "aren't I." For many teachers of English, however, "ain't" has approximately the same status as the four-letter Anglo-Saxon words, and since most of these are now the vogue of our novelists, the position of "ain't" is probably a great deal lower. Yet the man who wrote American English probably with greater fastidiousness than any other author, Henry James, used the word "ain't" regularly with "I" *when speaking in his own person*, not when he wanted to indicate the vulgarity of a character in one of his stories.

This confusion of what kind of language it takes to move upward a few rungs on the social ladder with the kind which shows the genuine force and power of English has often produced a species of distress in students. They never learn to be comfortable in verbal communication because they have been frightened; they are so afraid of saying the wrong thing that they say nothing at all or else cease to care altogether about the dialect of gentility which unfortunately among many of our teachers of English passes for "correct" English. The student who says "aren't I" may pass very satisfactorily the test of whether or not he should be admitted to the country club, but he should flunk cold the test of the teacher who knows something about the proprieties of language.

Students who have heard too many of the traditional language "don'ts" eventually lose patience and, as a result, may lapse into near-illiteracy and substandard language. Some knowledge of how English got to be what it is, some realization of its continuing state of change can dissipate these attitudes, can generate in the student real enthusiasm and pride, and thus increase both his comfort and skill in using English.

The student must begin, it would thus seem, with some respect for his language, as must you and I. For a long time we have been led to believe by academic snobs that there is something inferior about the English language, that it is barbarous and coarse and incapable of delicate shadings, meticulous nuances, and logical precision. Teachers of the classical and romance languages have taught us to be apologetic about English. We are made to feel a sense of shame because our verbs are not so irregular as those in French, our nouns not so rigidly declined as those in Latin and German, and our vowels and consonants not so liquid as those in Italian and Spanish. It's time we put a stop to such academic snobbery. English is in no sense inferior; for flexibility, suppleness, and even exactness it is unsurpassed anywhere in the world today; and its fluidity, grace and beauty are apparent to all who read it well or hear it used with skill and understanding. Furthermore, both its force and grace are accomplished with an absolute minimum of mechanical complexity. It is not necessary in English to change the ending of every noun, along with the endings of the article and adjective in front of it, every time the case use changes. Sensibly we have got rid of such cumbersome constructions in English, and our expression and our sanity are the better for it. Both the teacher and student of English must resist any attempt to make them feel that they work with a faulty vehicle for the statement of their thought; the study of English will get off to a good start if we begin with a deep love for it, for English is worthy of such love. Here is the statement of a man who loved it very much—Otto Jespersen.

English is like an English park, which is laid out seemingly without any definite plan, and in which you are allowed to walk everywhere according to your own fancy without having to fear a stern keeper enforcing rigorous regulations. The English language would not have been what it is if the English had not been for centuries great respecters of the liberties of each individual and if everybody had not been free to strike out new paths for himself. . . . The English language is a methodical, energetic, businesslike, and sober language, that does not care much for finery and elegance, but does care for logical consistency and is opposed to any attempt to narrow-in life by police regulations and strict rules either of grammar or of lexicon.

Jespersen and other students of the English language, as well as many of the writers of the past (Defoe and Swift are examples), have regularly reminded us that the strongest elements of English are the oldest words of all, the Anglo-Saxon roots and derivatives— the firm, solid transitive verbs, the unambiguous, concrete nouns, and the vivid adjectives of sensory perception. In introductory fashion, high school students can master material of this kind, and knowing it, they can develop a fine sense of discrimination in the choice of words. Obviously this is not to say that they must develop a feeling of resistance or hostility toward those elements of the language that are not Anglo-Saxon. That would be absurd at this point in our language history. If he is wise, today's student will use all the vocabulary which is available to him. But the character of a language, the quality of its vowels and consonants, the natural rhythms of its word order, and whatever inflections it may have, imposes a kind of verbal appropriateness whereby some words acquire a greater natural force than others; and it is this pattern to which a student of language is always sensitive, even though he may not always understand exactly the basis of such sensitivity. Yet there is nothing really mysterious about this pattern, as readers, and especially teachers, often infer. There are no chimeras about order, judgment, and reason in prose. If teachers of English help their students to learn how to listen and how to understand the linguistic significance of what they see in print—whether in James Joyce or on a highway billboard—the students will eventually see the exact character of their language.

The exercise will also entail for the teacher of English the obligation of helping students to resolve for themselves the question of their relation to what has traditionally been known as English grammar. A later chapter will study in detail the transformations and conflicts which make up the picture of the study of grammar in the high school today, but a general statement seems appropriate here. Today's student cannot ignore the fact that definitely established language conventions exist, and he must see the real necessity for order in language. Without the conventions of grammar, sentence structure, punctuation, capitalization, and the mechanics of English in general, we would expose ourselves to language chaos, and communication of an exact and honest nature would cease. Sensible language conventions, that is, agreements about the use of language which are based on a realistic scholarly, and humane analysis of the character of the language, serve an essential purpose and must be continued. There will always be a *prescriptive* side to language study in the school, and it would be folly to try to dispense with it. But in the term "sensible language conventions" it is the word "conventions" upon which the teachers of language must insist. Today's high school boy and girl must learn that it is highly inaccurate to speak of the "rules" of grammar, or "correct" English, if by the word "rules" we mean something fixed, unchanging, and immutable, like the rules or laws of mathematics and physics, for language does not always operate according to such rules. Laws of mathematics and physics are discovered; the "rules" of language are made, and man can and does change the "rules" of language frequently. Two and two will always and forever be four, but the day may come, if it is not already here, when no one will resist the use of an objective case pronoun after a copulative verb ("It is me").

The proper approach to grammar for today's secondary school student is the historical one. He should be taught that a really living language, a language which is doing the world's business, constantly and unpredictably undergoes change; that many of the forms and constructions which we approve today were once considered most improper; that "correctness" is finally determined by use, and that the fundamental law in operation here is that the conventions of language exist solely to facilitate communication and not that there is value in attention to the conventions without reference to communication. The teacher of English who presents grammar lessons as if they had some value in themselves, as if, as students were once told, the study of grammar would "help you to think better"—the teacher, that is, who leads students into sentence diagramming, verb conjugation, agreement or case drill, and parts of speech identification without demanding an instant performance in composition—serves the students falsely. Grammar books must exist for one purpose—to lead to something else, something more ultimate than grammar, namely, the organization of thought in language. Today's student should know what is in the grammar textbooks but, more important, he should also have his ears in public places, listening to the way people of his time are establishing meaningful verbal contact with one another.

Since any language which is being used by as many people as are now using English must regularly experience alterations, transformations, and variations, it is wrong to attempt to crystallize or solidify that language into rigid codes of "correctness." Professor George Lyman Kittredge once wrote that "scholars have always consistently averred that good usage is the only conceivable criterion of good English, but most people still clamor for a heaven-sent 'standard' to measure their words by. The best established idioms are continually put upon their defence merely because, since they *are* idioms, they differ from somebody's *preconceived* and *ill-instructed* notions of what ought to be correct."* Kittredge

* *Italics mine.*

is asserting that an effort to establish a rigid language authority with standards of "correctness" from which there can be no deviation is an error of great cultural magnitude. Many teachers of English no longer speak of "correct" and "incorrect" English, for they feel that to talk this way is to subject language to false disciplines which obstruct the processes for which language was made. Even the term "good" English is suspect if we mean by that term a kind of English which follows an unyielding series of principles and rules. The position of these modern teachers is effectively summarized by Richard K. Corbin and Porter G. Perrin in their recent high school text *Guide to Modern English*. The statement could scarcely be more succinct.

For good English is simply English that does what the user wants it to. When you talk or write, you have a purpose—you want to make others understand what you are thinking or feeling, or let them know what you have seen or done or explain what you want them to do. If the language you use carries out your purpose, if it gets your ideas across to others *in a way that pleases both you and them*, it is good. Otherwise, it is bad—no matter how fine it sounds or how "correct" it is.

Corbin and Perrin introduce then the notion of language appropriateness—the language must be right for the occasion. Language, in addition to conveying ideas, also conveys impressions, and depending on the nature of the impression which we wish to make in a particular situation, we will use our language. The teacher of English would not employ in reading a paper at a meeting of his colleagues the same kind of English which he would use in attempting to explain to his garage mechanic what was wrong with his car. Most teachers of English would be forced in the latter experience to use presymbolic language and fall back on making noises.

Speaking generally, *Guide to Modern English* tells us, there are two kinds of English: standard and nonstandard, though standard is divided into formal and informal. Formal English is almost exclusively a written English, the language of professional books, reference works, legal documents; informal English is both spoken and written, and nonstandard English ("the English used by people who do not have much formal education—or who have not been much affected by the schooling they did have") is mostly spoken. Informal English is the kind recommended for most of today's purposes. "In speaking," say Corbin and Perrin, "it is the comfortable kind of English that educated people ordinarily use," or, in writing, "the speech of educated people tidied up—with an eye to pleasing the reader."

This, for our students, is good advice. We live in an informal age, and all readers of modern literature have seen how writers like E. B. White, Mark Van Doren, and James Thurber have employed informal English for writing on subjects of profound seriousness. Informal English is probably never wrong in modern communication.

But though these distinctions are useful and instructive, there is danger that some students are likely to take questionable notions of social conduct from them. The inverted snobbism which leads a man to falsify his understanding of language precision in order to talk appropriately to "people who do not have much formal education" is offensive. Nonstandard speech can be moving and vigorous, but it can also be odious for a variety of reasons, and the student who has worked through to what he regards as an English of adaptable exactness and grace can scarcely be excused for corrupting that achievement in order to get chummy with the garbage collector. The garbage collector will sense the dishonesty and feel that he is being made a fool of. Varying one's kind of English ought, perhaps, to be solely a matter of the extent to which one varies idiom and word order—rarely a matter of vocabulary, unless one happens to be writing or speaking to persons who do not have the special technical vocabulary of a particular profession. Under no circumstances should we deliberately employ solecisms, barbarisms, profanity, or obscenity because of the notion that this is the way the persons we are addressing speak and write. They may or they may not, but, in either case, we would be guilty of insult.

Another danger in the position of Corbin and Perrin is that the recommendation of language appropriateness, or of a different English for different occasions, is likely to give the impression that there are no "wrong" kinds of English. This would be extremely unfortunate, for there was probably never a time in the history of the English language when there were so many wrong kinds. There *are* serious language failings in the modern world, far more serious than any of the past. They must be specified and courageously dealt with, for several of them present hazards for the future. A later chapter attempts to categorize them and to suggest ways in which we can keep our students from acquiring them.

But these are not the "faults" that traditional grammarians have been talking about. They are not, as Corbin and Perrin would probably agree, the failings deplored by old-fashioned grammarians and academic purists. As a matter of fact, the really serious language faults of our time are more likely to be heard in high places than in low, and the purists themselves would possibly be guilty of them. A letter recently received from a university professor read, "we are attempting ascertaining information concerning teaching of listening." There is some question, in my mind at least, about the ability of this professor to teach anything.

Man will never be free from some kinds of language abuse (at least, he never has been) and these change from one age to the next. Our day has seen a corruption of language rising from what we as a people have become through our service to material values. We have learned—and indeed in some places we actually teach— a language designed to deceive. It is a language which compounds abstractions without relation to real things, or a language which says that real things are something which they are not, or a language which attempts to make man something which he is not by creating in him artificial wants and desires. "Things are in the saddle and ride mankind," wrote Ralph Waldo Emerson, and in an essay on language, unfortunately not read very often now, he made a diagnosis and suggested a cure.

As we go back in history, language becomes more picturesque, until its infancy, when it is all poetry; or all spiritual facts are represented by natural symbols. . . .

A man's power to connect his thought with its proper symbol, and so to utter it, depends on the simplicity of his character, that is, upon his love of truth and his desire to communicate it without loss. The corruption of man is followed by the corruption of language. When simplicity of character and the sovereignty of ideas is broken up by the prevalence of secondary desires,—the desire of riches, of pleasure, of power, and of praise,—and duplicity and falsehood take the place of simplicity and truth, the power over nature as an interpreter of the will is in a degree lost; new imagery ceases to be created, and old words are perverted to stand for things which are not; a paper currency is employed when there is no bullion in the vaults. In due time the fraud is manifest, and words lose all power to stimulate the understanding or the affections. Hundreds of writers may be found in every long-civilized nation who for a short time believe and make others believe that they see and utter truth, who do not of themselves clothe one thought in its natural garment, but who feed unconsciously on the language created by the primary writers of the country, those, namely, who hold primarily on nature.

But wise men pierce this rotten diction and fasten words again to visible things; so that picturesque language is at once a commanding certificate that he who employs it is a man in alliance with truth and God. The moment our discourse rises above the ground line of familiar facts and is inflamed with passion or exalted by thought, it clothes itself in images. A man conversing in earnest, if he watch his intellectual processes, will find that a material image more or less luminous arises in his mind, contemporaneous with every thought, which furnishes the vestment of the thought. Hence good writing and brilliant discourse are perpetual allegories. This imagery is spontaneous. It is the blending of experience with the present action of the mind. It is proper creation. It is the working of the Original Cause through the instruments he has already made.

In short, a philosophy of language is unavoidably mixed with the philosophy of living to which the users of the language subscribe, and the language can be thoughtful and clear when the people are determined that their thoughts and perceptions shall not deceive them. "To thine own words be true" is a corollary to "To thine own self be true," and the study of language is inevitably moral. As Jespersen put it, "English grammar is the stirring story of the English people's long and constant struggle to create a fuller and more accurate expression of their inner life."

CHAPTER TWO

What Is English?

THE WORDS *pater* (Latin), *Vater* (German), *fater* (Dutch), *father* (English), *père* (French), and *Pitar* (Sanskrit) all name the same member of the family, and any group of high school youngsters asked to study the relationship of the words to one another as he sees them at the blackboard will at once notice their similarities in form. He will almost certainly be interested to know that this is no accident and that the six languages represented, along with some others not illustrated, are all descended from what once was the same language. It may come as no very great surprise to students to learn that much of the world's population once spoke the same language, and that language differences as we observe them today developed when various groups broke away and moved into remote regions where they lost contact with the parent group and with other groups who went in other directions. Thus a series of *dialects* was developed. The American schoolboy will be intrigued to learn that he and the French boy speak only dialectically different forms of the same language. He knows already what dialect differences within his own country can mean. He knows what a Southern accent is, what "Bronx-ese" is, and what a Western drawl sounds like. Television comics exploit the dissimilarities. Students living in our present world of mobility will undoubtedly have incidents to relate of being misunderstood when traveling with their parents in various parts of the United States.

We are at present encouraging our secondary school students to attempt more and more language study as part of our efforts toward world peace and international understanding. To know another nation well, we tell our students, we must know its customs, its geography, its literature, and, of course, its language. Thus as students acquire a closer and closer sense of language relationships, their adjustment to language study is made easier. To undertake German or French or Spanish, or even Russian, will not seem so formidable a task. Pointing out language similarities whenever possible ought to be a regular practice of the teacher of English.

Establishment of these similarities can be prepared for in lessons in which the English teacher discusses the origin of English, showing that it is derived from a hypothetical language which scholars generally refer to as *Indo-European* (some, like Jespersen, prefer the name *Aryan*, now in disfavor because of Hitler's usage). Indo-European is prehistoric; no record of it exists. Nor are scholars entirely certain where it was spoken; though most agree on central Europe, in the area between Germany and Russia, some give it an Asiatic location.

There are nine principal groups of Indo-European, and setting up the table for students, possibly through duplicated sheets, will effectively assemble for them a great many names and places merely scattered and isolated in their knowledge before. The groups of Indo-European are

1. *Latin* (or Italic)—giving birth through the Latin Vulgate spoken by Caesar's troops to the *romance* (or *romanic*) languages: French, Spanish, Italian, Portuguese, Romanian.

2. *Germanic*—Anglo-Saxon, German, Dutch, and Scandinavian.

3. *Greek*—the single language of this group, though there are many dialects, ranging from classical to modern Greek.

4. *Celtic*—Gaelic, Britannic, Welsh, Old Irish, and other of the indigenous languages spoken in the various British Isles. (It is interesting for students to see that what we now call English was not, by any means, the first language spoken in England, or Great Britain. Of that language, Celtic, we have virtually no traces in English.)

5. *Balto-Slavic*—Russian, Polish, Bulgarian, Lithuanian, Old Prussian, Lettish; in other words, the languages of the Slavic peoples living in the region of the Baltic Sea.

6. *Indo-Iranian*—Sanskrit, Persian, Hindustani. (Dis-

cussion and explanation can lead here to both cultural and geographical clarifications.)

7. *Armenian*—spoken south of the Caucasus Mountains and at the eastern end of the Black Sea.

8. *Albanian*—spoken northwest of Greece on the eastern coast of the Adriatic.

9. *Hittite* and *Tocharian*—not now used but probably quite close to the original Indo-European. In fragmentary texts they were discovered by archeologists. Some students may remember the references to the Hittites in the Bible.

Students will see at once that the table does not account for many languages spoken in today's world, for example, Chinese, Japanese, Arabic, Hungarian, and Hebrew. Without going into a tedious and confusing amount of detail, the teacher of English might indicate what some of the other language families are—the Finno-Ugric, the Semitic, the Hamitic, the Sudanese and Bantu, the Sino-Tibetan, the Malay-Polynesian, and the American Indian. Enterprising youngsters who want further reading can be sent to a popular, succinct, and easy-to-use treatment like that of Margaret Schlauch in *The Gift of Tongues.* There they will find briefly but carefully detailed not only the names of the various members of the family groups but also the geographical areas where the various member languages are spoken. The almost certain classroom question of whether or not all of these language families were once related—whether or not, that is, there were parent languages before Indo-European, progressing ultimately backward to a final source—is one which the teacher will have to resist answering. Miss Schlauch says, "We know too little about the early history of the languages outside of Indo-European and Hamito-Semitic to commit ourselves too far on the matter of ultimate relationships. For one thing, change operates very slowly in some groups and with almost dizzying rapidity in others. . . . The question about a single origin for the diverse tongues of mankind must be tabled until we know more of their earlier forms; and that may be—forever."

Nevertheless the lesson, even though it may end on speculation which cannot be resolved, is a highly instructive one, opening up for students areas of understanding and study not even guessed at previously. This is fresh, pertinent, and exciting material for the English class.

The simple fact of when English began is known by comparatively few of the people who speak it daily. In America at present many young men and women acquire Bachelor of Arts degrees without ever being exposed to the most elementary course in the history of the English language, yet this would seem an essential kind of knowledge in an educated man or woman. The subject is not difficult, and in the secondary English program students can learn that English as we know and use it dates from about the middle of the fifth century A.D., when the barbarian tribes from the Germanic area of Northern Europe overran what we now know as England. These were chiefly the Angles, the Saxons, and the Jutes, and the combination of their dialects brought about what we call Anglo-Saxon, or Old English, the language which prevailed in England (students should see the origin of this name) from approximately A.D. 500 to A.D. 1100, though, of course, these dates are highly arbitrary and subject to much qualification. In literature, it is the language of *Beowulf*, of a group of short but very beautiful lyric poems ("Doer's Lament," "The Seafarer," admirably translated by Kemp Malone), and of the writings of King Alfred. The history of the English language is divided into three major periods, and this is the first one—the period of Old English, symbolized by *AS* in the dictionary. The second period saw the emergence of Middle English, which came about as the result of a historical incident, the Norman Conquest of 1066. Middle English was used roughly from A.D. 1100 to about 1500 and is the language in literature of Chaucer and the medieval romances. In the dictionary a word coming into the language during this period is marked *ME*. The third, and current, period we name modern or, as some prefer, *new* English, and it began in about 1500, the start in England of the Renaissance.

But the student will find much exciting material in the record of language activity in the British Isles and America, and of how language was changed by a variety of social, political, cultural, and intellectual influences. Though he has learned that the history of English begins with Anglo-Saxon, it is appropriate that he know something of what happened before the appearance in England of the Germanic tribes.

The first language spoken in what we now think of as England was, of course, Celtic; except for a few place names (for example, Kent and Cornwall) and a number of names for rivers and hills (for example, Avon, Dover, Wye) there are virtually no vestiges of it left in English. Scholars find dating the language difficult, some believing that it started about 800 B.C.

The dramatic event which ushered in the second era in the history of language in the British Isles was the Roman conquest, completed about 40 B.C. by the forces of Julius Caesar and Claudius. The story of the success with which the language of a conqueror affects the language of the conquered is generally a fascinating subject, but the Latin residue from this period is very slight. Baugh says that only a handful of words—perhaps not more than five, outside of a few elements in place names—remain in present usage from the period of the Roman occupation. An interesting piece of information for students is that the forms "chester" and "cester," which they see in many English place names, as in Winchester, Worcester, Dorchester, derive from the Latin word "castra," meaning, as many will know from first-year Latin, "camp," and that the places which now have the remnant of this word in their names were military fortifications.

Since much has been made in the secondary school of the Latin influence on English, the discussion of the first Latin influence on the language of the British people can serve as the occasion for indicating that the presence of Latin elements in our language today is a matter of a number of distinctly separate events ranging from the crude activities of Roman soldiers to the highly sophisticated word-borrowings of Renaissance scholars. What must be corrected, and even resisted, is the notion students pick up that Latin is somehow a *native* or *natural* part of our language. Words of Latin derivation are in English because of a number of events, some accidental, some deliberate, but students should be aware that these words have been *added to* English; English is not a Romance language and is not a member of the Latin family. The majority of words in current English have been taken from other languages—Latin, French, Spanish, Italian—but these are *additions* to the native stock, which still does most of the hard work.

The most important occurrence in the record of language in the British Isles was the Anglo-Saxon invasion, and with this event the real history of the English language, as we know it, began. As the tribes moved into England during the fifth century A.D., their dialects became fused, and the result is the structure of the language which serves us today. The Angles, Saxons, and Jutes were Teutonic peoples, and, as a result of their trade with the Romans on the continent, their dialects already contained Latin words, chiefly from the activities of war, trade, and everyday household affairs. Words like *camp, wall, street, mile, pound*, and *cheap* are examples. But this is a comparatively insignificant consideration alongside the larger matters of word order, inflection, pronouns, strong verbs, nouns, adjectives, and adverbs, which remain the backbone of our language and are indispensable to communication. It is easy to overvalue the strength and directness of Anglo-Saxon—in recent years these qualities have become almost an academic fetish—but certainly it can be safely said that the prose styles which we tend to value most highly are those which rely very greatly on Anglo-Saxon elements. The prescriptions of such writers as Sir Arthur Quiller-Couch, Sir Herbert Read, and George Orwell are especially interesting in this regard.

In the last years of the sixth century the Christianization of England began, with the result that perhaps half a thousand Latin words having to do largely with the practice of the Christian religion came over into English. The words are the expected ones; they include such very common terms as *priest, disciple, epistle, altar, deacon,* and *hymn.* Words having to do with education and household life also became part of English as a result of the Christianization, including such familiar terms as *school, master, grammar, verse,* and others. The whole subject of the relation of the Christian Church to learning in these early years and the extent to which monastic life and its studies and interests affected English can be pursued by more eager students. Also of interest in this connection is the manner in which native Anglo-Saxon words came to acquire new meanings as the Angles and Saxons accepted Christianity and made their own vocabulary perform new duties. The words *God, heaven,* and *hell* are Anglo-Saxon in origin.

High school students who come into English classes will generally have some knowledge of the Vikings—a favorite subject with Hollywood in recent years—but probably none of the youngsters will be aware that the plunderings of these sea-rovers left nearly a thousand words in our English vocabulary. From about 800 to 1000 the Vikings visited the east coast of England in what at first were only sporadic raids for the purpose of taking the possessions of their rich neighbors but eventually became efforts at conquest and settlement. Consequently the Scandinavian which they spoke became mixed with Anglo-Saxon, and invasion once again had its linguistic effects. For the most part, the Vikings were Danes, and they got on well with the Anglo-Saxons. Furthermore, their languages were similar, and the problems of assimilation, therefore, not really severe. The words we derive from this experience are of many kinds and can often be recognized through pronunciation. English words with an *sk* sound are usually from Scandinavian, as are many words with a hard *g* sound. As might be expected, a number of the words have to do with sailing and battle, but there are others of a nonpredatory nature. *Law*, for example, is a Scandinavian word; for that matter, so is *outlaw*. Once again, the more detailed record of this influence can be made a matter of special reports from students who will wish to pursue the subject further, and such students will exist. As every high school class produces its quota of young scientists, so every one of my experience has also produced its quota, appreciably smaller, of fledgling linguists.

The Norman Conquest was the next major event. Students with any experience at all in world history will know about William the Conqueror and the Battle of Hastings. The story of what happened to Anglo-Saxon as a result of this invasion is a vastly complicated one, and teachers of English must decide individually how much of it they consider essential to the secondary school discussion of language history. For teachers who themselves want to review the subject quickly, Chapters V, VI, and VII of Baugh's *A History of the English Language* are superb.

Generally, I have introduced the subject by asking students to try to imagine the difficulties which arise when a conqueror attempts to take over a defeated country—the difficulties, that is, of subjugation. Resistance is natural in the conquered people, and when that natural spirit of resistance is joined with a fierce sense of pride and will, as in the Anglo-Saxons, then the strategies of the conqueror must be especially shrewd. Certainly not in defence of William or of conquest, but only in order to present the situation realistically, I have usually tried to help students see the advantages of the imposition of the language of the conqueror, particularly in matters relating to government, the court, law, the church, and authority in general. The result in the nation is subjugation in the most positive sense, since the conquered people are without the instrument of communication which makes possible a recourse to any defender of their rights. In other words, William's imposition of Norman French in England was a political move, an effort to minimize resistance. I ask students to remember their reading of *Ivanhoe* and the hostility of Cedric the Saxon. I use Scott's discussion of the conflict between Norman French and Anglo-Saxon to show that we have in English the interesting phenomenon of one word for the animal on hoof in the field and another for the meat of the animal when it is dressed for table, for example, *hog, swine, pig, shoat*—*pork; cow, ox, calf*—*beef, veal; sheep, lamb*—*mutton.* This illustrates somewhat the position of the Normans in England.

Saxon words might be used for that which was common, dirty, crude, but Norman was the language of the nobility, and of the graces and modes of the civilization of which they considered themselves the most advanced representatives. As the Normans were a people of elegance and style, so their language brought into English a sharper sense of manners, of refinement and fastidiousness.

But though Norman French affected English so strongly as to usher in the second of the three major periods of English language history, it was Anglo-Saxon which eventually emerged as the dominant of the two tongues. There are various reasons for this—some political, some literary. The closeness of the contact between England and France diminished, and with the advent of the Hundred Years War, Norman French declined in importance, becoming eventually a thing of scorn. Hostility was intensified, and there is a dark period of language confusion and uncertainty amounting almost to language chaos. But this is the period when, throughout Europe, vernacular languages were coming into their own as proper vehicles for a national literature. The writer who was to make England conscious of the suitability of English for literary work was Geoffrey Chaucer, and he chose to write in the East Midland dialect of English, that is, the dialect spoken between the Humber and the Thames. Middle English was the result, and the language has retained its fundamental character.

This, to be sure, is a greatly oversimplified version of the state of affairs, somewhat inaccurate in the impression it is likely to give that English and French from 1100 to, say, 1400, were in a constant state of opposition. During this time many men, of both backgrounds and of all classes, spoke both English and French, particularly if their duties called for them to move on various social and professional levels. Undoubtedly there were many Normans who wanted to get along peaceably with the Saxons and many Saxons who wanted to get along peaceably with the Normans, and very likely the accomplishment of literacy in both languages was, to them, a means of effecting this peace. But it is nonetheless true that for much of this time the ability to speak Norman was regarded as a badge of superiority, a requisite distinction of the ruling class. That Anglo-Saxon survived at all is remarkable; that it triumphed is astonishing.

The explanation may lie in the sense we have that the Anglo-Saxon words of our heritage are somehow closer to our emotional responsiveness and our human needs. Otto Jespersen is illuminating here.

From what precedes we are now in a position to understand some at least of the differences that have developed in course of time between two synonyms when both have survived, one of them native, the other French. The former is always nearer the nation's heart than the latter, it has the strongest associations with everything primitive, fundamental, popular, while the French word is often more formal, more polite, more refined and has a less strong hold on the emotional side of life. A *cottage* is finer than a *hut*, and fine people often live in a cottage, at any rate in summer. The word *bill* was too vulgar and familiar to be applied to a hawk, which had only a *beak* (the French term, whereas *bill* is the A.S. *bile*). . . . To *dress* means to adorn, deck, etc., and thus generally presupposes a finer garment than the old word to *clothe*, the wider signification of which it seems, however, to be more and more appropriating to itself. *Amity* means 'friendly relations, especially of a public character between states or individuals,' and thus lacks the warmth of *friendship*. The difference between *help* and *aid* is thus indicated in the Funk-Wagnalls Dictionary: '*Help* expresses greater dependence and deeper need than *aid*. In extremity we say "God *help* me!" rather than "God *aid* me!" In time of danger we cry "help! help!" rather than "aid! aid!" To *aid* is to second another's own exertions. We can speak of *helping* the helpless, but not of *aiding* them. *Help* includes *aid*, but *aid* may fall short of the meaning of *help*.' All this amounts to the same thing as saying that *help* is the natural expression, belonging to the indispensable stock of words, and therefore possessing more copious and profounder associations than the more literary and accordingly colder word *aid*; cf. also *assist*. *Hearty* and *cordial* made their appearance in the language at the same time . . . but their force is not the same, for 'a hearty welcome' is warmer than 'a cordial welcome,' and *hearty* has many applications that *cordial* has not (heartfelt, sincere, vigorous: a hearty slap on the back; abundant; a hearty meal), etc. . . . Compare also *darling* with *favorite*, *deep* with *profound*, *lonely* with *solitary*, *indeed* with *in fact*, *to give* or *to hand* with *to present* or *to deliver*, *love* with *charity*, etc.

To clinch the matter, let students see that The Lord's Prayer, which, for many, is probably the most deeply touching utterance of daily life, is, in its present form, mostly Anglo-Saxon. Indeed the original Anglo-Saxon version can be read with very little difficulty.

The Renaissance was a cultural influence of great magnitude. Fired with the new learning, intoxicated with the revival of Greek and Latin classics, and overly industrious in their attempts to establish the Greek and Roman writers as arbiters of literary and linguistic propriety in absolutist form, Renaissance scholars in England, as elsewhere, set about borrowing many words from the classical languages and making native words of them. The new words came chiefly from Latin and were, for the most part, learned words—words having to do with philosophy, science, and literature. But the scholars also borrowed from other languages when they felt that English was deficient, when, that is, it had no word for an idea or experience. Sometimes the words were brought into English unchanged; at other times an "Englishing" process took place. Sometimes the words were unnecessary and even absurd, in which cases, they usually did not last very long; sometimes they were little more than scholarly or literary affectation. There was, unquestionably, a large element of pedantry in the enterprise, but even when all the excesses of the movement are allowed for, we are obliged to conclude that English would be a much poorer instrument of communication had not the Renaissance scholars made their contribution. Their work is the most important of the Latin influences on English, though it must be remembered that Latin words had come into our language in the Middle English period through the contact with Norman French, a Romance language; in the Renaissance period as well, many of the new words, though ultimately Latin in origin, were borrowed in their French form. Baugh tells us that the English vocabulary at this time shows words adopted from more than fifty languages, and the terms taken from continental languages are very striking. We could not now do without them.

But the authors who brought in Latin words through their writings were the most productive. For special mention Baugh singles out two, Sir Thomas More and Sir Thomas Elyot. More's contribution is startling. To him we owe the words *absurdity, acceptance, anticipate, combustible, compatible, comprehensible, concomitance, congratulatory, contradictory, denunciation, detector, dissipate, endurable, erudite, exact, exaggerate, exasperate, explain, extenuate, fact, frivolous, impenitent, implacable, indifference, insinuate, inveigh, inviolable, monopoly, monosyllable, necessitate, obstruction, paradox, pretext,* and various others. Denied these words only, we would have a considerably more difficult time trying to express our meanings today. What, for example, would we do without *fact?*

Changes in English since the Renaissance have resulted from such developments as the eighteenth-century attempt to "fix" or "ascertain" the language, that is, to subject it to an authority and discipline establishing definite standards which could be cited in controlling usage, change, and adaptability; from colonial expansion, and borrowings that resulted from contact with people speaking other languages; from American English (on the whole, very beneficial); from scientific and technological advancement, which, at present, gives us our largest number of new words, though many last for only a short time; and, finally, from closer international contact which, in its negative form, war (especially World Wars I and II), has brought into usage many new terms and idioms.

The language students of the eighteenth century, looking backward and seeing the many changes which English had undergone in the previous three centuries, were alarmed that changes might accelerate in the future, with confusion and lack of clarity compounded. They hoped for a grammar which would give them rules to go by, but instead of studying English and working out scientifically an adequately descriptive analysis of its operation, they chose instead to demand that English be regulated according to the principles of Latin grammar. Their aims were understandable, but the procedure questionable. They wanted, in short, as George Campbell said in the *Philosophy of Rhetoric* (1776), "(1) to reduce the language to rule and set up a standard of correct usage; (2) to refine it,—that is, to remove supposed defects and introduce certain improvements; and (3) to fix it permanently in the desired form." There were efforts to establish an English Academy, similar to the French Academy, a movement which had the support at various times of John Dryden, Daniel Defoe, and Jonathan Swift. But the movement failed, in great part because of the opposition of Dr. Samuel Johnson and the good sense of the Preface to his *Dictionary*. Johnson's words there are as final a dictum on the folly of attempting to regularize a language as teachers of English can need.

When we see men grow old and die at a certain time one after another, from century to century, we laugh at the elixir that promises to prolong life to a thousand years; and with equal justice may the lexicographer be derided, who being able to produce no example of a nation that has preserved their words and phrases from mutability, shall imagine that his dictionary can embalm his language, and secure it from corruption and decay, that it is in his power to change sublunary nature, or clear the world at once from folly, vanity, and affectation. . . .

(S)ounds are too volatile and subtile for legal restraints; to enchain syllables, and to lash the wind, are equally the undertakings of pride, unwilling to measure its desires by its strength.

Johnson hoped that the "spirit of English liberty" would "hinder or destroy" the workings of such an Academy. We hear again and again through the history of the English language this note that the language is a diligent guard of English liberty and that programs to subject it to rigid strictures are consequently doomed. At another time, Dr. Johnson said of the Academy that it was something "which every man would have been willing, and many would have been proud to disobey."

But the proponents of language stability were not villainous, and, by the principles of scientific language analysis, some of their aims were altogether reasonable. George Campbell, again in his famous *Philosophy of Rhetoric*, stated three concepts which we still employ in determining good usage. Is the word or expression "present, national, and reputable"? There is, to be sure, a kind of evasiveness here. Reputable according to whom? we want to ask. When Madison Avenue uses "like" as a conjunction, are we all justified in doing so? Is it likely, as James Thurber suggests, that acceptance of "Winston tastes good/Like a cigarette should" will eventually lead a brewery to advertise "We brew good/Like we used to could"? Campbell's criteria are about the best we have, and yet we are not fully satisfied. "Present, national, and reputable" are words that one would imagine ought to apply without question to the language of the President of the United States, and yet the English of our presidents has not always been a kind we would extol as standard.

Yet the eighteenth century was, on the whole, successful. The difference between the English of Chaucer and of Swift is immensely greater than the difference between that of Swift and of C. S. Lewis or E. B. White. General areas of agreement about usage were established, and most of these have been honored ever since. When the eighteenth-century grammarians were wrong, it was likely to be because they deserted reason, the criterion by which they usually set so much store, and followed the analogy of Latin instead. As Baugh puts it, "Their greatest weakness was their failure, except in one or two conspicuous cases, to recognize the importance of usage as the sole arbiter in linguistic matters. They did not realize, or refused to acknowledge, that changes in language often appear to be capricious and unreasonable—in other words, are the result of forces too complex to be fully analyzed or predicted."

Not much needs to be said to students about later influences. Students will readily understand the effects on language of colonial expansion, scientific and technological advancement, and world wars. In the matter of the vocabulary of scientific advancement they will probably be ahead of their teachers. Personally, I would not attempt to compete with a boy of twelve in either knowledge or understanding of the terminology of explorations of outer space. Students might be warned, however, that much of this terminology has a short life, as further research makes an earlier terminology obsolete. Similarly, the vocabulary which comes to us from war experiences disappears fast. What would *blitzkrieg, ersatz, kamikaze*, and *commando* mean to youngsters now, less than two decades since these words were on all our lips?

Discussion of the nature of English and its history might end with discussion of the differences between British English and American English. Our students pick up somewhere the notion that American English is inferior, even vulgar and crude, compared with the variety spoken by Englishmen; and this notion ought to be corrected in the American classroom. American English has been a wholesome, vigorous, and salutary development in the history of the language, and for the very best reason possible: our insistence on comfort in language, our demand, that is, that language serve us, rather than we it. Americans take risks with language, deplorable risks at times, with horrible results. But frequently our willingness to take linguistic chances results not only in greater freedom but in greater precision and fluency as well. The English are often astonished at our speech, but not necessarily alarmed. On the contrary, English scholars have applauded our language liveliness, the freshness of our idiom, the imaginativeness of our figurative speech, and often the ingenuity of our slang. It was a great treat in wartime to hear American recruits from various geographic areas talking together in the barracks. Their accents might differ, along with volume, modulation, and even vocabulary, but all had the same eagerness to use words with daring. The boy from the Bronx spoke only in the present tense ("I'm walking along Third Avenue, see, and I meet my buddy coming back from the ball game"); the boy from South Carolina had words no one had ever heard before, wonderfully expressive words like "We're going out *scooter-poopin'*," meaning "We're going to have a good time"; the boy from Vermont might indicate distance by saying that a place was "twice out of hearing," but in every case something inventive and exciting was happening to the language. This is the American contribution to the history of English, and it is no small gift.

Such contribution should be encouraged. Imaginative teachers of English sometimes allow their students as an assignment to make up a few words. Shown by their teacher how some words now in use were coined (for example, "snide" from "sneer" and "aside"), thus filling a need for words that did not exist, students are then asked to invent a few words of their own. In presenting the words the following day, the youngsters must be able to spell them, to indicate their origin, to define them, and to defend them as worth-while additions to our present stock. Students have a good time with this exercise, and some of their contributions are delightful. For example, think of the expressiveness of "goof-proof," a compound contributed to one of my classes by an eleventh-grade boy. It goes far beyond "fool-proof," and I use it regularly without hesitation. Some of the words that are presented may very well be the result of cooperative family effort the night before, but what difference does that make? The assignment is not to test inventive skill but to help students to see that in this exercise they are doing only what man has always done—constructing and adapting his language to fit his meanings. Perhaps, more than this, it will give students a sense of sharing in the history of their native English which, in turn, should produce a sense of ownership and pride.

"It must be a source of gratification to mankind," says Otto Jespersen, "that the tongue spoken by two of the greatest powers of the world is so noble, so rich, so pliant, so expressive, and so interesting."

Bibliography of Works on the History of the English Language

Baugh, Albert C. *A History of the English Language*. Appleton-Century-Crofts. New York, 1935. An excellent, compact, authoritative, and highly readable study, probably as thorough a treatment as the teacher of high school English needs.

Carroll, John. *The Study of Language*. Harvard University Press. Cambridge, Mass., 1955. An excellent introduction to the varieties of language study. Essential to teachers of English.

Jespersen, Otto. *Growth and Structure of the English Language*. Doubleday Anchor A 46. New York, 1956. A paperback book, this is one of the outstanding book bargains of recent years. It is indispensable to the teacher of English: solid, urbane, and reasonable—altogether charming, a kind of lover's tribute to the English language.

Jespersen, Otto. The essay on "Language" in *The Encyclopedia Britannica*, Vol. 13.

Roberts, Paul. *Understanding English*. Harper and Brothers. New York, 1958. Chapter 3, "Something about English." Fast-moving, succinct, and popular in tone, this chapter from a text designed for college freshman English can be very helpful to high school teachers, who might place several copies on a reserve shelf in the school library and ask students to read the chapter preparatory to class discussion of the history of English.

Sapir, Edward. *Language: An Introduction to the Study of Speech.* Harvest Book HB7, Harcourt, Brace and Company. New York, 1949. Not a study of the history of the English language but a major work on the way in which language operates in human speech. An essential work.

Schlauch, Margaret. *The Gift of Language.* Dover Edition T 243. New York, 1955. "A popular introduction to the science of language," the jacket calls it, and so it is. Miss Schlauch has written useful, authoritative and altogether delightful chapters on language history, etymology, grammar, structural linguistics, the special language of poetry, semantics, and phonetics. Excellent notes, with bibliographies, and some suggestions for exercises.

Whatmough, Joshua. *Language.* Mentor Books MD 209. New York, 1957. Scholarly, formal, and distinguished, this is, perhaps too advanced for the secondary school. Teachers will delight in it, however, especially in Professor Whatmough's lucid and elegant style.

CHAPTER THREE

What Is "Good" English?

ASKING STUDENTS OF HIGH SCHOOL, college, or graduate level to list cooperatively the characteristics of the English which they regard as the best they have heard—the English of friends and acquaintances—produces interesting results. They will tell you how *forceful* or *vivid* the English was, how *clear* and *lucid*, how *smooth* (a favorite descriptive term) and how *enthusiastic*, how *inventive* and *persuasive*, how *logical* and *precise*, but rarely will they talk of how *correct* it was. With graduate students preparing to teach English I have, taking their suggestions, listed as many as thirty characteristics of the "good" English they have heard their acquaintances use, without receiving from a single student the comment that the English was "good" because it was grammatically correct. Generally I start the exercise with a series of instructions or questions addressed to the prospective teachers:

1. What is good English? Think of the person of your acquaintance who uses English better than anyone else you have known. In this connection you will probably have to think of spoken English. Don't think of a public figure, and especially not a literary figure, but of someone whom you know or knew who uses English with real skill and competence.

2. What are the characteristics of that English? Why do you think it was good?

3. How do you think these characteristics were acquired? What, in your judgment, did the person do in order to be able to use English so effectively?

4. What English activities in the secondary school

would, in your judgment, bring about such competence? Think back to your own English study. What did you do that really promoted good English? What activities did not? What activities actually got in the way of or interfered with the acquisition of good English?

5. How would you try to arrange to bring about the use of good English? What activities would you favor?

We discover repeatedly that almost never in these discussions is good English described as that which observes the niceties of conventional grammar, or suggestions made that the way to promote better English in the schools is to increase grammatical drill. In assessing the English of their acquaintances, students think first of the *manner* in which the person of their recollection conveys thought. "He's interesting to listen to," the students say, or "He knows how to put his ideas across"; never "He always uses the correct verb tense or the right case with pronouns." If one is to judge by the contributions of students to these discussions, proficiency in the use of English is a matter of skill in seeing the reciprocal relationship between thought and language. The person who uses English well is the one who knows how to make his language say what he wants to say. Students are much less disturbed by occasional violations of established usage than by sentences from which we cannot accurately extract thought, sentences which are long-winded, and sentences which give a sense of affectation and insincerity. Gradually we discover in our discussion that it is probably easier to say what good English is not than to say what it is, so we shift our direction. What is *not* good English? What are the bad kinds of English for our time?

The sincere student of modern language, if he listens carefully enough, is bound to make a remarkable discovery: that, as I have said already, the really serious language faults of our time are more likely to be heard in high places than in low. The gardener who says to his employer, "I ain't hardly got no room for them tulip bulbs," will be understood, and in such a way that you can face his problem head on—you help him to find room or you do not plant them. But what can a reader do with a statement like this from a business letter written by a top industrial executive? "Gentlemen: In re your communication as to the expediency of our continued controls of merchandisable materials, may we state that, pursuant to many requests from patrons, we are endeavoring to expedite delivery of such materials along the line of equitable distribution."

The writer means, I take it, though I am not sure, that the order will be filled as soon as possible, but what reader could be certain, even after the five-hundredth reading? Or take this sentence from a textbook in educational psychology: "The basic patterns of behavior in this area illustrate failure of adjustment in the preadolescent period of emotional tension, where the compulsions of articulation predominant in our competitive culture produce a dichotomy of purpose." Bravo!—not a single one of the vogue words of the moment left out.

This form of outrage, as Sir Arthur Quiller-Couch warned us a long time ago in his very useful book *On the Art of Writing*, is *jargon*, and a dreadful kind of language it is. Says Sir Arthur: "To write jargon is to be perpetually shuffling around in the fog and cottonwool of abstract terms . . . to beat the air because it is easier than to flesh your sword in the thing. The first virtue, the touchstone of masculine style, is its use of the active verb and the concrete noun. When you write in the active voice, 'They gave him a silver teapot,' you write like a man. When you write, 'He was made the recipient of a silver teapot,' you write jargon."

Teachers of English will find an excellent discussion of jargon in *The Logic and Rhetoric of Exposition* by Harold C. Martin. His strictures are valuable to all in the educational profession, where, unfortunately, jargon abounds. Dr. Martin defines jargon as

a language peculiar to a trade or profession, what we sometimes call 'shoptalk'; and it is the use of that language outside the trade or profession, as well as the use of overgeneral, empty words and combinations of such words. Jargon is offensive when its purpose is to create effect rather than convey meaning: like euphemism and inflated language, it is verbal pomposity, parade stuff portentously empty. Most of the sinning is done with a small number of words, each so broadened that it has lost all definiteness and power: *field, element, factor, scale, degree, aspect, level, area.*

Jargon is all around us today; no profession seems immune. Undoubtedly some offenders are worse than others, and teachers of English should be alert to point out where the most flagrant instances of verbal pomposity arise. At times the behavioral sciences seem rapidly to be reaching the point of incommunicability. Here are two recent utterances; the first is quoted in Dr. Martin's book; the second comes from an educational journal:

However, to form a rule or formula so as to evaluate the causation of this bane of humanity, wars, one would have to evolve a psychometer, so to speak, with which the occurrences of certain attitudes and involved coordinating factors could be gauged, compared, and in the ultimate contrast made self-evident in a social science general rule.

In terms of comprehensive understanding of interrelatedness of the many aspects of an educational task in relation to a particular setting, the above approach would seem to make sense clinically.

In a now famous essay titled "Politics and the English Language," George Orwell illustrates modern jargon very forcefully. He quotes first the very beautiful passage from Ecclesiastes: "I returned and saw under the sun, that the race is not to the swift, nor the battle to the strong, neither yet bread to the wise, nor yet riches to men of understanding, nor yet favor to men of skill; but time and chance happeneth to them all." In jargon, says Orwell, this would come out, "Objective considerations of contemporary phenomena compel the conclusion that success or failure in competitive activities exhibits no tendency to be commensurate with innate capacity, but that a considerable element of the unpredictable must invariably be taken into account."

Orwell believes that much jargon in the modern world comes from our unwillingness to face the brutality of present-day political activity. No one wanting to defend Russian totalitarianism would be so blunt as to write, "I believe in killing off your opponents when you can get good results by doing so." Instead, clothing the same belief in dishonest abstractions, he might, continues Orwell, write: "While freely conceding that the Soviet regime exhibits certain features which the humanitarian may be inclined to deplore, we must, I think, agree that a certain curtailment of the right to political opposition is an unavoidable concomitant of transitional periods, and that the rigors which the Russian people have been called upon to undergo have been amply justified in the sphere of concrete achievement."

Five rules, thinks Orwell, will help us to avoid such indecency of language. (1) Never use a metaphor, simile, or other figure of speech which you are used to seeing in print. (2) Never use a long word where a short one will do. (3) If it is possible to cut a word out, always cut it out. (4) Never use the passive where you can use the active. And (5) never use a foreign phrase, a scientific word, or a jargon word if you can think of an everyday English equivalent.

So upset did the history department at Swarthmore College become recently about the amount of jargon appearing on student papers that it instituted a Jargon Control Program, with specific prohibitions on a number of words and phrases.

Robert Hoopes, when Vice-Chairman of the American Council of Learned Societies, was asked at the end of a conference of educators to comment on the proceedings of the meeting; he answered in exasperation:

One thing that invariably troubles me at gatherings of this sort is the depressingly humorless solemnity of approach to all of the questions, the deadly, bleak self-evaluations—such as those conducted during this very afternoon's session—of what we are trying to do, whether we think our conversations and discussions thus far have turned up anything good or operational, whether we think we ought to go on talking in the first place.

What I am trying to say, in short, is that we must stop talking to ourselves. Asylums and little poetry magazines are full of people who do that. To the extent that we do it, we fail to impress anyone except people who feel compelled to remake themselves in our image because, for whatever their strange reasons, they envy us our jobs. If education is to be taken seriously, it must become seriously, simply, and concretely articulate.

To that end, I must confess, this conference, judging from what I have heard this afternoon, has been something less than fruitful. Until the educator—and I mean all of us—can meet the "challenge of cultural complexity" with "simplicity," which includes a cleansing of the language he uses to talk about education from the gobbledygook which colors it, the "educator" will remain the greatest stumbling block to education. The very deadliness of the language that has become the exchange vernacular among members of the fraternity, its wooliness, its verbal constipation, is enough to paralyze any serious enthusiasm toward solution of the problems we claim to face together. What does it mean, for example, to float—as has been floated this afternoon—the airy generalization that we should meet the "challenge of cultural complexity by simplicity in the schools"? And if "this," whatever the grammatical antecedent of "this" may be, is "Plato's old problem of the many versus the one," then Plato must be glad he's dead and not here to witness such an uncritical, unphilosophical, and unforgivably oversimplified application—if it may be so dignified—of a profound philosophical concept.

Everything we try to do in a respectable course in freshman English is vitiated by the oatmeal idiom in which sociologists, anthropologists, and professional educators carry on their discourse. Consider the following jottings from this afternoon's proceedings:

"facilitation of learning"—teach
"local level"—locally
"learning process"—learning

"Our group chose to deal with social and cultural trends in terms of lumping them together"—untranslatable

"At the theoretical level"—theoretically

"We decided to meet the problems of secondary education by a nonhierarchical approach to priorities"—untranslatable.

The verbs and the adverbs, you will note, are conspicuously absent. They used to be what kept our language muscular. But let me draw your attention finally to the following point. One of the recorders reported that his group had agreed that the high school classroom should be regarded as a "miniature social system." The image is tempting: we can now play society instead of playing school. He went on to say that the teacher must, as a consequence, attend to "biological, social, and other determinants of behavior." One wonders what is so profound about a biological determinant of behavior. The teacher must further be concerned with "peer clusters, sub-group dimensions, and psychological, emotive, idiosyncratic behavioral tendencies." The teacher must also learn how to "capitalize on institutional role expectations in creating a favorable learning situation."

Beyond the vocabulary, does not this conception of the classroom as a play-society run the risk of ignoring that greater responsibility of teachers to cultivate in their students a respect for history, an ineradicable wish to acquire an ever-accumulating knowledge of the cultural heritage of the race to which they belong, an unending—literally—desire to know where Man started, where he has been, what prices he has had to pay for certain choices he has made, as against others he could have made? If education concerns itself exclusively with what have been called the felt needs of the children, with preparation for democratic living, with adjustment to the society in which they find themselves, will it not forever prevent the children from growing up? The person who knows only his own age—and I intend the pun—remains forever a child. I, for one, resist in all this what strikes me as a conception of education as a conditioning process. Totalitarian societies condition their young and call it education. I had thought we were different.

Not that I have any objection to commencing education with materials drawn from the youngsters' immediate environment, to starting as we say, with the "contemporary," and leading them outwards—back and forward—from there. No other kind of beginning makes sense, and I sometimes wonder why this simplistic truth need be intoned so solemnly and regularly as it is at conferences of this sort. But if education remains only the preoccupation with what is contemporary, if the study of the contemporary, as Howard Mumford Jones has said, does not lead to the study of greatness, then education has failed.

It is probably idle to complain about the use of specialized vocabularies within professions, and certainly it is true that words frequently acquire for members of a profession connotations which they could not possibly have for the layman. The doctor is probably justified in saying *carcinoma* rather than *cancer*, as the bureaucrat may have some particular kind of operation in mind when he insists on *finalize*. But what becomes offensive is the manner in which the specialized word catches on, so that finally every meeting of two teachers is a *workshop* or a *colloquium*, every random thought in a newspaper editorial has an *ideational* emphasis, every slightest human indecision is personality *ambivalence*, every mild statistical exaggeration represents a *maximization of data*. America, at the moment, is giddy with this linguistic pretentiousness. It is bad English, and teachers of English must resist it. They can begin most effectively within their own profession.

Closely related to jargon is the kind of verbal buncombe which the late Representative Maury Maverick called "gobbledygook." This, too, is a form of pomposity, an attempt to create effect rather than convey meaning. Gobbledygook is a deliberate or self-conscious straining for an official tone—the use of language to impress.

Gobbledygook is often the refuge of officialdom; as a matter of fact, Representative Maverick coined the word to describe the kind of language which he found in *The Congressional Record*. Various departments and bureaus in Washington have their special brand of "officialese"; a national magazine once carried an article on the peculiarities of the language used in the Pentagon, where a new clerk has to undergo a kind of apprenticeship before he can feel at ease with government documents and official forms. Margaret Nicholson gives an example of official gobbledygook: "Herewith are enclosed the requisite documents government employees are requested to submit subsequent to the termination of their period of probation." What an excellent starting place for an economy-minded administration! Gobbledygook is expensive—there are at least eight words too many in that sentence, and printing costs are high these days.

In writing, gobbledygook is the author's effort to be what he imagines the reader wants him to be. This applies, for instance, to the teacher's expectations in an assignment; high school youngsters are often guilty of gobbledygook. They write something in a wholly natural way, but before handing it in, they dress it up in the way they imagine the English teacher prefers it. Often they are right in their estimate of what the teacher wants. English teachers are frequently deceived by the student who has some facility with the manipulation of words and may applaud his unguided excursions into the dictionary. College instructors report that one of their greatest difficulties is to get the student to be himself. The student is so determined to impress that, after completing an assignment in the vocabulary and prose style which are perfectly natural to him, he is likely to reach for the dictionary and replace all the ordinary words with long or unusual ones. The unnatural results are often ludicrous, as when a student once wrote for me, "While still engaged in the efforts to pursue the values of the secondary school curriculum, I acquired the decision to embark on a career of university studies." He meant, of course, "While I was in high school, I decided to go to college," but he did not think that statement sounded quite grand enough. Another student had an unfortunate mother. After every piece of composition he turned out as an assignment, she insisted on going through it and substituting polysyllabic words for those which had clearly and directly conveyed what her son had to say. It was not until after the fourth or fifth failing grade that she began to understand. Even then she could not believe that she had been doing wrong. She had the impression—middle-class gentility again!—that any big word is preferable to any small one, that the educated man is the one who can stagger his hearers with "ten-dollar" words. Students must learn that there is no value in knowing the meanings of a large number of words unless they can master the words well enough to use them in the *natural* expression of thought.

Russell Baker's "Lexicon of Gobbledygookese," reprinted here in part, is intended as a humorous piece but there are such large quantities of truth in it that the reader winces. The definitions may be of the Ambrose Bierce *Devil's Dictionary* variety, but the terms are out of today's news stories, and most of us are still under the delusion that they stand for something real.

The National Society for the Preservation of the English Language to Say What You Mean has issued solemn warnings from its annual conclave here against the accelerating debasement of the mother tongue. All purists have been cautioned to exercise particular care in approaching terminology injected into the language by the ad man, the bureaucrat and psychiatrist—"those masters of the flatulent cliché, the deceptive euphemism, the meaningless polysyllabic, and pompous argot," to quote the society's interim report.

As a guide for its members, the society has also compiled the following dictionary of "dangerously corruptive" words and terms with accompanying translations or definitions in pure English. "Let the purist step with care in salons where these terms are in common usage," warns the society, "for he walks at the very fringes of civilization."

IMPLEMENT, v. (*bureaucratese*), what you do to carry out a decision, policy, or program when you are doing nothing.

FINALIZE, v. (*bureaucratese*), signifying formal adoption of a decision, policy or program, with tacit agreement that it be given a quiet burial, or "implemented."

TEAM, n., a mutual protection society formed to guarantee that no one person can be held to blame for a botched committee job that one man could have performed satisfactorily.

AN IMPORTANT ANNOUNCEMENT (*advertising phrase*), euphemism for a sales talk read into forty million deserted living rooms while folks out in Televisionland put fresh heads on beer.

BASIC RESEARCH, n., scientific activity dedicated to discovering gimcracks that magnetize green-backed paper.

WELL-ADJUSTED, adj. (*psychiatric*), in debt, heavily mortgaged on home with low house-power, passion for three martinis before lunch, occasional rendezvous with neighbor's spouse, undisturbed by fallout, eyeing snappy new television set with tailfins, convinced mankind has made progress since Age of Pericles.

KNOW-HOW, n., singular mental capacity peculiar to persons of United States residence (therefore commonly called "American know-how") which guarantees that Russia cannot put up an earth satellite until spies filch American secret of how to do it.

GREAT, adj., (a) theatrical; applied to a performance that will be remembered until second drink of after-theater party; (b) sports; any contest played before television cameras; (c) political; any candidate not in prison at campaign time.

MASSIVE, adj., a meaningless interjection placed before any noun for special emphasis, e.g., "That massive Secretary of State, John Foster Dulles, enunciated the policy of massive retaliation, which aroused massive fears in Europe, produced a massive Soviet penetration of the Middle East and brought the word 'massive' into massive abuse throughout America."

TOP PRIORITY (*cliché*), a precise translation would be: "This may be idiotic, but it's the boss's idea."

RECESSION, n., economic phenomenon characterized by business decision that rising prices are essentially unhealthy and would become fatal if accompanied by wage increases.

BIPARTISANSHIP, n., a political truce during which each party rifles the other's files for ammunition in the next campaign.

Tautology is an attribute of nearly all forms of verbal pretentiousness; students often think that many words sound better than few—and not just because they are padding, either. The *good* student, thinking that a special effort is expected of him, generally ends by saying more than was necessary, even in single sentences. Thus there appear on papers constructions like : "It was during the month of August that unemployment became a problem of great seriousness" for the simpler and more expressive "In August unemployment became a serious problem." High school students must be helped to eliminate the dead wood in a sentence. Not "It has seldom been the case that we have had so much trouble selling concert tickets," but "We have seldom had so much trouble selling concert tickets."

Secondary school students are not generally addicted to *euphemisms*, but our kind of civilization soon forces young adults into the practice, so the youngsters had better learn about them. It is easy to point out euphemisms in modern America. As has been shown many times, nobody dies in America—one "passes on," or "passes away," or "goes to his eternal reward." (Evelyn Waugh's hilariously savage novel *The Loved One* deals with our euphemisms at the time of death.) Middle-class gentility would profess horror at the thought of a lady having a shot of whisky or a jigger of gin, but she may take a *highball* or a *cocktail*. We go to any length to avoid using the word "toilet." School children ask the teacher's permission to go to the "bathroom," (when they do not want to take a bath) or to the "restroom," (when they do not want to rest). Ladies go to "powder rooms" and men to "the little boys' room," whatever that is supposed to signify. All of us go to "comfort stations." There would seem to be a giant linguistic conspiracy to avoid the facts of our bodily existence.

But, then, euphemisms are everywhere. The man who shines my shoes calls his place a "valeteria," my garage man calls his service station (this, too, is a euphemism) a "lubritorium," and any day now I expect my maid to start calling herself a "culinary technician."

Euphemisms result when we use what we regard as a mild, inoffensive indirect word or phrase for one that is more direct or harsh, or may seem to have unpleasant connotations for some people. Thus a college undergraduate once wrote for me, "After we had imbibed a sufficient quantity of liquid refreshment, we were desirous of partaking of solid sustenance." I imagine that what he really meant was, "We had had so many martinis that we thought we had better eat."

Wilfred Funk commented several years ago in *The Reader's Digest* on the practice of euphemisms.

Nowadays . . . the garbage collector may be called a "sanitary engineer" and his conveyance a "disposal truck." The old-fashioned ratcatcher is a "rodent exterminator" and the dogcatcher is a "canine control officer."

Publicity is no longer handled by a press agent: he is now a "public relations counsel." The poor are "underprivileged"; criminal children are "juvenile delinquents"; servants have become "help." And where do you go for a drink? To a saloon? Not on your life! That vulgar word went out before Prohibition. You now have one in a "cocktail lounge" or a "tavern."

Dictators have stopped killing their enemies; they "liquidate" them. And they never conquer a country; they "liberate" it. Big businessmen aren't fired, they "resign," or they have an "extended leave of absence." Radio and television programs aren't paid for by anybody; they come to you "through the courtesy of the sponsor."

At times, of course, the euphemism becomes a form of humor; the person who uses or concocts it has his tongue in his cheek, and we smile with him; similarly the one who deliberately uses clichés. In these cases we recognize the intentional nature of what is being done, and we have a laugh together. No harm done. But when the euphemism and the cliché are used with seriousness, as a means of asserting one's special linguistic superiority, when, that is, they become verbal pomposity, twisting the user into an absurd caricature of himself because he has a mistaken conception of what constitutes language power and distinction, then, from the teacher of English especially, they must receive rough treatment.

Jargon, gobbledygook, tautology, euphemisms, and clichés—these are the serious language failings of our day, the really bad English. But they have very little to do with what has traditionally been regarded as correct and incorrect grammar. In many high school textbooks, they are not even discussed. Nevertheless they are far more serious than what has usually been regarded as bad English, for they indicate fuzzy thinking, social pretensions, literary affectation. As such, they are a corruption of language, forcing English into something other than the directness, purity, and concreteness of which the language is capable.

May we as teachers of English, then, concentrate only on these abuses and forget all about what the grammar books contain? Can we ignore altogether what the books have to say about sentence structure, word usage, agreement, and position?

Not in the least. Many of the conventions of grammar are still functional safeguards against confusion and imprecision. We have by no means outgrown grammar or the need for exact analysis of the ways in which sentence parts fit together. But we need to acknowledge that not all problems in sentence order and word usage are of equal seriousness. We waste students' time with elaborate attention to case, for example, at the expense of rigorous consideration of the position of modifiers. In the study of a language which inflects hardly at all, drill work in nominatives and objectives is largely irrelevant, but constant work with the problems of word order and position is not.

The most serious mechanical errors in the use of English are obviously those which interfere with communication, which set up obstructions between the writer and the reader or between the speaker and the listener. A number of these are so serious that the reader or listener is unable to overcome them, and the exact meaning of the statement is never known. Errors of this kind can and do produce misunderstandings and uncertainties of such importance that law suits are sometimes required for clarification. Not infrequently experts in English are called into court to advise the judge or members of the jury about sentence meanings; the position of a comma has been a deciding factor in the outcome of numerous civil cases. It can be said, therefore, that those conventions of grammar which reduce the number of errors causing incomprehension in the reader or listener are imperative materials for the secondary school English class. In my judgment, the following errors are among the most serious in modern usage.

1. *Faulty reference of pronouns.* Faced with the sentence "Fred's father said that he could not use his car for a few days," what can the reader do? On his own, he cannot possibly penetrate the meaning. Who cannot use the car—Fred or his father? For that matter, whose car is it?

There are three kinds of faulty reference: (a) ambiguous reference, which is the kind in the sentence above—possibly the most frequent and certainly the most serious; (b) no reference—"In Holland they keep the streets of the cities very clean"—not quite so serious, perhaps, until we see what happens in modern usage with the demonstrative "this"; and (c) wrong reference —"In order to vote, a citizen must be twenty-one years of age; they must also be of sound mind"—a solecism we would expect to encounter only in the most relaxed conversation, where, presumably it would not cause very much distress.

Let me return to the careless use of "this." Certainly the convention which asserts that every pronoun must have a definite antecedent, definitely expressed, is rather severe, judged by modern usage. We regularly use "this" and "which" to stand for larger units than single words, and no confusion results. For example, if I write, "He worked hard to assure the success of the school bond issue, and this caused him to neglect his business somewhat," there is slight danger, if any, that the reference of "this" will be misunderstood. At times, however, serious ambiguity results when "this" is made to stand for a large unit. "Tod knew that keeping fit was essential to his success as a member of the crew; this gave him much personal satisfaction." What gave him satisfaction? The keeping fit? The success? His membership in the crew?

When this kind of ambiguity enters discussions of public policy, science, art, education, law, medicine, the results, if not disastrous, can produce much bewilderment. The following statement, taken down at a conference, is more typical than we may be willing to admit: "This problem of selecting students for advanced courses is a difficult one. I don't know if this makes any sense, but it seems to me that we have to give this much more thought. Many people in the community are watching this carefully, and whatever this proves, it certainly means that we've got to proceed cautiously with this."

2. *Inaccurate use of modifiers,* that is, modifiers in positions that make the meaning of the sentence uncertain. As the textbooks say, these modifiers can be dangling, squinting, or misplaced, but all types are serious, since all will get in the reader's way. What do you do with "Carrying his report card, while going down the stairs, I saw Frank with several of his friends"? In speech, stress and intonation might make this sentence clear, but why take the chance?

All of us know the howlers from the joke books: "For Sale—a grand piano by a lady with mahogany legs." Dean Francis Keppel of the Harvard Graduate School of Education tells of the experience of Mr. R. B. Merriman, a former Master of one of the Houses at Harvard, who found a portrait of Sir Robert Downing, the former owner of 10 Downing Street. He sent the portrait to the then prime minister, Neville Chamberlain. Mr. Chamberlain wrote back to thank Mr. Merriman as follows: "I shall hang it on the walls of 10 Downing Street when I retire for the benefit of mankind" (all of this sentence without the benefit of commas). I have frequently demonstrated to students what happens with each shift of the word "only" in the title of the popular song "I Only Have Eyes for You" (it is, of course, in the wrong position to begin with). "*Only* I Have Eyes for You" (I and nobody else); "I *Only* Have Eyes for You" (I have them but I don't plan to do anything with them); "I Have *Only* Eyes for You" (eyes, but nothing else); "I Have Eyes *Only* for You" (now he did it); "I Have Eyes for *Only* You" (poor thing all by herself on that desert isle); and "I Have Eyes for You *Only*" (a kind of booster shot here—he really means it).

Writing about Hester Prynne in a test on *The Scarlet Letter*, a student at the University of Cincinnati once came up with "Hester was forced to stand on the scaffold and show the scarlet letter to the community that was hanging on her breast." His instructor's comment, inspired, was in the margin: "I get it—Miss Community Chest of 1620."

Humor aside, the position of modifiers is an acute matter in modern usage. The squinting modifier, the one that can modify either the element before it or the element following it, is especially troublesome. What does "boldly" modify in this sentence? "I urged him boldly to express his opinion." What is being done boldly—the urging or the expressing? Or consider this sentence: "By the terms of the contract, the company is obliged immediately to construct the bridge." Which is to be immediate—the obligation or the construction? There is a considerable difference. The squinting modifier often results from our efforts to avoid splitting an infinitive, but it is far better to split the infinitive than to leave the meaning uncertain.

3. *Incorrect punctuation*, particularly misplaced commas, or omission of necessary commas. Often the insertion of a comma is nothing more than a gesture of assistance to the reader: "When they started eating, the dog started barking." The comma gets everything straightened out in the first reading. But punctuation often controls meaning. Let students discuss Quince's speech as Prologue to the play of Pyramus and Thisbe in Shakespeare's *A Midsummer Night's Dream*, where inaccurate punctuation makes him say exactly the opposite of what he intends. At the present time, partly in

the interests of economy, there is a movement among publishers to eliminate as much punctuation as possible, and certainly publishers are able to argue effectively that many of the marks are unnecessary (the period after an abbreviation, for example), but where punctuation is the most expeditious means of asserting relationships, the writer should not dispense with it. No one would deny the necessity of the comma in the following sentence: "Henry, James spoke to a group of young writers in Paris once." A rare sentence?—perhaps. But how about this one: "Doctors Frank, Wilson, Earle, Carter, Joseph, Tyler, and Crawford attended."

Besides faulty reference, inaccurate use of modifiers, and incorrect punctuation, there are other kinds of serious errors which attention to the established conventions of English usage can help us avoid, but those given here suffice to demonstrate that the teacher of English must be aware that some of the conventions are more useful than others. The bad English which is produced by our failure to observe these conventions is an English that does not communicate, or communicates only ambiguously, and as a result the reader or listener is powerless to respond to the statement. Nothing has been gained by our effort to establish contact with him, and when this contact is essential to desired cooperative action, the loss can be grievous.

Good English, then, avoids the pretensions of jargon, gobbledygook, tautology, euphemisms, and clichés, just as it also avoids that disregard of language conventions which causes distress in reader and listener. Not all of our students will become brilliant speakers or accomplished prose stylists, but it is given to all of them to express themselves clearly, to *nearly* all of them to express themselves logically, to *most* of them to express themselves persuasively, and to *more than we may be willing to acknowledge* to express themselves eloquently. The English which serves them in each or all of these tasks is good English.

CHAPTER FOUR

Traditional Grammar: Purpose and Problems

AT THE YALE CONFERENCE ON THE TEACHING OF ENGLISH in March, 1957, the Committee on Grammar defined its position with admirable clarity:

> Let us begin, then, by stating unequivocally that this Committee believes grammar should be taught in the secondary schools. This statement is not so unnecessary as it might first appear: there are teachers today who seem to deny that grammar should be taught. Some profess not to teach grammar because they believe it is not necessary. Upon examination, we discover that they do teach grammar, but under a different name: "sentence structure," they call it, or "mechanics." They mean only that they do not teach grammar as they were taught it. Nevertheless their statement "grammar is unnecessary" is quoted in the press, and has a pernicious effect: it misleads inexperienced teachers, and misrepresents our position before the public.

The statement affirms, as the preceding chapter of this book attempted to do, that traditional grammar, or at least some of it, is under attack. Teachers of English find themselves in a period of critical evaluations, of exciting new orientations, new perspectives, new adjustments where grammar is concerned. As the statement of the Committee indicates, there is even some confusion about what the word "grammar" means; some teachers who profess to be abandoning it are, in reality, abandoning only some sections of it. Particularly interesting is the comment that teachers "do not teach grammar as they were taught it." Certainly the kind of grammar taught twenty or thirty years ago is under sharp attack indeed, with a group of increasingly numerous and increasingly vocal linguistic scientists asserting that traditional grammar does not give an adequate description of English, especially of English as it is used in today's world. For the first time in perhaps a century and a half, the English teacher is questioning what was once thought of as the most stable material of the curriculum. Is a noun *really* the name of a person, place, or thing? Is a phrase *really*, or *only*, a group of closely related words without a subject and predicate? Is a sentence *really* the expression of a complete thought—or are there complete thoughts which are not sentences?

Possibly the teacher of English can work out his own position by facing a series of questions:

1. How much grammar do you think the secondary school student should know—right now, in today's world?

2. Should all students in high school be taught the same amount?

3. At what grade levels should it be taught? (Teachers or prospective teachers should be very realistic here and try to recall at what age grammar became really meaningful to them. Traditionally, students have received their largest doses in junior high school. Was this where they should have received it?)

4. How much of the teaching of grammar should come out of books and workbooks and how much should be taken from students' own composition work and from literature they are studying?

As used in this chapter, the word "grammar" will mean the theory and principles guiding attempts to describe word forms and functions, and to show the relationships among words and units of words. Included, therefore, in the definition are parts of speech, syntax, sentence structure, word inflections, and punctuation. Not included are diction, word usage, spelling, capitalization, and, of course, pronunciation. Yet the distinction is not altogether valid. The areas of linguistic discussion and analysis frequently cross, so that our discussion of, say, parallelism is conditioned by our consideration of idiom and current usage. The chief emphasis of this chapter, however, will be on the parts of speech and how these work separately or together to shape the English sentence. The teaching of the parts of speech in the traditional manner is still a major segment of the English curriculum in most of our schools.

Let us address ourselves to the question of how it is being done and what it may be accomplishing.

The ability to make such an investigation requires that the teacher or prospective teacher of English have a very secure knowledge of traditional grammar. Whatever the final position which the individual teacher may take about the continuing validity of traditional grammatical instruction in the secondary school, the very uncertainty of the hour demands that the teacher know intimately and thoroughly what is under discussion. Most emphatically will this be true for the teacher who decides to abandon the traditional variety; there can be no authority worthy of professional respect behind his support of a new approach to language study if he has a faulty understanding of the old approach from which he is departing. The Yale Committee might very well have included in its statement that some teachers avoid grammar, and even take a strong position against teaching it, for the simple reason that they do not know it. A college program of nothing but literary study has erased what they had of grammar in the secondary school, and resistance now seems easier than review.

The teacher of English should know that the structural linguists who are leading the attack on traditional grammar are thoroughly acquainted with it. The reader will not find in any of the books by those who now question the old position a single statement that today's teacher of English does not need to *know* the old position. The structural linguists know traditional grammar very well indeed; their own writings are models of correctness in the traditional manner. In reading Bloomfield, Fries, and others, one is struck by the attractiveness of their writing styles and the clarity of their verbal forms and constructions, but even more so by the degree of their familiarity with grammatical exactness of a highly specialized nature. The questioning of traditional grammar is not being done by a group of insensitive philistines. Structural linguistics is in no sense anti-intellectual. Whatever he might object to in what the structural linguists have to say, the language conservative could find no fault with the way they say it. The lesson for the teacher of English is plain: *he must know formal grammar and know it well.*

Knowing it, what does he do with it? How does he bring it into the course of study in such a way that he can count on its serving the language skill of his students?

First of all, both teacher and students must realize that they work with a vehicle inadequate to their purposes. The structural linguists are right: formal English grammar is not a wholly valid description of the English language. The definitions and the terms are only semifunctional; they do not do the full job. Every one of the assertions of formal grammar needs immediate qualification; anything presented as a rule has at once a list of exceptions appended to it, and, even then, the analysis is not complete. Yet, up to a point, all of the traditional declarations work and are practical. The teacher of English will have to keep his classes alert to the constant need to supplement and refine traditional materials in the light of modern usage and practice.

Second, the teacher of English will insist on some attention to the origin and derivation of the terminology itself. Only a few of our teachers, saddled as they are with the Latin terminology of grammatical study, devote any time at all to seeing just what the words mean, and especially where the older grammarians got them. The elementary school youngster studies adjectives, but does his teacher help him to look at the word *adjective* itself? Derived from *ad*, meaning "to", and *jacere*, meaning "to place next to," or, for the youngster, more interestingly, "to hurl at," the word becomes through its derivation an accurate, and even metaphorically vivid, description of what the thing does. Continuing with his study of adjectives, the youngster learns from his book that it is "a word that *modifies* a noun or pronoun." Probably, he is asked to commit this to memory, and he goes through the remainder of his school career repeating it whenever called upon to do so, but with a very hazy notion of what it means, because no one has given any attention to the meaning of the word "modify" in this connection. Suppose the teacher were simply to present to the class a sentence like "Because it was raining we had to *modify* our picnic plans." At once the students would be able to tell the meaning of the word *modify*—to change, to alter. This is precisely the meaning of the word in the definition of an adjective: the adjective changes or alters our understanding of the noun. If I announce the single word "tree," my hearer has a vague, indefinite impression, but if I say *green, maple* tree, immediately the concept of the tree is changed. This is what all adjectives do, whether they be descriptive or limiting—they change the concept of the object which is named by the noun.

Attention to the terminology itself has been slighted, and a moment or two spent on the terms can be highly instructive. Why, for example, is the *verb* called the *word*, from the Latin *verbum?* And what is the significance of the preposition *trans* in the word *transitive?* Why should a verb form be called the *subjunctive,* or *joining-under mood?* Why *mood? Mood,* in what sense? What do such simple words as *pronoun, tense,* and *voice* mean? Surely many of the difficulties which our students have with these words can be dispelled if we take time to discuss the descriptive appropriateness of the word to what it names.

Third, the teacher of English must constantly demonstrate the relation of each item of grammatical study to other items. Personally, on the senior high level, I tried always to teach as much grammar *simultaneously* as I could. I am aware of the difficulties here—of trying to teach too much at once and thus accomplishing nothing well—but I would risk these in order that students should see the whole picture of grammatical relationships. Thus when I teach the noun I like to teach the noun as word, as phrase, and as clause; and I go on to do the same thing with the adjective and the adverb. This brings separate parts of study together, and the study of parts of speech is at the same time serving the study of sentence structure and syntax. Let me illustrate.

Through observation of a number of sentences, the definition of a noun is induced as the *name* of a person, place, thing, action, or idea. The fact that it is a *name* is insisted upon. (As semanticists have demonstrated, one of the major errors in modern thought is the confusion of the object named with the name itself.) Examples are then given in class:

> person—mother, Ted
> place—city, California
> thing—table, Empire State Building
> action—swimming, speaking
> idea—honor, duty, beauty

The noun as the name of an *action* is carefully considered. Several of the structural linguists insist that the gerund is a source of confusion for students because youngsters are unable to distinguish it from a verb, since both contain action. In the discussion of the definition of the noun, the difference can be made clear: the gerund has to have an additional word, an auxiliary or helping word, before it can be a complete verb—*was swimming, is speaking.*

Returning to the sentences in which the nouns have been located, the students then observe the way in which the nouns are functioning in the sentences and construct a list of noun uses:

> subject of a verb
> direct object of a verb
> indirect object of a verb
> predicate nominative (or subject complement)

object of a preposition
appositive
subject or object of a verbal
object complement

Using nouns other than those in the sentences, the students then give examples of each of the uses:

subject of a verb—The *clown* dances.

direct object of a verb—The clown sang a *song*.

indirect object of a verb—The clown sang his *friends* a song.

predicate nominative—The clown is a *comedian*.

object of a preposition—The clown is in the *circus*.

appositive—The clown, a famous *comedian*, once made a movie.

subject or object of a verbal—We wanted the *clown* to sing a song. Knowing the *clown*, we enjoyed the circus more.

object complement—Tom called me a *clown*.

Having established and discussed these uses thoroughly, the teacher turns next to a group of sentences in which not a single word but a group of words, or a phrase, is performing these functions, and after careful analysis of the sentences, we then construct a single phrase of our own which we attempt to use in all of the noun functions. Let's say that we choose "singing in the bathtub."

subject of a verb—*Singing in the bathtub offers* pleasant relaxation.

direct object of a verb—I always *enjoy singing in the bathtub*.

indirect object of a verb—Hal *gives singing in the bathtub* a top rating among things he likes to do.

predicate nominative—Helen's chief vocal exercise *is singing in the bathtub*.

object of a preposition—I am perhaps too fond *of singing in the bathtub*.

subject or object of a verb—We know *singing in the bathtub to be* relaxing.

Describing singing in the bathtub, Clare made an amusing speech.

object complement—Charlie considers *a waste of time* the *singing in the bathtub* of his brother.

appositive—His only *vocalizing, singing in the bathtub*, will never get him into opera.

Whether or not these phrases will be named as gerund phrases is a decision for the individual teacher to make. From grade ten onward, with classes of average, or better-than-average, ability, I would certainly name them as such. But if they are named, then further work in identification and analysis is necessary.

Furthermore, students should see that there is another kind of noun phrase, which can be found in most of the regular uses. This is the infinitive phrase (again, whether or not it is named as such should be the decision of the individual teacher), and it can be effectively introduced with a sentence like "To know him is to like him," where infinitive phrases are being used as subject and predicate nominative. It is not difficult to elicit examples of the other uses from students, where examples are possible.

direct object of a verb—I *want to learn French.*

indirect object of a verb—A very unlikely construction, but possible:
I *gave to learn French* the number-one spot on my summer activities.

object of a preposition—Very unlikely because of the double preposition.

appositive—His *ambition, to learn French,* was finally realized.

subject or object of a verbal—*Wanting to learn French,* he attended night school.

Any discussion of the verbals must, of course, reveal that, since they are part verb, they continue to act like verbs—that is, they may themselves take objects, or be completed by predicate nominatives. They may even have other verbals in these various positions—for example, "*To enjoy learning French* seems impossible to me. Students should see the overwhelming frequency of verbals in modern communication, and the intricacy with which they tie together various sentence parts. Many teachers of English have shied away from verbals in recent years, considering them too difficult for many of their students. Such teachers might very well reconsider their decision in the light of the frequency of verbals and the use that can be made of them to demonstrate principles of compact sentence order.

The dependent clause as noun is also a favorite in modern usage, particularly as the object of a verb. Virtually every indirect quotation uses this order: "He said that the plane would be on time." For students who are having difficulties with dependent clauses, the scheme proposed here, developing as it does from seeing words and phrases in specific noun functions, often clarifies the fact that every dependent clause functions as a part of speech.

As with words and phrases, students first see some dependent clauses operating as nouns in sentences. Then, as with the gerund phrase, a dependent clause is offered by the class for testing in the various noun uses, for example, "whoever knows the answer."

subject of a verb—*Whoever knows the answer* will be rewarded.

direct object of a verb—We will applaud *whoever knows the answer.*

indirect object of a verb—He will give *whoever knows the answer* a complimentary ticket.

predicate nominative—The honor student will be *whoever knows the answer.*

object of a preposition—Give this prize to *whoever knows the answer.*

subject or object of a verbal—I want *whoever knows the answer* to speak at assembly next week.

Calling *whoever knows the answer* to the platform, the principal will reward him.

object complement—I consider a brilliant man *whoever knows the answer* to this problem.

It might seem that this scheme presupposes some previous work with phrases and clauses, as well as with verbals, but it has been used successfully with students who had not had such experience. In that case a greater amount of time was given to the unit, with careful analysis and discussion proceeding inductively from example sentences offered the students on the blackboard or duplicated sheets—whenever possible, their own sentences—and with additional examples always elicited from them. Invariably the student comments following exposure to this scheme ran, "I understand grammar better now than I ever did before," or, more encouraging to the teacher, "Grammar begins to make some sense now. I see how it all fits together and how it's supposed to make better sentences."

The course activity must not stop with sentence analysis. Immediately the students should be asked to demonstrate in impromptu composition that they are able to improve sentence variety in their work as a result of being able to place phrases and clauses in the different noun roles. The writing exercise is, to be sure, somewhat artificial, but there is a positive carry-over value; and students are ready to go on to a similar consideration of the adjective as word, phrase and clause, and the adverb as word, phrase, and clause.

To arrive at the definition that an adjective is a word that modifies a noun or pronoun, students should be presented with examples that show adjectives operating in a variety of ways. Easiest to recognize are the descriptive adjectives in the position immediately preceding the noun (the *red* barn), and after brief work with these, teachers can go on to predicate adjectives, "the weather is *warm*," adjectives which follow the noun, "He used a form of the lie *direct*," or "He dug the well *deep*," and then the whole range of limiting adjectives: numerals, demonstratives, interrogatives, indefinites, possessives, and the articles. Students should see, in every case, how the adjective has an effect on the noun—how it modifies or changes the concept which the noun has given us: *this girl* is different from *girl*.

Descriptive adjectives are expressed in degrees of comparison—positive, comparative, superlative—and these normally present no difficulties to students. Occasionally they may have trouble remembering whether or not a particular adjective adds the suffixes *-er* and *-est*, but the dictionary can solve the problem in an instant. For the most part, all adjectives of one syllable add the suffixes, and all adjectives of three or more syllables prefix the adverbs *more* and *most*. Adjectives of two syllables may do either, and here is the area of doubt. In connection with the comparison of adjectives, students might be warned against the modern fondness, particularly in advertising, for the incomplete comparison: "Eight out of 10 housewives say Spoofy Puddings taste *better*." Not better than anything or better than they used to taste—just *better*. The statement, of course, says absolutely nothing. A pinnacle in this sort of noncommunication was reached several years ago with the cigarette slogan: "Always milder, better tasting, cooler smoking."

The barbarisms of the double comparative ("more tastier") or double superlative ("most tastiest") need only to be mentioned, but it is interesting to the class for the teacher to point out that these were once not altogether frowned upon. They were seen only as a more emphatic or intensive form of the comparison. Thus Shakespeare wrote, "the most unkindest cut of all."

While working with the adjective as word, teachers should introduce the participle. This is best done by putting at the blackboard the four principal parts of a common verb, like *tear, tearing, tore, torn*, and then showing how the second and fourth parts, which we call the present participle and the past participle, can be used in the regular adjective positions: "The *tearing* cloth indicated that the fabric was old." "The *torn* jacket lay on the chair." No matter how complicated the subject of the participle may become, this is fundamentally all that it amounts to: one of the principal parts of a verb is used not as a verb but as an adjective; however, the word does not lose its verb properties. It can go on doing and being everything a verb can do and be—take an object, have adverbial modifiers, be expressed in tense and voice, and so on.

The simplest kind of adjective phrase is prepositional. Students might learn at once that every prepositional phrase is either an adjective or adverb. In short, every prepositional phrase is a modifier. Classes will have little trouble with adjective prepositional phrases, chiefly because of the usual position of such phrases: "The tall building *on the corner* has been leased by a bank." To the student who has learned that words and phrases which answer the question *where?* are adverbial, the teacher may have to demonstrate that this is true only in relation to the verb; an answer to the question *where? after* the verb is adverbial but not otherwise. In the sentence given, "on the corner" is both descriptive and limiting—it points out *which* building we mean. Half a dozen examples of the adjective prepositional phrase should suffice to make this construction clear, but teachers might assign the composition of sentences containing such phrases.

Other adjective phrases are participial and infinitive, though the latter are not common. The greater amount of class time should be spent on the participial phrase, and the work should begin with observation of sentences in which the participial phrase can be found used in a number of ways.

He looked at the tree *broken by the storm.*

Seeing him at the window, I hurried inside.

The city, *damaged severely by the tornado,* was almost deserted.

I could not appreciate the church *built by a modern French architect.*

Being an orphan, he was deprived of a mother's care.

In every case students should see the adjective function of the entire phrase—it is *modifying* or *changing* a noun or pronoun. Similarly, students should see what the other elements in the phrases are doing: "by the storm" modifies the participle by telling *how*—that is, it is a modifier of a word which is an adjective and part verb and therefore adverbial; "him" is the object of the participle "seeing"; "severely" is an adverb modifying "damaged"; "orphan" is a predicate nominative after the copulative "being."

Discussion of the participial phrase should deal at some length with the dangling participle. The first examples should be of the clearly recognizable kind, those which cause a laugh:

> We were delighted to see a beautiful garden of tulips turning a bend in the road.
>
> Quietly lapping milk from a saucer in a corner of the kitchen, Howard found his sister's pet kitten.
>
> Looking out the window, a parade could be seen.

With just a bit of help, the writer or speaker would probably recognize such blunders as these and correct himself, but there is a kind of dangling participle which is much less obvious and, for that reason, much more common. This is the kind which results almost entirely from the use of the passive voice; making the finite verb active will, in virtually every case, correct the dangling construction.

> Having spent all my money shopping, my purse was found to be empty.
>
> Before arriving at La Guardia Airport, the Statue of Liberty could be seen.

Class work with this kind of sentence will reveal not only the error of position, or, more logically, of a modifier without anything to modify, but also the weakness of the passive construction in English. Active verbs *work;* passive verbs *evade.* There are, to be sure, legitimate uses for the passive voice, most of them having to do with problems in naming the actor—for example, "Three dollars were stolen from the drawer"; we don't know who did it. There are more passive verbs in the chapters of this book than I would normally use, since in using the singular noun "teacher" I did not want to use a possessive pronoun or adjective of either gender; thus instead of writing, "The teacher will discover the difficulties of her students," I have often written something like, "The student's problems will be discovered by the teacher."

The infinitive phrase as an adjective often expresses purpose with a noun; it tells what the noun is used for. "Dr. Clark's wife has plenty of time *to give to the Red Cross drive.*" "Tod has extra heavy shoes *to keep his feet dry.*" "This is the best club *to join.*" Notice that the verbs are not words of action. Action will make the infinitive phrase adverbial, as "Tod wore extra heavy shoes to keep his feet dry." This, however, would almost surely be a matter of considerable confusion for high school students of any but unusual skill in grammar, and the matter should be avoided. Infinitive phrases may dangle, too, but because most infinitive phrases are adverbial in nature, it is best to discuss them with the adverb and ignore them altogether at this point.

Adjective clauses are known also as relative clauses because they are introduced by relative pronouns: *who, whose, whom, which*, and *that* are the common ones. We use *who* for persons, *which* for things, and *that* for persons or things, except that we very seldom use *that* with a proper name.

To see these clauses as modifiers of nouns, students should begin with a number of example sentences.

We drove for almost ten miles a car *that badly needed oil.*
I never before had a teacher *who could make math so interesting.*
Clare Morris, *whom we have elected class secretary,* knows how to type well.

In each case the whole clause gives additional information about a noun. Furthermore it must be seen as a *clause.* Several observations should be made about the relative pronoun: (1) the significance of its name, *relative*—it relates back to a noun or pronoun in the main clause, its *antecedent;* (2) *its work in its own clause*—that is, since it is a pronoun, it must have one of the regular noun or pronoun uses, subject of a verb, direct object, object of a preposition, and so on. Drill here can be very profitable for all phases of sentence structure. Students should work with sentences in which they are asked to pick out the adjective clause, underline the finite verb, circle the relative pronoun, indicate with an arrow its antecedent in the main clause, and then give the use of the relative pronoun. Class recitation on these sentences should follow to assure clarification for all students.

Obviously this is the place to tackle the problem of "who" and "whom." When students see the relative pronouns functioning in the clauses, then they will see that the choice of *who* or *whom* is simply a matter of recognizing its use—*who* for subjects and predicate nominatives, *whom* for objects of all kinds.

A final difficulty with relative clauses has to do with punctuation: when do we put commas around them, or which are *restrictive* and which are *nonrestrictive?* Again, some work with terminology first. A clause is *restrictive* when it has a limiting, or restricting, effect on the meaning of the sentence; remove it and the sentence means something different. It is *nonrestrictive* when it gives additional detail which, though informative, does not limit the meaning of the main clause; the relative clause can be added or left off without changing the principal thought.

Restrictive: All water *that is boiled* is safe to drink. (Students will see immediately the danger of removing *that is boiled.*)

Nonrestrictive: Columbus, *which is the capital of the state*, is located in the center of Ohio. (The relative clause gives interesting, and even important information, but it is not essential to what the main clause says. Remove it, and the main clause is unaffected.)

Students should see, from work with sentences, that the majority of our relative clauses are restrictive, for the simple reason that we use so many of them for purposes of identification: "The TV program *that we watched last night before studying* was a Western." This is the means of identifying a particular program and consequently the clause is restrictive. When, however, the clause is a second means of identification, then it would be nonrestrictive: "Frank Sinatra, who appeared in *From Here to Eternity*, was once a singer with a dance orchestra."

Restrictive: My brother who lives in Chicago will be here for Christmas.

Nonrestrictive: My brother Bob, who lives in Chicago, will be here for Christmas.

Some recent studies of English grammar prefer to abandon the terms "restrictive" and "nonrestrictive" modifiers and to see the restrictive modifier as a modifier of the noun which precedes it, and the nonrestrictive as a modifier of the entire sentence. (See Roberts, *Understanding English*, pp. 286–8.) The justification for the distinction, according to Roberts, is that "it gets closer to the structure of the sentence." Very possibly. In this chapter, however, where my objective has been a review of traditional grammar, I have preferred to use the terminology and definitions which are more or less general in secondary school textbooks.

The work with the adverb can follow this same general pattern, though students will have to see that adverbs have more uses than adjectives. Observation of sentences should reveal the adverb as a modifier of verbs, adjectives, and other adverbs.

The salesman worked *patiently* to convince the customer.

The playground was *too* muddy for the little children.

The pilot speaks to the passengers *quite often.*

Students are generally told that adverbs can be located if we ask a number of questions after the verb: *how, when, where, why, how long, how often.* Any element which we get as an answer—after the verb—be it word, phrase, or clause, is adverbial in nature. "We drove *through the city*" tells *where*. "He will speak *at three o'clock*" tells *when*. Similarly, students have often been told that many adverbs which modify verbs end in *-ly*, and this is true. But they must be warned that not all words ending in *-ly* are adverbs, not even those that look like adverbs, such as *only*. *Only* is more frequently an adjective. The point to stress with every kind of aid or clue which we give to students of grammar is that it may not work all the time. Far more important than aids or clues is secure understanding of the construction of the sentence—what are the words, phrases, and clauses doing?

Like adjectives, some adverbs are compared, but there are relatively few problems here. Adding *-er* and *-est* to a word ending in *-ly* may create a few spelling hazards, but we change a *y* to an *i* in forming many noun plurals, as well as in comparing a number of adjectives.

Adverbial phrases are prepositional or infinitive. The former are so frequent in English that it is scarcely possible to speak a sentence without at least one, and a few exercise sentences should suffice to indicate their prevalence. Infinitive phrases used as adverbs to modify a verb generally answer the question *why:* "She wrote to the clergyman to get her birth certificate"; when they modify predicate adjectives or other adverbs, they often act as intensifiers: "The children were too sleepy to watch the late show," or "He talked too fast to be understood." Adverbial infinitive phrases can dangle; in sentences which give directions or reasons, dangling phrases are especially common:

To get the best results, a soil conditioner should be used.

To be sure of a table at the prom, reservations should be made early.

Again, students should notice that the dangling construction results from the use of the passive voice. An active verb immediately corrects the error.

The adverbial clause is formed when we subordinate one idea to another in a sentence through the use of a conjunction which establishes a subordinate, or dependent, condition. The clauses answer the same questions words and phrases do—that is, they are clauses of time, place, manner, reason. Teachers frequently approach the work with adverb clauses by introducing the common subordinate conjunctions and then asking students to bring pairs of sentences together by using these conjunctions. The word *subordinate* might require some explanation for a few students, but they will see its meaning clearly in a sentence like, "A first lieutenant is *subordinate* to a captain."

The great advantages of subordination should be insisted upon; students should see the dramatic relationship of ideas which results when they use words like *because, although, since, when, if,* and others. The punctuation of the adverbial clause is easy to handle; it amounts to little more than seeing that when the clause is not in the normal order of the complex sentence—principal clause first, subordinate clause second—the subordinate clause should be set off by commas. The exception is the nonrestrictive clause which gives the impression of being tacked on after the principal clause. Of course, punctuation of adverbial clauses often occurs simply to prevent misreading.

Important facts for students to retain, then, as they complete their work with adjectives and adverbs as words, phrases, and clauses are (1) that all prepositional phrases are either adjectives or adverbs; (2) that participial phrases are adjectives; (3) that infinitive phrases are nouns, adjectives, or adverbs; (4) that subordinate, or dependent, clauses are nouns, adjectives, or adverbs. Establishing these relationships, even if we use the new terminology of the structural linguists, is essential to student understanding of what lies behind the construction of various kinds of effective sentences.

Many teachers of English prefer to begin each year's study of grammar with attention to the verb, presenting it, rightly, as the backbone of the sentence and even, if they carry the matter far enough, the basis for what might be called the *philosophy* of traditional grammar. The simple subject-predicate relationship which must exist before a sentence can make any assertion about the condition of man begins with a recognition of the fundamental nature of man; the finite verb attests man's mortality. The purposes of traditional grammar emanate from man's discovery that no statement about himself was possible unless it dealt with *time,* unless it made clear that every action and condition of his existence has a beginning and an end. A sentence is not so much the expression of a complete thought as it is a reflection on the state of our being or a compulsive account of the limits of our capability. The finite verb is measured in tense; its very definiteness in time establishes the completeness of the sentence; the verb makes clear our identity as men. It is, therefore, rightly named the *word.* A grammar commensurate with our humanity is impossible without it.

It makes good sense, therefore, to start with the subject-predicate relationship, and teachers, on any grade level, can afford to be overly explicit here. The traditional definitions of subject and predicate are not very helpful to the students who are most baffled by sentence order—what really have we said when we define the subject as "the person, place, or thing about which an assertion is made"? Could this not apply with logic to any noun or pronoun in the sentence? "The minister made a weekly visit to his relatives in New Jersey." The subject of the sentence is "minister," but our definition of a subject will seem to some students to apply equally well to the minister's relatives. Doesn't the sentence assert that they live in New Jersey?

The definition of a predicate is even more inconclusive: "the word or words used to make a statement about the subject." On the basis of this definition, what will many students take to be the predicate in our sentence about the minister? Quite a few of them will choose "visit." And if we insist with them that the predicate must contain a verb, they will tell us that "visit" is or can be a verb: "I visit my grandmother every Sunday."

Once again, attention to the terminology itself may help us. What does the word "predicate" mean when it is used in other than grammatical connections? What do we mean when we say that "his actions were *predicated* on the assumption that he knew the truth"? Actually, an act of affirmation is taking place; the individual is proclaiming the sensibleness of what he does. The predicate of a sentence is also an affirmation—it attaches a fitting action or condition to a person, place, or thing: man builds, baby cries, weather changes, property deteriorates, God is. (To the objection that the action or condition is sometimes not fitting to the subject, we can answer that the incongruity is generally made clear by the remainder of the sentence or paragraph: "Joe barked like a dog in providing the sound effects of the play." In the most general sense, however, whatever an individual can do is *fitting* to him, and the objection is irrelevant.)

But the most instructive manner of dealing with the predicate is to see it as a verb—that is, as the word which fixes the time of an action or a condition. More important than the nature of the action, for syntactical purposes, is the duration of it. Precision of time gives us the predicate.

Let the teacher, therefore, begin with a verb and, in building a sense of the sentence, see all other words and sentence units in relation to it.

growls
bear growls
bear growls loudly
big bear growls loudly
big bear growls loudly in the cave
a ferocious big bear growls loudly in the cave near the lake

And so on. The possible additions to this basic pattern are end-less and, as they are attached, can be named in relation to what they are doing. From single parts of speech, adjectives and adverbs, chiefly, the sentence building can move to prepositional phrases, then to verbal phrases, finally to dependent clauses. Eventually the sentence might look something like this: "Angry because he can find no food, a ferocious big black bear, pacing restlessly to and fro, growls loudly in the cave near the lake." A high school class that has cooperatively formed such a sentence and can see the relationship of the sentence parts to one another is well on its way to better sentence construction. Needless to say, the pattern can be repeated many times.

No doubt teachers make too much of the parts of speech. (What, by the way, does *that* term mean—*parts of speech*, surely a very sophisticated language concept, and yet we ask seventh- and eighth-graders to master it?) Instead of the seven different categories, noun, pronoun, adjective, verb, adverb, preposition, conjunction (I omit the interjection, which is an independent sentence element and gives no one any trouble anyhow), why not a more economical grouping according to relationships; for example,

Group A	*Group B*	*Group C*
noun (a name)	verb (an action or condition with exact time)	connectives:
pronoun (stands for a name)		prepositions (always with a noun)
adjective (describes or points out the thing named)	adverb (the how, when, where, why, how long, or how often of the action or condition)	conjunctions (general joining words)

The number of terms is not diminished, but the grouping makes function stand out more clearly. The parts of speech do not seem to exist in isolation from one another.

The verb, naturally, demands much more attention than we have thus far given it. The kinds and properties of verbs, the principal parts, agreement, tense sequence—all these must not be slighted. Textbooks in the traditional grammar are generally quite thorough in these matters, but the teacher of English learns over a period of time how to supplement the text in the interests of quicker student mastery of verb functions. For example, most texts give only three principal parts for verbs—the present, past, and past participle—yet the teacher knows that because of the constant use of the progressive form of the verb, particularly in the present tense, inclusion of the present participle is a great help. We say to our friend, "What are you doing?" not "What do you?" and he answers, "I am writing a letter," not "I write a letter." The further advantage of having the -*ing* form printed is that it is an aid to correct spelling, showing students when a final *e* must be omitted before the addition of the suffix.

In the discussion of regular and irregular verbs, the texts might offer enough language history to indicate that users of English have generally tended to regularize verbs. It seems natural to us to want the past and past participial forms to be alike and to end in *ed, d,* or *t*. With this explanation students can understand why they sometimes slip and say "throwed," or "drawed," or "knowed." They should also see, however, that we occasionally reverse the process and make regular verbs irregular: probably more people now say "dove" than "dived," though the verb remains regular.

Terms like *voice* and *mood* are bewildering to many students, and, again, some attention to the words themselves should be given. Both are somewhat metaphorical, yet metaphorically they mean about the same thing—manner, treatment, arrangement. By voice in verbs we mean approximately what is meant by the voicing of a musical arrangement, but this parallel should not be pushed too far. Verb properties have to have names; operational definitions are, therefore, probably better here: voice is that property of a verb which indicates whether the subject is acting (active voice) or being acted upon (passive voice); mood is that property which indicates whether the verb is making an assertion (indicative—that is, indicating a state of affairs), giving a command (imperative, from *imperator*—that is, like an emperor), or expressing a condition contrary to fact (subjunctive—to subjoin, that is, to attach or append, as something contingent or possible).

A simple table can clarify for many students the difference between transitive, intransitive, and copulative, or linking, verbs. (Most textbooks now favor the three categories to facilitate student understanding, though the copulative is, properly, a form of intransitive.)

> transitive—shows action and requires an object to complete its meaning.

> intransitive, or intransitive complete—shows action but does not require an object; generally a word of motion, as *walk, go, travel*. Sometimes mistaken for a transitive, as, for example, "He ran a mile." The verb, however is intransitive; the meaning is "He ran *for* a mile." The action of running cannot be performed on the mile.

> copulative, or linking—does not show action and does not take an object. It does require some word, a noun, pronoun, or adjective, to complete its meaning. There are, of course, violations in idiom, as "He is here," though this is in actuality an intransitive complete in the passive with the past participle understood. The construction is intended as something like "He is situated, or located, or found, here."

Several cautions ought to be introduced: (1) English verbs are generally stronger in the active voice. The passive all too often removes the doer from the sentence and thus weakens its force; in addition it seems to evade the responsibility of naming the actor. (2) Whether a verb is transitive, intransitive, or copulative depends entirely on its use in the sentence—verbs can move from one category to another. In the sentence "The soup smells good," *smells* is copulative; in "I smelled the flowers," *smelled* is transitive. (3) The verb *be*, particularly the form *is*, should be resisted as much as possible in favor of verbs that do a good day's work, preferably transitive verbs of action. *Is* is flabby and denies the pleasure of exactness; the adjective following it should be strong and decisive.

Study of the verb should not overlook problems of tense sequence, the logic of time relationships. The sentence horror that we hear all too frequently today—"We would have liked to have gone with you"—does violence to the hearer's sensibility and judgment: how could the two actions possibly have occurred simultaneously? Two solutions exist, depending on our meaning: "I would like (right now) to have gone with you (then)," or "I would have liked (then) to go with you (the liking took place before the going)." Verbals present some difficulties in tense sequense, also. The absurdity of the following sentence can easily be seen. "Locking the door, he ran down the hallway." Mastery of tense sequence in relation to the perfect tenses can be greatly facilitated for our students if we clarify the word "perfect," which, as applied to verb tense, means "perfected" or "finished," "completed." Thus the present perfect tense indicates action which started in the past but is being perfected or finished or, for that matter, merely continuing at present ("I have written her a letter every day for three weeks."). The past perfect tense represents action that started in the past, continued for some time, and then was perfected or completed in the past ("I had written her three letters before I discovered that she had moved."). The future perfect tense shows action that started in the past, is starting at present, or will start in the future, and then continues until it is perfected in the future ("When you arrive at five o'clock, I shall have completed the letter."). Tense sequence need not be baffling once students have a clear picture of the patterns in chronology which our tenses are equipped to handle.

Such, then, are some of the problems in teaching formal grammar, and, let us be quite honest about it, for many of our students grammar will always remain one of the great academic mysteries. Partly this is the fault of the grammar, partly the fault of the teaching, partly the fault of the students. The traditional grammar which we have been using since the origin of American education is unmistakably faulty, and certainly, for some of our students, it does increase the perplexities of communication. Yet many learn it quite fast and quite well and, what is more important, learn to make it serve the full, forceful shaping of their thought. The Yale Committee is right to suggest that teachers of English proceed with caution as they are presented with new schemes of language analysis. We are fond in America of throwing the baby out with the bathwater (the expression has even become cliché) but, as someone observed, one man's baby is another man's bathwater; and a sign of maturity for us all would be that we stop solving our dilemmas on an either-or basis. Because we have a new and exciting way of approaching language study, we are hardly justified in tossing away hurriedly a system of analysis which apparently did not seem cumbersome to the philosophers, scientists, statesmen, and artists who used it to bring into our civilization the ideas which support us. In any case, the teacher who deals with those ideas must know well the formal order of the language in which they are expressed.

CHAPTER FIVE

Structural Linguistics: Purpose and Promise

THE COMMISSION ON THE ENGLISH CURRICULUM of the National Council of Teachers of English in *The English Language Arts in the Secondary School* (1956) comments near the end of the chapter "Developing Competence in Grammar" on important new developments in the teaching of English.

Traditional English grammar, which at the present time is the grammar of English that has been adapted for use in secondary schools, has been justly criticized as not a scientific analysis of the English language, not adequately descriptive of the English language, too prescriptive and authoritarian in attitude, and tending to interfere with careful study of the actual structure of English. Such critical analysis has led both to the attempt to improve the traditional program of grammar and to the formation by students of linguistics of a new, scientifically based structural grammar. At the present time, there is no one analysis of the grammar of English which is universally accepted. In the years immediately ahead there will be seen (1) further attempts to improve the traditional description of grammar, (2) further critical analysis and refinement of the new structural grammar, and (3) experimentation with the adaptation of the new structural grammar for the secondary schools. The effort is not to avoid grammar but to find the most truly descriptive grammar of English.

In an earlier publication of the National Council of Teachers of English (*The English Language Arts in the Secondary Curriculum*, 1952), five basic concepts evolved by linguists were announced.

1. *Language changes constantly*. Changes, however, have too

often been deplored or ignored. It became the task of the linguists of the present century to point out the nature and significance of these changes.

2. *Change is normal.* In *Growth and Structure of the English Language,* Otto Jespersen says, "Change in language is not corruption but improvement: changes which take place in all languages, but especially in English, are in the direction of simplification and clarification."

3. *The spoken language is the language.* Speech determines usage more than the written word. As a matter of fact, the written word is really a form of dialect. Changes in speech precede morphological change. In the essay "The Status of Linguistics as a Science," Edward Sapir writes, "Historical and comparative linguistics has been built up chiefly on the basis of the hypothesis that sound changes are regular and that most morphological readjustments in language follow as by-products in the wake of these regular phonetic developments. There are many who would be disposed to deny the psychological necessity of the regularity of sound change, but it remains true, as a matter of actual linguistic experience, that faith in such regularity has been the most successful approach to the historic problems of language."

4. *Correctness rests upon usage.* Grammar should be descriptive, not prescriptive. According to the structural linguists, one of the fundamental errors made by eighteenth-century grammarians was that they saw grammar only as prescriptive. "With the impact of linguistic studies in the twentieth century, the relationships of correctness to use has been made clear."

5. *All usage is relative.* The distinction between "good" English and "bad" English should give way to the recognition of the levels of usage. The appropriateness of language to a social situation rather than a single standard of usage should be recognized. [This has already been discussed in Chapter One.] "A teacher is not to teach any one form of speech as correct or incorrect but to develop in the pupil the same sensitivity to the appropriateness of language in each situation which he himself has developed."

To these five basic concepts, several others would now be added by linguists.

Stress, intonation, and pitch are of major importance. Stress, insist a number of the linguists, is often a better indication of meaning and syntactical relationships than the traditional parts-of-speech terminology. Writing on "The Importance of Phonology in Grammar" in the Reports and Speeches of the Third Yale Conference on the Teaching of English, Henry Lee Smith, Jr., said, "Through them [intonation patterns] we receive over and over again signals as to when subject stops and predicate begins, when complement starts and verbal material ends, when 'adclausal' material joins on to complement or is 'interjected' before a principal sentence starts. And this is accomplished whether we have normal word order or whether one of the many inversions are used which abound in the written language, especially in poetry."

In a clever and illuminating section on the uses of the preposition "to," Smith demonstrates "how stresses can serve unerringly to differentiate the 'same word' in different grammatical functions. For instance, there are five syntactic uses of the little word 'to,' but our written language distinguishes only two." He comments also on the importance of his investigation for student writing. "The fact that in certain cases the written form of English has no regular way of representing certain relationships that are carried by phonological signals in the spoken language is one of the main causes of the mistakes we find in our themes and compositions."

Form is often more revealing than meaning. For this reason, structural linguists give a great deal of attention to sentence patterns. To demonstrate the primary importance of form, they use nonsense words in regular syntactical patterns. Though we do not know what the words mean, subject, predicate, object, object of preposition, and modifiers are all clearly identifiable. The structural linguist prefers to reverse the pattern of the traditional grammarian who went to meaning to get at the form. The structural linguist studies the form and then goes on to meaning.

Traditional sentence analysis does not deal accurately, or at least not adequately, with the structure of the English sentence. The sentence is *not*, or at least it is *not always*, a group of words expressing a complete thought. Complete thoughts are often transmitted in something less than traditional sentence arrangement. Furthermore, many word arrangements which we would accept without hesitation as having satisfied the proprieties of a complete thought defy syntactical analysis altogether. The structural linguist demonstrates that this situation is particularly evident in spoken English. Communication of thought is carried out quite effectively in many more diverse ways than are allowed for by the dicta of traditional sentence structure. The linguist asks us to be alert to the many patterns of verbal communication characteristic of our language today. He is not antagonistic to the analytical insights which are provided by traditional study; he merely insists that it is not adequate, not sufficiently comprehensive, not genuinely scientific. As we would not want an inadequate chemistry, biology, or physics to describe natural phenomena, so we do not want an inadequate science of language. Thorough and diligent investigation must always be going on, and it must supplement in the classroom the somewhat limited grammar upon which teachers of English have traditionally insisted.

Recently William G. Perry, Jr., Director of the Bureau of Study Counsel at Harvard College, permitted me to see printed versions of interviews with Harvard freshmen. These young men represent verbal aptitude at probably the highest student level in American education. Their College Board scores are very impressive indeed. Yet in speaking to Mr. Perry's counselors about academic problems, they used, casually and naturally, a kind of English for which there would be little textbook prescription or approval. The situation of the interview was one in which clarity of thought was of major importance if the student was to be helped. That his remarks were entirely comprehensible to the interviewer was apparent from the interviewer's responses and suggestions. Completeness of thought was coming through in word patterns which would be the despair of someone intent on traditional sentence diagramming.

To summarize, the linguists are saying, as Karl Dykema puts it in an article titled "Progress in Grammar," "The trouble with classical formal grammar as a description of English is not so much that it is wrong as that it is incomplete. Worst of all, it is an incomplete description which pretends to completeness, and that is its fatal weakness."

It is scarcely possible to do justice to structural linguistics in a single chapter; the subject is large and complex. Teachers of English who are interested—and all should be—ought to become thoroughly familiar with the material and even, if possible, enroll in a course in linguistics in a nearby university. Only now are the books and articles on the implications of structural linguistics for the classroom beginning to appear. In Harold B. Allen's collection of essays titled *Applied English Linguistics*, there are important sections on "Linguistics and the Teaching of Grammar and Composition," and "Linguistics and the Study of Literature." A basic contention of the structural linguists is that skill in language will be more easily acquired by our students when we have a system which truly describes the way in which the English language functions. They are concerned, therefore, to set up a system which *will* be fully descriptive. This involves them naturally in the construction of new terms and new definitions, and the teacher who has been brought up traditionally, like most of us, is likely to be somewhat bewildered and confused at the outset.

Structural linguistics is still in its infancy, and many clarifications and refinements must still occur. Some of the linguists themselves are doubtful of the advisability of bringing linguistic considerations into the secondary school classroom, except in very elementary form, until much more research has been accomplished. A few disciples have been too zealous, a few teachers have been too enthusiastic, and the result has been a number of unfortunate and something less than fair-minded and informed attacks. The strictures of J. Donald Adams in the New York *Times* Book Review and of Mortimer Smith in the Bulletin of the Council for Basic Education have much less to do with the science of language than with etiquette and social manners, but their impatience stems very likely from their seeing wholesale adoption of programs in linguistics which are not yet sufficiently understood. Quite simply, much work needs to be done, and the first job is that of clarification of terms. It is, of course, doubtful that the efforts of the structural linguists to construct a reasonable description of how our language operates will provide the impetus to language anarchy, yet this is one of the most persistent charges against them. No student of language in his right mind ever said, "Whatever is, is right." When the charge was made in a responsible and informed manner several years ago by I. A. Richards, answers were offered by a variety of language scholars, and Mr. Adams and Mr. Smith should know what they said. They ought also to know Otto Jespersen's theory of energetics, restated in Jespersen's *Efficiency in Linguistic Change*, 1941.

Many teachers of English are not willing to surrender the prescriptive prerogatives of language study, and the structural linguists would not insist that they do so. The reasonable position is merely that the linguist would ask the teacher to know thoroughly what is being prescribed and what it is being prescribed for. Obviously this will require the teacher of English to be a more diligent student of language than he has usually been in the past, for he must begin with firm renunciation of the convictions of the purist, namely, that the rules of grammar and sentence structure are absolute, final, and fixed.

We do the structural linguists an injustice to think of them as being concerned exclusively with a new grammar—with word groups, syntax and the structure of sentences. Their interests are much broader. One of these is to show how languages are related to one another, so that some attention to linguistic science will help in the mastery of all languages. As a matter of fact, some of the major advances in structural linguistics have occurred in teaching English to foreign students.

Furthermore, a number of the structural linguists are interested in what their discoveries may contribute to the study of literature. As Margaret Schlauch points out in *The Gift of Language,* their work can assist very effectively in the study of modern writing, where the obscurities of such writers as Joyce, Eliot, Hart Crane, Gerard Manley Hopkins, and even Gertrude Stein are dispelled by careful attention to linguistic findings. Language is, after all, the sole material with which the literary artist works, and he is thus severely the victim of its history. It is the rare artist, like Joyce, who tries to extricate himself from this history and extend the boundaries of language. Even then he is securely bound. The daring verbal pyrotechnics of *Finnegans Wake* are possible only because there is a discipline to depart from, a rationale which makes the departure into magic believable.

Chiefly under investigation, of course, is the possibility of a dynamic new relationship between structural linguistics and composition; and linguists and teachers of English alike, though cautious, are hopeful. More than anything else, this means a positive approach to the student's writing as we notice and applaud every one of his demonstrations of language achievement and as we make him constantly aware of language achievement in the world around him. The teacher who knows linguistics will understand that the student comes into the class with a high degree of language skill, in ways that many teachers are unable or unwilling to recognize and honor. The composition program must seize upon the language success which is already his, compliment it, and then build positively beyond it.

To know the evolutionary character of language, to understand something about the processes of change, to see that man constantly adjusts his invention to his needs and joys is to begin to be more comfortable with it. To look at language positively in the classroom—to analyze a passage of literature rhetorically to see how the author accomplishes his success; to hear and applaud the theme of a classmate because it made a strong point to which the whole class responded; to be in an English class in which the teacher, through informed linguistic study, is always making the student aware of how well he can already use language and of how much better he can use it after increased understanding and practice of it—this is to begin to learn to write.

The negative approach begins with the way in which the teacher's attention to a student's theme is described. We say that it is being "corrected," that is, made right. We start, in other words, with the conviction that it is faulty or full of errors. These errors the teacher marks precisely and then refers the student to an appropriate section of a handbook for review of the "rules" covering his defections. Usually, also, the student is asked to correct a few exercise sentences filled with errors of the kind to which he is prone, and then to hand in the corrected theme and the corrected exercise sentences. This is not to teach composition. We cannot teach good writing by showing students bad writing. Let us work positively and show them good writing everywhere that it is to be found. But, most of all, let us show it to them in their own work. They are probably more accomplished than we think. The linguist helps us to see that accomplishment.

But, apart from these functional considerations, there is a humanistic prerogative for linguistic study. Near the end of his book *The Structure of English*, Charles Carpenter Fries writes of it eloquently.

The chief use and value of a descriptive analysis of the structure of English, however, does not seem to me to lie in any of the five matters just discussed, or in all of them together [the teaching of English as a foreign language, avoidance of ambiguous constructions, more accurate punctuation, greater variety in sentence structure, better grasp of the devices for communicating meaning]. I believe fundamentally in *education* as distinct from *training*. Training seems to me usefulness or value in terms of output or product, with the individual person as the means. His skills are developed so that he can do things. Education, in contrast with training, seems to stress the individual himself as the end, and measures usefulness and value in terms of the contribution to the freedom and development of individual personality. From this point of view, I should insist that the chief value of a systematic analysis and description of the signals of structural meaning in English is the insight it can give concerning the way our language works, and, through English, into the nature and functioning of human languages.

In an article "Grammar or Gramarye" James Sledd asks the most important question of all: "What is the purpose of grammatical instruction? Is it only the narrowly practical purpose of enabling students, in their writing, to conform to some arbitrary set of rules, or is it also the humanistic purpose of advancing the study of man as proper to mankind?" His answer: "I teach [grammar] for a good reason. The proper study of mankind *is* man, and there is nothing so basic to our humanity as our language."

Mr. Sledd's book *A Short Introduction to English Grammar*, which he describes as an "interim" book, that is, a book for the condition in which we now find ourselves, the condition of being somewhere between the traditional and the modern linguistic points of view, has specific and valuable suggestions for the English class. Most realistic is his appraisal of what must immediately be done and of the cautions we must observe in doing it.

What now, in summary, does the present situation demand of a grammarian who believes that English grammar should be an important part of the general education of American citizens and of the special education of English teachers? The general direction in which he should move is clear: the conventional schoolroom grammar is defective and must be brought more nearly in line with the principles and methods of contemporary linguistics. The movement in this direction is already too strong to be resisted, even if resistance were wise. Yet the schoolroom tradition is the only grammatical tradition which many teachers, students, and laymen now know; it is not totally false or misguided; and since contemporary linguistics is not monolithic but various, alive, and changing, no one can offer a new description of English as a grammatical faith in which the untutored may finally and safely rest. Only the lightminded opponents of *any* grammatical training will profit if the change from old grammars to new is attempted too arrogantly or too rapidly.

In "Grammar or Gramarye" Mr. Sledd indicates what a truly descriptive grammar of English would be. It includes, he tells us, phonology, morphology, and syntax. Of the first two matters, many teachers of secondary school English today would know little. The whole subject of English grammar is enormous.

An adequate phonological statement involves, among other things, the distinction between phonetics and phonemics and the description of the English vowels, consonants, stresses, pitches, and junctures. The morphology can be separated from the syntax only by some kind of definition of the word as distinct from larger forms, and within the morphology one must deal with such thorny questions as the distinctions between inflection and derivation and between the native and foreign derivational patterns. In the syntax, one must establish a number of "parts of speech," some of them large open classes like nouns, others small closed classes like prepositions; one must somehow relate these syntactic classes to morphological classes defined in terms of inflection or derivation or both; one must establish a concept of modification or expansion and state the positions of modifiers of noun heads and verb heads; one must describe the favorite sentence patterns for statements, questions, and requests; etc., etc. The barest outline of such a description is a lesson in modesty . . .

The purpose of structural linguistics, then, is that we should know the whole domain of language, and the promise is that this knowledge will be, for the first time, accurate and constructive, and that our knowing it and caring about it are measures of our humanity. Reading what the structural linguists have written, some teachers of English are still cautious. They await what Mr. Sledd proposes and, in his own book, has, to a very great extent, brought about: the joining of the old and the new. Their position is best expressed, perhaps, by a comment which was made in *The American Scholar* several years ago by Jacques Barzun in writing about H. W. Fowler. Said Mr. Barzun, "Fowler showed by his precepts and by his style what it could mean to take a reasoned view of the democratic citizen's duty toward language. It meant making an effort to be understood but also to seek the best; it meant forgetting ego but not distinction. To that extent Fowler was aristocratic. The word *usage* once conveyed the combined obligations—the social one of pleasing by simplicity and clarity and suitability of language; and the intellectual one of respect for tradition and reason through a conscious choice of the best forms."

To know the subject of structural linguistics adequately, teachers of English need acquaintance with some of the following books:

Allen, Harold B., ed. *Applied English Linguistics*. Appleton, 1958.
Bloomfield, Leonard. *Language*. Holt, Rinehart and Winston, 1933.
Carroll, John. *The Study of Language*. Harvard, 1955.
Chomsky, Noam. *Syntactic Structures*. G. Lounz, 1957.
Francis, W. Nelson. *The Structure of American English*. Ronald, 1958.
Fries, Charles. *The Structure of English: An Introduction to the Construction of English Sentences*. Harcourt, 1952.
Fries, Charles. *The Teaching of the English Language*. Nelson, 1927.
Hall, Robert A. *Leave Your Language Alone*. Linguistica, 1950.
Hill, Archibald A. *Introduction to Linguistic Structures*. Harcourt, 1958.
Lloyd, Donald J., and Warfel, Harry R. *American English in its Cultural Setting*. Knopf, 1956.
Pooley, Robert. *Teaching English Grammar*. Appleton, 1957.
Pooley, Robert. *Teaching English Usage*. Appleton, 1946.

Roberts, Paul. *Patterns of English*. Harcourt, 1956.

Roberts, Paul. *Understanding Grammar*. Harper, 1954.

Roberts, Paul. *Understanding English*. Harper, 1958.

Sapir, Edward. *Culture, Language, and Personality. Selected Essays edited by David G. Mandelbaum*. Univ. of California, 1956.

Sapir, Edward. *Language, An Introduction to the Study of Speech*. Harcourt, Harvest Books, 1949.

Sledd, James. *A Short Introduction to English Grammar*. Scott, Foresman, 1959.

Smith, Henry Lee, Jr. *Linguistic Science and the Teaching of English*. Harvard, 1956.

Trager, George L. and Smith, Henry Lee, Jr. *An Outline of English Structure. Studies in Linguistics:* Occasional Papers, No. 3, 1951.

Whitehall, Harold. *Structural Essentials of English*. Harcourt, 1956.

Whorf, Benjamin Lee. *Language, Thought and Reality*. Technology Press, 1956.

A brief, though useful, sketch of some of the general principles of structural linguistics is "The 'New Grammar,' " the reprint of five short pieces which appeared in the Scholastic Teacher Edition of *Practical English* in 1958. It can be secured by writing to Scholastic Magazines, Inc., 33 West 42nd Street, New York 36, New York.

CHAPTER SIX

Writing Is for _All_: A Practical Program

A BASIC APPROACH

ON THE SUBJECT of English composition Dr. James B. Conant, in _The American High School Today_, is clear, direct, and positive.

The time devoted to English composition during the four years should occupy about half the total time devoted to the study of English. Each student should be required to write an average of one theme a week. Themes should be corrected by the teacher. In order that teachers of English have adequate time for handling these themes, no English teacher should be responsible for more than one hundred pupils.

To test the ability of each student in English composition, a school-wide composition test should be given in every grade; in the ninth and eleventh grades, these composition tests should be graded not only by the teacher but by a committee of the entire school. Those students who do not obtain a grade on the eleventh-grade composition test commensurate with their ability as measured by an aptitude test should be required to take a special course in English composition in the twelfth grade.

Many teachers of English have long hoped for just such a statement as Dr. Conant's. In only a very few schools do we find students writing a theme a week, and the principal reason why they do not is that teachers of English at present meet too many students in the course of a day. The number of pupils in a high school class now ranges from, in most public schools, a minimum of twenty-five to—there is no maximum—forty or forty-five. Most teachers of English have a five-period day, and by simple multiplication, one can see that a theme a week for this number of students means approximately 150 to 200 papers. If the theme-writing exercise is to have any value at all, the paper must be carefully marked and returned to the student, who should then revise it and, ideally, have a conference with his teacher about it. All of this takes time, and in many places teachers long ago gave up any hope of ever trying to accomplish it. The result is that many students write only occasionally—perhaps once or twice a semester; some never write at all.

But for the neglect of composition there are reasons other than the large numbers of students. Many teachers remain unconvinced of the primary importance of writing. They see composition as something which only the college-bound student needs, and they feel that he will pick up compositional skill somewhere along the way, probably from his reading. Altogether too many of our teachers of English still have the scientifically fallacious notion that a great deal of reading or abundant drill work in grammar will produce effective writing. They assume that their responsibilities to the student are discharged if a large number of elegant essays in his literature text are assigned and a number of faulty sentences in a grammar workbook corrected. If the student writes for them at all, they give attention only to mechanical errors on his papers. His themes come back dripping in red ink, every misplaced comma marked, an innocuous grade (usually a C+) at the top, with some noncommittal remark like "Shows improvement" or "Interesting in spots." The student takes a cursory glance at the grade, shrugs, and throws the essay into the wastepaper basket. What difference does it make?

In other schools, composition is neglected for what I would regard as the most unfortunate reason of all: the teacher's feeling that to teach composition is somehow beneath his professional dignity. This is part of what we might call the "marching-band" movement in American public school education, the imitation of the college all the way down into the elementary grades. Colleges have immense, dramatic marching bands; we see them at football games between the halves; people who have never actually seen a game watch the bands on television. The result: six-year elementary schools now have marching bands. For what reason? So they can play between the halves of football games; for the grade school has a varsity football team, too, complete with coach, professional-type equipment, playing field, locker room, showers, and hydrotherapy. The student's advancement into junior high school sees an intensification of this activity, and of course the pageantry in senior high school has now advanced to homecoming celebrations with downtown parades, the return of old grads, and the crowning of a king and queen. The aping of the college is complete.

What this means to the teaching of composition is that many teachers of English cannot seem to put aside their college experience in literature. They insist on bringing it down into the junior and senior high school with them. Teaching English means teaching the literary classics they studied in college. So ninth-grade students read *The Turn of the Screw* and discuss its symbolism; *The Young Manhood of Studs Lonigan* appears on the seventh-grade reading list (I have seen it there), and eleventh-grade boys read *The Immoralist*. A recent book on the teaching of English recommends as appropriate high school reading *Samson Agonistes* ("nothing in all Milton's prose or poetry is as easy as *Samson Agonistes*"), *Prometheus Unbound*, and *The Cenci*. The serious literary scholar who knows these works intimately is likely to shudder. The difficulties of all three poems are enormous. Such professors of literature as Douglas Bush and I. A. Richards have confessed their inability to solve to their satisfaction many of the problems of meaning in *Prometheus*. The high school youngster who could read this poem with any degree of secure understanding and esthetic satisfaction would be a rare student indeed—rare to the point of not needing a teacher in the first place. The eleven-year-old daughter of a friend of mine was recently given by her seventh-grade teacher *St. Mawr* by D. H. Lawrence to read. "I hear it's a wonderful story about a horse," the youngster's teacher had said. My friend returned the book to the teacher with a note. "Kate doesn't have time for this right now," he wrote. "She's reading *Black Beauty*."

The traditional literary materials of the secondary school can certainly stand reassessment; a number of them need to be replaced with fresher, more stimulating works, but let us by all means keep our sanity. Let us not insist upon Proust before puberty.

It is easy to see how composition suffers at the hands of such a teacher as I describe. Composition, he feels, is something which ought to have been done somewhere else—before the students got to him. If his students write at all, they are asked to do "creative" things or, what is often worse, "critical exercises." Little imagistic poems flow out of the room on a conveyor belt ("The birch tree/In a dust storm/Is a Russian ballet dancer/In the tawdry dressing room/Of an Indiana high school auditorium"), and boys and girls are sent searching for death symbols in Edgar Allan Poe.

Never do students experience the systematic writing *unit* which begins with discussion of an issue or an observation wholly within their understanding and interest, which proceeds then to consideration of problems of organization, which requires the writing (in class) of the student's thoughtful reaction to the question, which returns to the student the teacher's analysis of his paper (largely a matter of the questioning of the student's assertions or the suggesting of further clarification); which asks the student to make an appointment to talk the paper over with the teacher, who, in conference, suggests a date when the revised paper should be returned to be made part of the student's permanent-record folder which will indicate what progress, or lack of it, the student is making in the written expression of his thought. *This* is composition. *This* is the kind of activity which the Conant report advocates.

Dr. Conant does not say that the work in composition he recommends should be limited to certain kinds of students—the "gifted" or the college-bound or the above-average or, for that matter, the below-average. Writing is for *all*, for the most brilliant as well as the most limited. If we look at the matter only in an exclusively practical way, we must acknowledge that communication in a technological age demands clarity and precision above everything else. The status of the individual matters very little: clear, straightforward expository expression is as much the need of the steelworker as of the corporation executive or research scientist. Experience in composition is experience in the shaping of thought. The composition program in the schools must develop from the fundamental understanding of the reciprocal relationship between thinking and writing. The effort to put a thought into words is a means of discovering what we want to say.

Several years ago, I asked my tenth-grade students to write paragraphs of personal experience indicating how a significant event in their lives had been quite the opposite of what they had expected. We had read a story or two of this variety and had talked the stories over carefully, and I felt that the students might profit from an assignment of having to search through their lives for an occasion which, because it was so very different from what they had imagined it to be, probably had some part in helping them to understand the world better. Here is a paragraph submitted by a Negro girl.

They said all facilities would be separate but equal. At nine I couldn't have objected to separation. I didn't even mind the inequality—then.

I had come from New York where from kindergarten through the second grade I had gone to school with all kinds of children. I remember that on my street a little Italian girl who ate a big plate of spaghetti or rice for dinner walked to school with my brother and me. In our school yard just about any language could be heard—and each child was understood. I don't remember noticing a distinct change when we moved to Dallas. I was a big attraction at school because the children always begged me to talk. "You talk and act proper," my school mates used to say. I didn't even mind the wooden steps all through the school—the auditorium that was the same size as a classroom. All this I didn't mind until one day when Daddy took us riding and I saw *their* school.

And they had said separate but equal.

By almost any standards that could be applied to it, this is a remarkable paragraph. It is excellently shaped, it moves with a fine sense of both logical and chronological order, and, as the sports writer would say, it "packs a terrific punch." A fifteen-year-old could scarcely be expected to do better with the assignment.

I insert the paragraph for several reasons. First, there is a widespread opinion in some academic circles that, for reasons never clearly specified, today's student cannot be taught to write; that he is incapable of learning precision and clarity of statement, let alone fluency and grace of style, through instruction; and that we waste our efforts in hoping for logical force and rhetorical ease. Faced with such a paragraph as this which I have reproduced, the critics would only grudgingly admit that the student must have been a superior one, a "gifted" child, with a special talent for writing. But this is not true. When I first encountered this student, she was barely able to put a sentence together. Whatever she acquired in the ability to write was gained through careful practice and attention. Nothing should anger teachers of English more than the view that only a few students can learn to write well and that the achievement of clear, expository prose must forever remain impossible to others. Sir Herbert Read says, "Poets are born, not made, but the ability is given to every man of average intelligence to write clear, orderly prose."

The reason why today's students do not write well is that composition has been taught too little and too unsystematically. Not that there has not been a considerable amount of writing done in some places; on the other hand, some—a few—schools, mostly the private ones, have been fulfilling the Conant aim and have had their students writing at least a paper a week. But even here the results have not been all that was hoped for. For just to write is not enough: the composition program must proceed in a systematic way through high school years. It must be a sequential study, like mathematics or science; the youngster must learn to crawl, then to walk, then to run, and then—if the Muse touches him—to fly. The syllabus for composition work should be carefully planned, carefully detailed, and carefully followed, with the whole perspective of the high school English program, even the whole perspective of the high school curriculum, in mind.

It goes without saying that writing should be a part of every activity in the English class. Writing experience should grow out of the lessons in sentence structure, grammar, usage, and especially literature. We must encourage students to write on what they have read: give them topics which will require an interpretation of a story or poem or a section of a longer work. Again may I insist that the topics be kept within the range of student understanding—let's avoid topics like "The Symbolic Presentation of Narrative Epiphany in *Dubliners* by James Joyce." (I hope it will not seem to the reader that I am inventing these esoteric topics. I have seen assigned to high school students every one which is quoted in this chapter.) But certainly students can write clear expository paragraphs about evidence of conflicting economic classes in *The House of the Seven Gables,* or whether Macbeth really sees or only imagines that he sees the witches, or where Huckleberry Finn stood on the question of slavery. However, students must do more than write merely on literature. This practice gives the course an air of professionalism, as if the only function of the English class is to turn out writers, teachers of literature, or literary critics. The high school English program must serve the complete man and the whole curriculum. Expository and persuasive writing, with exercises on a wide variety of subjects, are essential.

To repeat, the kind of skill we want can be accomplished only through constant practice. Ability in the written expression of thought cannot be achieved through sentence structure or drill in grammar or through the reading of essays in the hope that a sense of paragraphing will filter through from the stylistic charm of Lamb or Macaulay. The student can be helped through the analysis of good pieces of writing to see what their successes are, but knowing these is no guarantee that he will be able to use them. He must sit down before a blank sheet of paper and struggle—there is no other way.

He must, furthermore, be given some sensible motive for writing, and in this connection an excellent statement is to be found in

Chapter 4, "How To Write and Be Read," of Jacques Barzun's *Teacher in America*. Professor Barzun rightly says that there is only one valid motive for writing: the desire to be read. And let us be honest enough to admit that we generally do not care to read what the youngster writes, that we regard the reading of his paragraphs as a chore or a violation of our esthetic souls, and that, like as not, we make our boredom obvious when we assign the writing exercise or return the papers.

Barzun is equally helpful on what the student should write about. He says quite succinctly, "A child should select a topic that truly engages his interest. To eliminate pretense he must be helped to do this by means of questions and suggestions." Don't ask for "A Vacation Experience" or "My Favorite Aunt" or "A Pet I Once Had" or, to take one of the howlers from Barzun, "I Am the Mississippi River." Once I had to read a batch of themes, handed in on the first day of the fall term, on "Time To Read during the Summer." Of course the themes were written the night before they were due and had no relation whatever to a summer reading program. Even worse were the themes I read some years ago for an American Legion essay contest on the topic "What American Freedom Means to Me." May I suggest to all people who assign such topics that one of the surest ways to lose freedom is to make a constant demand that young people say what it is. What Edgar Allan Poe once called "the imp of the perverse" is likely to start its operations, and young people will run for relief to something which freedom most certainly is not.

In my judgment, the high school writing program should avoid *long* papers, papers of more than 1000 words. Generally these are a signal for running to the encyclopedia or the library—the impetus to plagiarism, borrowing, paraphrase, and quotation. Short papers of not more than 300 words are enough—at least at the start. At the Yale Conference on the Teaching of English several years ago, Arthur Mizener said, "The single paragraph of five or six sentences raises all the problems of a longer composition." Certainly it gives instruction in organizing and shaping a single thought. For the first year or two composition in the secondary school, in grades seven and eight, that is, ought to be limited to very short pieces, chiefly to paragraphs. The teacher must insist that in each paragraph a single, clear, orderly thought be presented to the reader. This is enough at first. As a matter of fact, the colleges would be very happy if *only* paragraph writing were accomplished in *all* of the students who come to them.

I have insisted already that papers must be marked carefully, returned, corrected, revised and made part of the student's record of progress, and that his composition work be a matter of regular conference. Today's teacher of English simply must have time to talk individually with students about their writing. This is an educational imperative, and if it means fewer classes and fewer students, so be it. That a large part of the composition work should be impromptu is also generally accepted now—personally, I think one-fourth a desirable amount. Teachers may make the impromptu theme an exercise in analysis, supplying the students with a "springboard" quotation and then requiring comment on it in the way of elucidation and interpretation. Equally effective is the extemporaneous exercise which grows out of interest in a problem which has excited the public imagination at a given moment, something, that is, which is in the news.

In this connection it is easy to help the student see that composition is not a technique limited to the uses and interests of the English class; he learns that skill in writing is to serve him in every activity he undertakes. For this reason we must insist with our colleagues that composition cannot be taught exclusively in a course in English; it can be taught only by the united efforts of the entire teaching staff, for this is the only way to assure accuracy in every subject. If the student is writing badly in English class, then he is writing badly in history, physics, geometry, if, in this day of the objective test, he is writing in these courses at all. Perhaps one of our first efforts should be that of getting our colleagues in other subjects to require some writing in their classes.

But the teaching of compositional skills must ultimately concern itself with the manner of dealing sensibly with grammar, sentence structure, the mechanics of English in general. Here the teacher of English ought to be conscious always of a simple truism easily lost sight of when one uses manuals, workbooks, and drill exercises, namely, that the conventions of language mechanics exist solely to facilitate communication and not for their own sake. This simple assertion cannot be made too frequently. The question of verb agreement, let us say, is best raised *after* the need for clarification has been demonstrated in composition work. From the first themes of the year the teacher can select various errors and discuss these with students in class. Again, it cannot be said too often that attention to grammar should become a positive and constructive performance, demonstrating through language success how the so-called "rules" affect the expression of thought, rather than negative and analytic. The "rules" are honored because they help the clear and forceful communication of ideas. Studies have demonstrated that pupils who were taught English in this manner and those who were taught by the more direct method of manuals, workbooks, and drill exercises score about the same on tests and examinations, but the advantage for the pupil of the first experience is that his training goes on beyond the examination—it becomes a functioning part of his whole existence.

Work in the writing of paragraphs can include the analysis of other paragraphs, not necessarily by the great writers of the literary past, but by the professional authors of the daily paper and the weekly magazine. This is an inductive approach which will bring about the definition of a paragraph as the rounded development of an idea; students will see that the paragraph is effectively formed when a thought is fully or exhaustively explored; that a paragraph is not a group of sentences loosely hurled together, but that it represents the thoughtful shaping of an idea which is generally expressed at the opening of the paragraph. In this exercise the topic sentence is introduced, and, again by studying the paragraphs of others, students see how topic sentences have a shaping effect on the method of paragraph organization. The idea which the paragraph is to explore determines the method of exploration. Students list what seem the most frequent of these methods of development: (1) examples, illustrations, anecdotes, (2) particulars and details, (3) definition, (4) comparison and contrast, (5) cause and effect, (6) enumeration, (7) repetition, (8) analogy, and various combinations of these methods. Often I have given the class sample topic sentences, and we have discussed the way in which the method of paragraph development is announced by the sentence itself. As an assignment I have given them additional sentences, asking them to indicate which method the sentences would seem to indicate and then to take any two of the sentences and develop them into full paragraphs. Here are ten sentences which I have occasionally used:

1. No one should have been surprised by the recent election results.
(Cause and effect. Why not surprised? I was.)

2. Trying out for a school play is a grueling experience.
(Examples, illustrations. Is it? Show me.)

3. Though on the surface they might seem to have much in common, the soldier and the sailor have vastly different responsibilities.

(Comparison and/or contrast. How are their duties different or alike?)

4. The term "nonobjective painting" has been subjected to many nonobjective misinterpretations.
(Definition. What do *you* say it is?)

5. The quality of mercy is not strained.
(Analogy. Remember how Shakespeare did it: "It droppeth as the gentle rain from heaven"?)

6. Someone has said that social conditions in the South are the result of two races sharing half a loaf of bread.
(Cause and effect probably. How did things get that way? Still, there are other possibilities—maybe a combination of methods would be best.)

7. The personality differences between Patton and Montgomery were always apparent in the military tactics they used.
(Particulars and details. What were they like? Also, perhaps, comparison and contrast.)

8. The epic poem is nothing more than a highly sophisticated folk tale.
(Repetition preferably. A challenging idea should be restated in different words.)

9. Does today's student need more or less grammar than his parents received?
(Tricky—tossing in a question. How about cause and effect? The paragraph would have to give reasons for one position or the other.)

10. Courage and wisdom often go hand in hand.
(Analogy. Get these abstractions down to earth where we can see them.)

The objectives of this study of the paragraph are clear enough: the teacher wants students to see that an idea must be worked with, shaped, explored, exhausted of its full potential; that the development of the idea must have a logical beginning, middle, and end. Students' paragraphs, as a rule, are woefully underdeveloped; an idea is no sooner stated than dropped. It stands out isolated and alone, with nothing to support it or lead it toward other ideas. Constant work in paragraphing will, above everything else, make the student aware of how much development ideas are worth—of how much more attention than others some ideas deserve—and of how much revision and refinement ideas require to emerge with clarity, accuracy, and conviction.

True, when we sit down to write, we do not, as a rule, figure out what method of development we will use for individual paragraphs. As we have seen, the nature of the development is generally predetermined by the idea itself. Furthermore, teacher and students will often disagree over what method of development might be most effective in a particular case. There is every reason why they should disagree. But no student can come out of this unit without the realization that there is more to writing good prose than he imagined—but, equally, that the writing of good paragraphs *is possible for him*.

Some teachers of composition caution against too much work with the topic sentence. They demonstrate that many paragraphs get along perfectly well without one, and that in paragraphs of narration and description the topic sentence is likely to be a rarity. Besides, they reason, the skilled writer almost never plans his work in the self-conscious way of putting a topic sentence together and then building his paragraph around it. Too much explicit instruction in writing can be harmful, they feel; the sensible procedure is to arouse the child intellectually or emotionally so that he will not be able to resist expression.

There is a great deal to what they say, and work with the topic sentence can certainly allow for the kind of paragraph, in any form of writing, which avoids the single organizing statement. And we have already faced the objection that skilled writers do not plan paragraphs so explicitly as the suggestions here might seem to indicate. Attention to the structure of the paragraph need not deny the value of good motivation; on the contrary, motivation and organization should be complementary. But it is difficult to see how composition can proceed in anything other than an aimlessly impressionistic fashion unless repeated attention is given to the processes of logical development. The analogy of the automobile driver is perhaps apt. The skilled driver no longer operates his car in such a way as to be fully aware of what he is doing; he does not say, Now I release the brake pedal; now I press the accelerator; now I put the car in "Drive," and so on. These operations have become automatic; he does them without thinking. Yet there was a time in his preparation to drive when these acts were separate and deliberate and he had to give them conscious thought. Practice has made them automatic.

So it is with the writing of paragraphs. With practice, the writer acquires an automatic paragraph sense which guides him *almost* without thought. But only—as with the car driver—*almost*. The moments inevitably arrive when thought must take over, when the driver has to prove that his manipulation of the vehicle is something more than impressionistic guessing, when he has to show, in short, that he has the vehicle under control. In these moments the student who has worked diligently with the topic sentence as an instrument of control has something to fall back on.

MARKING STUDENT PAPERS

If there is order in the syllabus, if the writing moves progressively from assignment to assignment and from year to year, students will be able to observe their progress, and a sense of achievement will prompt them to move forward in eagerness. In order that they can see this progress, the marking of their papers should be thorough and informative. The following suggestions may be of some benefit.

Make the comments direct and personal. Insist that the student give you plenty of marginal space or space between the lines so that you can talk with him, question him about meaning, tease him a bit about blunders. The very best kind of marking is that in which the teacher sets up a marginal dialogue with the student, the remarks to be discussed more fully and resolved in the conference. Barzun's suggestions about the kind of marginal comment to make are excellent. In a manner that demonstrates that you care about what the student is doing, get under his skin. Show him where and how he has slipped and that you know he can do better.

Compliment him wherever and whenever possible. Some teachers, rightly, in my judgment, feel that a paper should never be returned unless the student receives some word of encouragement and praise. Remember that nothing which the student does for you or anyone else is so much a product of his own effort as a composition. It is his *creation;* no part of it existed before he sat down at a desk with a pencil. With all of the solecisms, tortuous constructions, and upside-down logic which it may contain, he is nonetheless proud of it. Don't massacre him. Of course, this determination to compliment the student may set you to scratching your head at times. You will feel that in some cases about all you can say is, "That's an interesting shade of ink you're using," or

"I like the way you observe margins." Most of the time, however, something stands out—a clever use of idiom, a colorful comparison, an unexpectedly mature judgment. Show the student that you approve.

Unless you are working with very advanced students on the highest grade levels, don't try to mark every error on every paper. Some teachers prefer to concentrate on one or two kinds of error per theme. A paper all covered over with the reader's marks can be woefully discouraging, particularly to the student who is trying hard for the first time. Concentrate on one or two difficulties and let the student work for a paper or two to correct these. When he does, he will see that he has accomplished *something*, and you can go on to something else. But when you mark every single blunder, he is overwhelmed by the number of mistakes and gives up trying.

Find a good but not too ingenious set of symbols. This will save you a great deal of time. Do not ever rely exclusively on symbols; your personal remarks mean far more to a student than a "k" or a "d" in the margin. But certain kinds of errors do not need to be specified over and over again, and symbols will teach the youngster to help himself. Every composition text on the market will offer you a set of symbols to consider. Select an easy one and supplement it with your own marks. Some teachers do not like to use red ink or a red pencil because of the associations with blood, deficit, and so on. Personally, I don't see that it makes much difference. You can scarcely use blue ink if the student has used it—your comments will not stand out well enough—and pencil for me is ineffective for the same reason, if the paper has been typed. Red has at least the advantage of being seen.

Give themes letter grades—students want them. And one grade is quite enough. Avoid the wishy-washy practice of one grade for thought and one for grammatical correctness. If the composition is successful, all parts of it serve one another—the paper is a successful *whole*.

Rewrite for the student occasionally. Your phrasing of what you can see that the student intended can often be the quickest and most effective means of instruction. These rewritings of yours should be discussed in conference, however.

Return the papers quickly, the sooner the better. In composition especially, students like to see how well they have done, and if the paper is held for a long time, they will lose interest. If the theme has been the result of a lively discussion, then their interest in the subject at the time of writing the paper was presumably high. If the papers are not returned for a week or two, interest is lost and the subject is forgotten.

Be amenable to student disagreement with your interpretation of what he means. At any cost, be sure that *he* knows what he means, and if his writing indicates the slightest uncertainty, then be adamant in your own view. But all of us err occasionally in reading, and it is certainly possible that we can be wrong. Remember, however, that our reading too fast or with distraction may have been the result of the writer's inept handling of his subject.

Select a number of faulty sentences from the papers, present them anonymously at the blackboard on the day when the themes are returned, and make them the subject of a language lesson. The rewards are many. Language study now has a sense of immediacy: students are working with their own sentences.

Read—or have students read—some of the best papers. It's a good idea to do both. Which ones you read will be determined by a number of factors—your reading of the paper of a student who is making his first fumbling efforts may do much to encourage him.

Relate the paper being marked and returned to the previous composition work and to the writing exercises which are to follow. Keep the students always aware of the syllabus they are following and what your arrangement of the writing program hopes to accomplish *for them.*

Suggest that students read one another's papers and discuss them among themselves.

Ask the student's permission to pass his paper on to other teachers and to administrators if it is distinguished, particularly if it happens to deal with a subject of school interest or improvement.

Use every resource to get good themes in print—the school paper or literary magazine, church or social club bulletins, the local newspaper, even, if the theme is good enough, as student essays sometimes are, professional magazines. Teachers of English should be aware of writing contests, like those of *The Atlantic Monthly* and *Scholastic,* and attempt annually to interest students in submitting work in these competitions. Remember: in writing, nothing succeeds like publication.

In the whole academic year there is no hour quite so dark for the teacher of English as that in which he takes the first look at the results of the students' initial assignment in paragraph writing. One is tempted to abandon composition in the course—at least for a while—and go back to the handbooks and drill exercises to teach the parts of the sentence and the forms of verbs. The possibility of getting across to an entire class the notion of a paragraph as a structural unit, the rounded development of an idea, seems so remote that one is inclined not to try. Maybe a sense of paragraphing will filter through from their reading, the teacher says to himself, as he adds a few extra essays to the reading list. Maybe they can learn to write good paragraphs by not writing any.

But of course they can't. Some few students, unusually sensitive to the rhythms of rhetoric, may improve their writing skill demonstrably as a result of subconscious limitation of prose pieces they have read, but for the others—if they are to acquire the simple techniques of exposition and persuasion—there must be the agony, the exhaustion, and the desperation which accompany *all* efforts to put thought into prose, but especially the first.

The first papers of the year always give evidence of student distress, but of the wrong sort. The kinds of exhaustion and desperation which accompany this beginning exercise make themselves apparent in the tortuous constructions, the multiple tautologies, and the flagrant solecisms which are found on nearly every paper. Faced with such immensities of disorder, what does the teacher do next? To point out all lapses in unity and coherence, to specify all slips in clarity and logic, and to mark all errors in usage, grammar, sentence structure, and diction is a task of such frightening proportions that the teacher begins to cringe—sometimes literally. Is there another way out? Can we, in some other way, though with these same pieces of composition, work to the same effect?

Teachers might consider the possibilities of the cooperative method of correction, which can be used somewhat as follows: In the first few theme assignments the teacher would not ask for more than one paragraph, of perhaps five or six sentences. In this initial paragraph the student is free to write on any subject of interest to him, though he is limited to composition of an expository or persuasive nature, no narrative or descriptive paragraphs.

When the papers come in, the teacher reads all of them through carefully and then from a class of, say, thirty students selects about twelve or fifteen paragraphs which he considers representative; generally he would choose an equal number of good, mediocre, and poor pieces, which are then reproduced by duplicating machine so that every member of the class has a copy of each of the selected paragraphs. Then, together, the class goes to work on them, a paragraph at a time.

The students read the paragraph silently; when they have

finished, the teacher questions them about its meaning. Are they able to say without hesitation what the paragraph is about? Can the thought of the paragraph be expressed in a single sentence? If so, is there one sentence already in it which seems to convey the central idea around which the paragraph is built? Are all other sentences closely related to the central thought? If not, which ones are out of line? This is a very revealing exercise as the students see, in specimens of their own work, the difficulty for anyone other than the author in discovering what the paragraph is trying to say. The paragraphs are always presented to the class anonymously of course, but I have known the author of a paragraph under discussion to become so distressed with the inability of the class to penetrate his meaning that he has blurted out, "Now this is what I meant," giving then a clear and straightforward statement, recognizable at once as the topic sentence he ought to have written.

Thus the class is stimulated into a consideration of the whole problem of unity in a paragraph, and the discoveries which they make about a particular piece of work will be either that the unity of the paragraph is substantially good and needs no significant changes, or that the deletion of one or more irrelevant sentences will greatly improve matters, or that the material is so unrelated that complete rewriting is demanded.

If the finding is of the first or second nature, the class goes on to consider the order of the paragraph. Are the sentences in the right place? Does the second one follow from the first, the third from the second, and so on to the end? Is there a smooth transition from one sentence to the next, a natural, flowing line of development? If not, what, first of all, are the possibilities of rearrangement? What words, phrases, or clauses could be suggested to improve the ease of passage from one sentence to another? Thus, without even introducing the terms, the teacher leads the class into a sense of paragraph coherence and standard transitional devices.

Next students look at the grammar, spelling, sentence structure, diction, in short, the mechanics of the paragraph. Obvious errors are spotted at once and corrected. More complex matters—parallelism, dangling modifiers, vague reference—will probably be discovered by perceptive students, but the teacher sometimes has to direct their attention to these faults through leading questions. The teacher is ruthless about sentence fragments and comma faults, insisting that though there may sometimes be a stylistic excuse for a fragment, early exercises in composition demand that it be marked as intentional. Whatever in this whole area of mechanics any student objects to, he must oppose authoritatively; that is, he must specify in terms of established conventions why he should make a particular correction.

After mechanics the class is ready to talk about the "logic" of the piece—the accuracy or inaccuracy of the views presented, the quality of truth and the general validity which the paragraph contains. If the paragraph is persuasive in character, the class should be especially careful to evaluate the soundness of the argument. They examine critically the assertions of the author; they analyze his proposition and test his definitions. Above all, they inquire into the reasonableness of what he has said. Is his conviction acceptable to them? If not, what are their recommendations? Can the paragraph, with a few sentences, be "saved"? Or is its logic so questionable that nothing less than a complete rethinking of the proposition is required?

If the class feels secure in proceeding, they go on to talk about the rhetoric of the paragraph. How can it be improved stylistically? How can it be made more exact and economical, more forceful and effective, more fluent and graceful? Here the class might experiment with sentence variety and attack jargon, gobbledygook, tautology, and general awkwardness, for students soon learn to detect stylistic pompousness and, better still, to avoid it in their own writing. Coming upon jargon in paragraphs studied under the cooperative method of correction, they suggest at once a straightforward and unpretentious diction which *says* honestly what it *means* honestly.

Improvement of the rhetoric of the paragraph is nearly the last step in the cooperative method, and, as one might expect, students by this time have come out with something quite different from the paragraph with which they started. Let me illustrate. When I performed this exercise once with a group of high school juniors, one of the original paragraphs read as follows:

In choosing a college after completion of high school it is necessary to first consider entrance requirements. While considering this, decide whether a coeducational, religious, or military school is most desirable. Of course the field of study which you wish to pursue must be considered. If a specific field is of interest, the facilities of the school on this field must be ascertained. In connection with the facilities, endowments must be considered. If there are few endowments, either by alumni or interested organizations or families, there will be less equipment available. Also if the endowments are few there is less chance of attracting better teachers. The faculty should always be considered because it determines indirectly the quality of the education you receive. Another matter to be considered is whether it is a small or large college and its location. Of course of greater importance is whether or not it is an accredited school, because if it is not, your degree will mean much less. Last but not least, cost must be considered. This will include tuition, living expenses, supplies, and other essentials. The number of available scholarships in your field should be considered.

We were agreed after we read this paragraph that it is seriously defective in a number of ways, its major fault being that its author has crowded too much into it; there is sufficient material here for an entire theme, with the various "considerations" serving for development into small paragraphs themselves. The crowding produces a repetition which is made even more objectionable by the eight repetitions of "considered." The paragraph has no "shape"; there is apparently no order to the arrangement of these "considerations," there are several shifts in person, and the ending is abrupt, giving neither summary nor conclusion. The class was not sure that the paragraph was worth working with, but decided to try to reconstruct it anyhow, largely, I suppose, because the challenge was so great.

Tackling mechanics first, getting rid of the shifts in person, and adding a conclusion, we came up with this version.

In choosing a college after completion of high school, one must first consider entrance requirements. While considering these, one should decide whether or not he wants to attend a coeducational, religious, or military school. Of course one must consider the field of study he wishes to pursue. If a specific field is of interest, with the facilities, endowments must be considered. If there are few endowments, either from alumni or interested organizations or families, less equipment will be available. When the endowments are few, there is less chance of attracting competent teachers. One should always consider the faculty because this determines indirectly the quality of the education one receives. Other matters to be considered are the size and location of the college. Whether or not the school is accredited determines the value of the degree. Finally, the cost of tuition, living expenses, the possibilities of a scholarship if necessary. Attention to all these matters will result in a wise choice of college, which, in turn, will benefit one's later life.

We could see at once that we were still some distance from a good paragraph, so on we trudged. A few slips in logic next caught our eye. Choosing a college is probably best accomplished *before* one leaves high school. The division of colleges into "coeducational, religious, or military" not only does not exhaust the possibilities but also does not set up distinctly separate categories. The faculty of a college will determine the quality of an education *directly* rather than *indirectly*, and we could not feel very confident that "attention to all these matters" would automatically result in a wise choice of college, as the conclusion we had just added seemed to assert. These were minor difficulties, however, as we proceeded to attack the big problems of order, sentence variety, coherence, and vocabulary.

But there was just too much to do, and effective oral discussion and remedy would have taken too much time. Plainly the thing to do at this point was to let each student go to work on the paragraph himself, reshaping the material as a written assignment. Next day, therefore, we had about thirty versions to consider, each of which was a marked improvement over the original. Here is the one which the class selected as best.

When one begins to think about choosing a college, he should be careful to evaluate the schools in terms of his own particular interests and needs. He should decide, first of all, whether he wants to go to a private or state-supported institution, and if he prefers the former, there are other considerations: whether or not it is denominational, co-educational, or limited in the kind of curriculum it offers, many private schools being only liberal arts colleges. Where one goes will undoubtedly be affected by the facilities of the school in a person's field of interest, and since the quality of both faculty and equipment is often determined by the size of endowments, the prospective student will try to learn how the college receives its support. Very few people will give a second thought to a school which is not accredited, but this matter should certainly not be overlooked. Size and location are important, but these are problems of individual taste and judgment. Finally, the cost of tuition, living expenses, supplies, and other essentials must be given some thought, along with the possibilities of a scholarship grant if necessary. Only when he has considered each of these subjects carefully is the student ready to make a wise choice of college.

The writer here might seem much more gifted in composition ability than the author of the original version. But this is not true. The author of this revised and improved version and the author of the original are the same person. Obviously in a few days' time he had learned something about the construction of paragraphs.

Here is another piece of writing from the first assignment.

Several factors have contributed to the use of musical interests of the past decade. The most notable being in the technical branch. Radio has been (and is being) widely exploited as a means of providing musical entertainment, for nearly everywhere you go, there is a radio. Also in this field is the phonograph, which has been improved greatly in the past few years. Probably the development which has most influenced the serious listener of music is the long-playing record. Before this invention, listening to records was hampered by the interruptions occurring when a record must be turned over, or a different record started. An ever-increasing number of musicals have been produced in Hollywood recently, and Broadway is never without its hit musical shows such as "Kismet" and "Pajama Game." Even the harsh medium of television has been used to present musical plays and operas in the past year. Those are the major reasons for the increase of interest in music.

Attacking this paragraph cooperatively, students agreed that though it was generally poor, it was not altogether hopeless. In the paragraph as a whole a thought was available to them, although the first, and, presumably, the topic, sentence was meaningless. They realized at once that the major failure here is that of vocabulary rather than of thought: "the use of musical *interests*," "radio has been *exploited*," "the *harsh* medium of television." Nevertheless, the class approved the unity of the piece and saw also that the problem of coherence was solved somewhat automatically by the means of development which the topic sentence demanded, that is, naming the "contributing factors." Students then observed at once the sentence fragment and the unnecessary punctuation, went on to attest the general correctness of what the author said, though noticing that he had omitted important musical activities, and then made their suggestions for improved rhetoric. This is what resulted from the oral reconstruction.

Interest in music has been growing rapidly during the past decade, largely because of improved methods of presentation and reproduction. Radio has been providing universal musical entertainment, for radios are everywhere. Another contributing factor, the phonograph, has been made consistently better in the past few years. The serious listener gladly welcomed the development of the long-playing record, because, before this invention, listening to records was hampered by the interruption occurring when a record had to be turned over or a different record started. An ever-increasing number of both light and serious musicals have been produced in Hollywood recently, and Broadway is never without its hit musical shows, such as "Kismet" and "Pajama Game." For audiences of more serious tastes there are always many concerts and recitals. Even the highly commercialized medium of television has been used to present musical plays and operas during the past year. All of these activities have greatly increased the pleasure of listening to music in America.

Though this new paragraph represents a marked advance over the original, my students were still not satisfied with it, and for the very best reason of all. They felt that it was "jerky," and when I pressed them to explain what they meant, they said that, upon reading it, one could tell that it had not been written by one person but by a number of persons. In short, they had learned for themselves that though the discussion and correction of paragraphs can be a cooperative enterprise, the successful writing of them cannot. A paragraph must be written out of the experience, intelligence, and sensibility of one human being, for no group of people can do his thinking for him or go on to order his thought in the firm structural outlines of a good paragraph. The re-formed paragraphs always dissatisfied them finally; for they were learning the lesson basic to an understanding of what good prose is, the organic relation of thought and language. "The thought and speech are inseparable from each other; matter and expression are parts of one: style is a thinking out into language," John Henry Newman told us in *The Idea of a University*. My juniors learned this practically, out of their own experience.

Here is a paragraph which they rejected as being virtually meaningless, too confused in its thinking for rewriting.

In this argument the author is referring to federal scholarships. These scholarships would be given to qualified high school graduates, according to need for college training. Since there is lack of space, the author will only attempt to mention the main points. First of all, many of the present scholarships are negligible. They average only two hundred and seventeen dollars apiece. Obviously that amount is not going to help a person who can't afford to spend any money for college. Also, we must give equal opportunities to the smartest people for their benefit and also for ours. For every smart person in college there is one person who hasn't got the resources to attend college. Some people who are not as smart as these people are in college because their parents make enough money. If colleges are forced to admit students on a basis of wealth rather than on academic standards, then an intellectual aristocracy will result. This situation only increases the serious shortage of technicians and scientists necessary in our turbulent world. The best thing that the United States can do is to set up a program of federal scholarships and thereby improve the American academic standards.

Here, on the other hand, is one which students were inclined to leave almost as the author wrote it.

Short-wave listening is an entertaining and educational hobby. It is usually practiced by a prospective "ham," or radio amateur, who is learning Morse code and radio procedure in order to obtain a license. Furthermore, he probably also listens to talking "hams" to learn their various styles of patter, for it is interesting to note the different accents and phraseology of "hams" from many sections of the country. Radio amateurs do not constitute all of short-wave radio, however. To the layman it is a thrilling experience to tune in commercial stations from the other side of the world. The simplest receiver can "pull in" the BBC and usually will be able to get Mexico or Venezuela. Of course many times the reception will be in a foreign language, but most countries have

English broadcasts beamed at the United States at one time or another. An average set can receive the English propaganda broadcasts from Moscow, which are very interesting and sometimes amusingly ridiculous. With a little effort one can pick up countries as far away as Australia or Japan. Short-wave truly brings the world to your ears.

There are weaknesses here, but the students could see the rounded development of an idea stated clearly and comprehensively in the opening sentence. They observed the use of details and examples, the coherent means whereby the paragraph moves, with a fair degree of smoothness, from point to point, and the sense of style which brings the paragraph to a natural and at the same time artful conclusion. It was a fairly easy task to travel onward from their approval of this paragraph to a rudimentary though fairly precise notion of what skill in composition is. To clinch the matter, we did similar cooperative laboratory work on paragraphs from a few pieces of effective modern writing, expository paragraphs by successful professional writers like John Gunther, Elmer Davis, and Corey Ford. Students had access to a pocket-book selection of modern expository essays, and from these books we took paragraphs which we broke down for evidence of the very characteristics of good organization and construction seldom found in the student work. The comparison did not discourage the students, however, but rather made them want to try for the same kind of effectiveness. A good paragraph was no longer a mystery.

They were ready then for the next assignment in theme writing. When the results came in this time, the hour for the teacher was not nearly so dark.

THE DIFFICULT STUDENT

In a comprehensive high school, teachers of English generally meet with a certain amount of student resistance to the composition program. Some students will insist that they cannot write and a number will simply not want to. The reasons are various, and student reluctance is not to be related to delinquency or near-delinquency. Many students do not see a sensible motive for writing, others are so deficient in writing skills that they are embarrassed to put words on paper, and others feel that they have nothing to say. Most difficult of all, in the large city schools, of course, is the student whose disaffection is so acute that he is antagonistic and offensive. How will the teacher get him to write? Or, for that matter, should the teacher bother? Does he need composition? Should he write? Why?

I am going to assume, for the time being, that he really does want to write and that his insistence that he does not is only a manifestation that the teacher has not reached him, has not given him any sensible motive for writing. I believe, further, that he has a great deal to say, is often able to say it more graphically than his classmates, and that he needs to write for the simple reason that he thinks. If I am wrong on all of these points I will still feel justified in trying to get such a student to put something down on paper. He is a human being, and I am determined that he will accept his own dignity.

How, then, do I get him to write? Let me speak first of what I must *not* do.

I must not use the "regular guy" approach, try to get chummy and attempt to speak his lingo, or what I imagine that lingo to be. I have seen distressing examples of teachers trying to be one of the boys. The minute the teacher starts trying to use expressions like "cool," "Daddy-o," "walk tall," and "rumble," the student will know that he's being tricked, and he'll laugh, as he should. The teacher will accomplish nothing by trying to be a carbon copy of Marlon Brando.

I must not serve his violence or sense of violence. The smoking pistol, the switch-blade knife, the speeding hot rod do not belong in the school as subjects of themes or otherwise. The school need not compromise with the leather jacket, the motorcycle, the sideburns, and the rock 'n' roll juke box. When teachers have attempted this kind of compromise and asked the student to write about such matters, the results have generally been dishonest or phony. In a number of cases the students were genuinely shocked and had to try to imagine for the purposes of the assignment a world of violence which the teacher was wrongly assuming they knew.

I must not use social problems too frequently. This is where the student knows how to trick the teacher. He knows the stereotype responses. He's heard them all so often that he will tell the teacher exactly what he's sure the teacher wants to hear and thus force himself into a pose. If the teacher wants him to write on integration, or capital and labor, communism versus democracy, then the teacher must be sure that the material is presented in a fresh and somewhat disguised manner.

What should I do for the difficult student?

First, through a sympathetic interest in all people I can attempt to know what he is really like. The values of his world are actually not very different from those of the teacher's, but teachers often assume that they are. They create for the youngster a kind of background which is altogether untrue and see him as either the victim or defender of it. If they think of him as victim, then there is a danger of sentimentalizing his predicament to the point of excusing him from responsibility, a serious disservice to him. If they think of him as the aggressive defender of the blackboard jungle state of mind, then their own defenses tighten in a way which prohibits communication altogether. The tragedy, of course, is that, in both cases, the teacher's attitudes are likely to be based on a false picture of the student's world. Our large cities are probably somewhat less the areas of gang violence than our newspapers would have us believe, and our students come to us with notions of human dignity which they rightly expect the school and the teacher to serve. Several years ago I saw an apprentice teacher, very young and very small, leading a class composed entirely of boys who looked like the hoodlum stereotypes. She was teaching poetry, Amy Lowell's "Patterns," and getting not only superb attention and maximum courtesy but perceptive and well-phrased answers as well. How was she doing it? By realizing the closeness of the subject of the poem to the experience of everyone in the room, including herself—the loss of a loved one in war and the difficult adjustments that follow, such as the necessity to go on with the pattern of life when we want to give up altogether. In complimenting her students, this young teacher was bringing out the best in them. She was using no language different from that which was natural to her. But her poise and her warmth said, "This piece of writing is about something very important to all of us. We would suffer equally in such an experience. This poem means as much to you as it does to me."

To impress on the difficult student the value of the work in composition, I can help him to see, through the practical affairs of the world he knows, the necessity for clear, orderly *direction*: the inconvenience, the danger, and even, sometimes, the tragedy which result from the wrong directions given to a tourist, the wrong directions of a shop foreman, the wrong directions to a plane pilot from a control tower. Let him study the sharp clarity of road markers and direction signs on a turnpike or superhighway. Let him see that the world we live in, in the interests of quick, decisive action, forces a constant refinement of what we say or write. Let him experiment in writing directions or improving some already in use.

To stimulate discussion prior to writing, I can call his attention to lively but accomplished motion pictures and television programs, pictures like "On the Waterfront," "The Harder They Fall," "The Sweet Smell of Success," "Pajama Game," and others. These are films with excellent screen plays, written by first-rate authors, and their production was a matter of care and sensitivity. I once saw a difficult class come alive for the first time during the year because of an imaginatively led discussion of how certain repeated objects in "On the Waterfront" helped to carry the meaning of the picture. The transference to the analysis of a story was easy, and there was an appreciation of the tasks of the writer. However, in recommending motion pictures and television programs, the teacher must be careful. Do not send students to "arty" offerings— they don't want to see "Blossom Time" and neither, probably, do you. I would be hesitant about anything too obviously "cultural." Surprise the student by showing the accomplishments in what he might naturally go to first, though this does not mean insisting that he search for accomplishment where none is likely to be.

I can keep my demands of him small, at least at the outset. A theme of one or two hundred words is quite enough.

I can try to get him to read a story or two of a kind which he has not previously read—stories of genuine literary merit with themes and ideas which will probably surprise him: "The Short Happy Life of Francis Macomber," by Hemingway, or "The Rocking Horse Winner," by D. H. Lawrence, or "Noon Wine," by Katherine Anne Porter. These are stories which will present few, if any, problems in vocabulary or syntax, and students will want to talk them over, in discussion which the teacher can direct toward a writing assignment. Some years ago a recalcitrant young man showed up in one of my classes and, on the first day, informed me that he would not do any of the reading. "I never read books," he said. "I have never read a book through in my life." I told him I was afraid he didn't know what he was missing and asked him if he would try to read a book which I would choose for him. Possibly the idea of the personal interest appealed to him, and he said he would. I gave considerable thought to the choice of the book and presented him the next day with *All the King's Men,* by Robert Penn Warren. He came in several days later shaking his head about it. "It's great," he said. "I didn't know there were books like that."

He read it through and wrote a fine short theme on why he thought Warren wrote the novel.

Through vigorous class discussion I can get the student to *think* about something—on his own, outside class, before the writing assignment is given. For this reason I prefer to use with difficult students not theme topics, but theme problems based on human situations close to the student's interest and experience. I have used the following three problems successfully.

Joey Adams is one of the most popular boys in school. Everyone likes him. But Joey has a problem.

Joey, who is sixteen, has a younger brother Chris, who is fourteen and in the first year of high school. Chris has never been very healthy. When he was a baby he had rheumatic fever and it left him with a bad heart. He's thin and delicate and isn't allowed by the doctor to be too active.

But Chris is very talented. He always gets 'A' in Art because he can draw and paint very well. His teacher has said that he should be an artist. Chris is proud of his talent and spends most of his time drawing.

A few days ago Ben Reardon, Joey's best friend, came to Joey to tell him that he heard some of the other boys at school teasing and tormenting Chris and calling him a "sissy." Until Ben came along they were even pushing Chris around a little and laughing at him because he likes to draw. "That's only for girls," they said.

You can see Joey's problem. He likes his brother and wants to help him. But he has to do it in a way that Chris won't hear about. Rough stuff is strictly out. Chris would hear about this and be embarrassed.

In about a hundred words tell what you think Joey ought to do.

Mrs. Tucker has three children: Sue, 15; Robert, 13; and Betty, 12. The best friend of the family is a next-door neighbor, Mrs. Grimes, who has always been very nice to the children, giving them presents at Christmas and on their birthdays and helping Mrs. Tucker in every way that she could.

In return, at Christmas the Tuckers have always bought Mrs. Grimes a very special gift, for which they usually spent from five to ten dollars. The whole family enjoyed shopping for this gift, especially Sue and Betty.

But this year Mr. Tucker has been off from work a good deal because of sickness, and Mrs. Tucker doesn't see how they can afford the present for Mrs. Grimes. There will be scarcely enough for the Tuckers' Christmas.

In about a hundred words tell what you think Mrs. Tucker ought to do. She knows Mrs. Grimes will have fine presents for the Tucker children, and she knows they will feel bad about not being able to shop for her. Is there any way you can think of in which they could give Mrs. Grimes a present this year?

Terry Martin is an unusually fine trumpet player, even though he's only sixteen. Already he's had an offer to play with one of the best jazz combos in town, Fred Rayburn's Quintet.

But the members of the Quintet belong to the Musicians' Union, which won't take new members until they're eighteen years old. Fred Rayburn went to the business agent of the Union and talked it over, because Terry is so good that Fred knows he would be a big attraction. And Terry really wants to play with the group, at least on week ends so that he won't have to quit school.

The Business Agent said the Union could probably put Terry on an apprentice status. He wouldn't make the same scale as the regular members until he was eighteen. In order to do this, the Union would have to have the signatures of both his parents.

Terry's father would gladly sign, but not his mother. She knows that the combo will be playing in taverns most of the time, and she doesn't think a boy of sixteen ought to be in these places because of the drinking.

Is there any way in which this problem can be worked out so that everyone will be satisfied? In about a hundred words tell what you think Terry ought to do.

The solutions to the problems were usually just about what one would expect and about what one would receive from any class. Some were ingenious and some were pedestrian. But there was never any doubt that the work represented an honest effort on the part of the student. To be sure, he had discussed the problem with his classmates—it was encouraging to see him talk with them about it at cafeteria tables—and a number of boys and girls had frankly sought the advice of their parents. This was nothing for the teacher to object to. When the student sat down in class the next day to write, what he wrote was the result of an exchange of thought, and he wrote what he knew and meant. And, almost as if by magic, the number of his errors was greatly diminished.

THE JUNIOR HIGH SCHOOL

As a result of their language experience in the seventh grade pupils should

1. Have a sense of the importance of *order* in all communication. To this skill will contribute (a) exercises in sentence analysis of a very elementary variety, as students look at their own sentences to discover essential sentence components—subject and *verb* and the order in which these parts generally occur. (Pupils should learn

as early as possible that English is, above all, a word-order language and that the writing of a sentence is a matter of orderly structure). From student sentences teachers can select various patterns for class analysis. Attention in the seventh grade, however, should be focused on basic parts: subject, verb, object. Phrasal and clausal units should be left to a later year, unless the class is a particularly able one in composition. (b) Sentences should then be joined to other sentences in simple paragraphs which will require *chronological* order, that is, paragraphs of direction (how to get from one place to another), paragraphs of process (how to do something or make something), and paragraphs of simple narration (what happened to me one day).

2. Have a sense of the *interrelatedness* of all language activity.
To this end teachers will arrange that the writing activities specified above grow out of units which include literature and grammar. The discussion of a story should include attention to sentence patterns, and the writing of various kinds of paragraphs should be prompted by the content of the selections in literature. In turn, the sentences of the students will be analyzed in class for any evidences which they may contain of creative or imaginative distinction: figurative language, sharpness of image, sense of style or rhetoric, and so on.

3. Have a sense of the importance of *accuracy* in communication.
This skill will be promoted partly through attention to chronological order in the paragraphs but also through attention to the importance of correct spelling, punctuation, and pronunciation. Again, attention to these matters should develop from the students' own work, as the teacher helps them to see what confusion may result from misspelled words, sentences incorrectly punctuated, and words wrongly accented. The selections in literature can be studied as spelling, punctuation, and pronunciation lessons when unusual or commonly misused words occur. Emphasis in acquiring this skill should always be on the dangers and confusions which may result when spelling, punctuation, and pronunciation are careless. This is a simple matter to demonstrate in a language of such spelling disorders as English.

4. Have a sense of the *evolution* and *development* of language.
This skill should grow out of an increasing sensitivity to *words*. As they are required to write, students should be asked constantly

to refine or revise what they have written, searching always for the more accurate, the more graphic, and the more specific word. Class exercises can develop around attempts to supply more effective words in selected student sentences and from here the movement is a natural one to a discussion of the origin of some of the synonyms offered and their interesting stories. Similarly, attention can be given to striking words in the literature selections. Students can be encouraged as a "fun" exercise to invent and define a few words of their own; this attention to words and their origin and development will grow into vocabulary study which is not isolated from other parts of the English course.

5. Have a sense of the *varieties* of English in writing and speaking.

This understanding should not be pursued at length on the junior high school level, but there can be introduced and briefly discussed the fact that different levels of communication exist, and that such matters as time, place, and audience determine which levels are appropriate. *The notion of one, final, and absolute standard of correctness should be dispelled* as pupils are helped to see that language is in a constant state of change and that what has traditionally been referred to as "correct" English is no more than a set of conventions loosely agreed upon as a means of promoting clarity.

Eighth Grade

As a result of their language experience in the eighth grade pupils should

1. Have a sense of the importance of *observation* in all communication.

To the development of this skill will belong a discussion of the process of *seeing* well and of seeing objects in relation to other objects. Simple paragraphs of description will be written, resulting from class discussion of what we should notice when we describe objects and places. This is the first step of transition from chronological order to *logical* order, and again students can give attention to successful paragraphs of observation and description in the literature selections they read.

2. Have a sense of the need to *interpret* experience or find meaning in what they observe.

Literature can be of major assistance in preparing the writing assignment here, as students discuss stories where the reader must extract meaning from the narrative events (for example, "After You, My Dear Alphonse," by Shirley Jackson; "Clothe the Naked," by Dorothy Parker; and "A Visit of Charity," by Eudora Welty). Class discussion of personal anecdotes and experiences might precede the writing of a paragraph or two in which the pupil is asked not only to relate a personal experience but also to tell what special meaning it had for him.

3. Have a sense of the importance of *transition* in communication.

Through analysis of their paragraphs and of paragraphs in the literature selections, students can discover the value of certain transitional words and phrases in establishing logical order. The simplest words and phrases should be introduced first: words like *but, however, although,* and the adverbs of time (*then, now, next,* and so on). In their writing students should be encouraged to experiment with these words and phrases, even in a self-conscious manner, so that the use of them will eventually become automatic.

4. Have a sense of the importance of *emphasis* in communication.

Through analysis of their paragraphs and of paragraphs in the literature selections, students can discover the value of placing major elements of narration and meaning in the more dramatic areas of the paragraph (usually at the beginning or end), can see how putting sentences together can lead up to a point of highest interest and how a careless arrangement can destroy the strong interest which a paragraph might otherwise contain.

5. Develop skills in spelling, punctuation, pronunciation, and vocabulary in the manners specified under seventh-grade skills.

Ninth Grade

As a result of their language experience in the ninth grade students should

1. Have a sense of the paragraph as the *rounded development* of an idea.

To this understanding contribute class exercises in the writing and analysis of expository paragraphs introduced through a study of how a single idea (the topic sentence) is developed into a paragraph. Topic sentences of all kinds (other than narrative) are experimented with, as pupils see the kind of development appropriate to each. In other words, the objective here is to see the shaping effect which the topic sentence has on the logical order of the paragraph in which it is contained. Again, attention should be given to the selections in literature, but these should be essays or articles, not stories.

2. Acquire the ability to do a *simple analysis* of what someone else has written or said.

To develop this skill teachers can present the class with statements of famous personages, political or scientific figures, and ask the students to write, without discussion, a paragraph showing that they know what the statement means and, further, of how it could be applied to them. The statements should, of course, be especially lively and challenging, and the results of the student writing should be compared as further experience in sharpening and vivifying expression.

3. Learn the distinction between *concrete* and *abstract* language.

Through simple exercises in definition pupils will discover the difference between words which name tangible objects available to sense perception and those which name ideas or things of the mind. Analysis of literature will reveal that both kinds are effective, but that the nature of the writing determines which of the two will be generally more appropriate. Students will experiment with the various ways in which we define something and will be helped to see the great importance in the modern world of defining *accurately*. They should also be helped to see what happens in the political, social, and international worlds because men are not using definitions in the same manner.

4. Acquire a sense of *coherence*, or transition from one paragraph to another, through the experience of writing two longer compositions (three or four paragraphs—not more than 150 to 200 words).

Once the sense of paragraphing is secure, the teacher can go on to demonstrate, through the pupils' reading and discussion, the manner in which paragraphs are joined together in order to continue the development of an idea or explore another aspect of it. Assignments might profitably return to the analysis of a statement, or, if the class is a slow one, to the process exercises of the seventh grade, this time carried to composition length.

5. Develop skills in spelling, punctuation, pronunciation, and vocabulary in the manners specified under seventh-grade skills.

THE SENIOR HIGH SCHOOL

Here, in outline form, is an attempt to give some sort of order to the high school program in composition. Only objectives and writing exercises are suggested; the classroom activity which might precede the writing is not specified. Teachers have many ingenious ways of provoking discussion, but if further suggestions are wanted about what the class might do in preparing to write, particularly helpful ones can be found in the Reports and Speeches of the Yale Conferences on English, 1955, 1956, 1957, 1958, 1959.

The only kinds of writing allowed for here are expository and persuasive. This is not to denigrate the excitement or the instructive value of "creative" writing, though I think that such writing above the ninth grade should be done infrequently and never as a compulsory exercise, but only to insist that the imaginative exercise, this is, the writing of stories or poems or even plays, be thought of as supplementary to that work which centers on the organization and expression of thought. It is assumed, of course, that writing opportunities will be provided in many ways other than straight composition—in quizzes, in vocabulary study, and in assignments dealing with the reading of literature.

Tenth Grade

Objectives:
1. To help students see the importance of order in the expression of thought.
2. To help students acquire a sense of narrative progression or chronological sequence.
3. To continue the work of seeing the paragraph as the rounded development of an idea, as something shaped or designed, a unit which exhausts the potential of a single idea.

Writing exercises:
1. Paragraphs of straight description, using the method of centering attention on one object in a room or landscape and seeing other objects in orderly relation to it.
2. Paragraphs of straight narration detailing a single incident of climactic power; the emphasis here is on arrangement of sen-

tences in the sequence which best supports the narrative build-up.

3. Discussion of the more-or-less standard methods of paragraph development, an exercise which can effectively begin with the listing of a number of topic sentences on the blackboard, followed by discussion of what methods are seemingly made inevitable by the nature of the sentence itself.

For example:

A. "College homecoming celebrations are colorful affairs." (Examples, illustration, anecdotes.)

B. "Emerson's appearance was that of a scholar." (Particulars and details—essential to description and characterization.)

C. "As a result of recent Soviet activity, the word satellite has acquired new meanings." (Definition.)

D. "Some people want to be out in front and others are willing to work in the ranks." (Comparison and/or contrast.)

E. "Ivy is injurious to brick buildings." (Why? Cause and effect.)

F. "There were three main causes of the Spanish-American War." (Enumeration.)

G. "I consider a human soul without education like marble in the quarry." Addison. (Analogy—assertion of a resemblance between two or more things which in other respects are quite different; often like an extended simile or metaphor.)

H. "We probably cannot say too often that government becomes daily a more expensive process." (Repetition.)

In such exercise it is effective to give students in class a number of sample topic sentences and ask them to determine which method of development seems appropriate to each, and to follow the discussion of their answers with the assignment that they select any two of the sentences and develop them into full paragraphs.

4. Several brief pieces of critical analysis based on the literature of the course or outside reading, the compositions to be evaluated chiefly for the sense of paragraph order and development. Students should here be cautioned against attempting too much. A single observation or two about the story, poem, or play, fully and logically presented, should suffice.

Eleventh Grade, First Semester

The first half of the eleventh year is planned as a review of the writing practices of the junior high school, but these are developed in a more intensive and sophisticated manner.

Objectives:

1. To help students see the importance of accurate and complete observation.

2. To make students aware of the differences between concrete and abstract language, *and the relative merits of each.*

3. To help students acquire a sense of transition and coherence in the paragraph and in the longer theme.

4. To give students practice in the interpretation and analysis of statements and quotations.

Writing exercises:

1. Short pieces of writing based on the student's observation of something which has interested him because of its unusual qualities or conditions. The value of this exercise can be demonstrated by all sorts of stunt activities: for example, one teacher's class is interrupted by the unexpected visit of another teacher on some out-of-the ordinary activity, which the class cannot help noticing. After the visit the class continues, but some ten or fifteen minutes later, the students are asked to write an account of what they observed. Their observations are then compared, and the variety of the reports discussed. What accounts for the variety, since everyone saw the same thing? What is the importance of good observing and accurate reporting?

2. Careful discussion of the difference between concrete and abstract language and the advantages and disadvantages of each, particularly a consideration of the kinds of writing for which each is appropriate. The writing of fairly long paragraphs in which students are asked (a) to write a paragraph consisting entirely of concrete nouns, active voice verbs, and adjectives of sensory perception; (b) to write a paragraph in which abstract nouns and passive voice verbs greatly predominate; (c) to write a paragraph in which concrete and abstract nouns alternate, the concrete nouns being used chiefly as a means of bringing the meaning of abstract nouns closer to the experience of the reader. Many additional, non-writing lessons in language can, of course, grow out of these activities.

3. Discussion of standard transitional devices in composition, both those which are syntactically natural (pronouns, repetition of

nouns, rearrangement of word order) and those which are stylistic devices (conjunctive adverbs, parenthetical expressions, adverbs of time, and so on). Writing of fairly long paragraphs in which these methods of transition are deliberately employed; then the writing of paragraphs in which orderly transition must be arranged without the use of any transitional devices whatever—that is, the transition must be a matter of the logical development of the thought, with the ideas flowing naturally and freely from one to the other.

4. Short pieces of analysis in which students are asked to work with quotations or attention-getting statements of public officials. In the writing students must (a) demonstrate that they know what the quotation or statement means, (b) discuss its validity, and (c) apply it to human experience as they have observed it. This exercise can be used in connection with the writing which students are asked to do on the literature of the course.

Eleventh Grade, Second Semester

The whole semester will be given over to practice in sentence variety. Starting with the basic sentence patterns, teachers will proceed to consideration of various kinds of modifiers, leading eventually to demonstration of the varieties of subordination and their advantages. Phrasal and clausal units will be experimented with so that the full range of the English sentence is explored. The stylistic differences between subordination and coordination will be analyzed, and the various connectives studied. Students will take shorter sentence units and combine them to achieve greater flexibility and rhetorical ease in their writing.

While this work with the sentence is going on, students will be asked to hand in one two-paragraph theme each week, preferably on any subject of their choice, though the teacher had better be ready from week to week to make some specific suggestions to those who "can't think of anything." These papers will be rigidly marked *for two things only*—how well the thought comes through and how much sentence variety is demonstrated. Students will be encouraged to take stylistic risks, to have fun with words, to say exactly what they want to say, *just as they want to say it*. Penalties for errors in grammar and spelling will be at a minimum. The injunctions will be two: "Say something which you think is interesting, and say it in what you think is an original way." The grade will be cumulative—the grade on the last paper will be the grade for the semester's composition.

Twelfth Grade

Objectives:

1. To provide as wide a variety of writing experiences as possible, though chiefly within the patterns of exposition and persuasion.

2. To intensify writing exercises of analysis and interpretation of literature.

3. To prepare for the successful fulfillment of writing assignments in college.

Writing exercises:

1. Process theme—the detailed explanation of a mechanism or organization: its purpose, its parts, the method of its operation.

2. Impromptu paragraphs—analysis of a simple statement directly out of school experience, something controversial based on an editorial in the school paper or in current events.

3. Critical report—a full-length paper (750 to 1000 words) based on a book read.

4. Definition I—Short, very concrete. The student must define something he knows well.

5. Definition II—slightly longer, abstract. The student must take an abstract concept and make it truly meaningful. One of the objectives here is that he will learn how to introduce his own views without prejudice, emotion, or vagueness. In short, he will begin to learn how to use abstractions responsibly.

6. Impromptu exercise. Have a little fun: definition which is also a kind of character sketch, in the manner of the seventeenth-century characters: "the life of the party," "the big wheel," "the steady dater," "the worrying parent," "the political candidate," and so on.

7. Critical report—second full-length paper based on a book read.

8. Character sketch I—this to be done on someone whom the writer knows intimately. The person must be presented chiefly through action and speech—"don't tell, show"—with no adjectives of judgment or criticism.

9. Character sketch II—famous personality, celebrity, public figure, someone the writer has studied or read about; the picture of this celebrity in an unusual or unexpected role or situation.

10. Impromptu analysis. Students write on a characteristic utterance by someone in public life, the statements supplied by the teacher. Students must reveal the extent to which the statement is revealing of personal characteristics. Thus the author of the state-

ment should be well known, and there should be a variety of statements and persons.

11. Critical report—Third full-length paper on a book.

12. Composition combining narration and analysis. The student must give a carefully detailed account of some actual experience which he later realized to have special meaning for him—the kind of experience which aided the growing-up process. The objective here is that he will learn how to abstract from an account of experience, to generalize and take coherent meaning from narrative detail. Before he writes, he should be provided with some examples; otherwise a good deal of writing is likely to be sentimental moralizing.

13. Assertion and persuasion—three full-length papers (750 to 1000 words) the writing of which is preceded by discussion of principles of argumentation, the fallacies of argumentation, simple logic, and irresponsible use of language.

> Paper One—the writer recommends some change in school policy.
>
> Paper Two—the writer recommends some change in community policy. (Probably this would have to be altered for students in independent schools.)
>
> Paper Three—the writer recommends some change in national or international policy, demonstrating some simple research to support his views.

14. Source theme or research paper, preferably on a literary topic. Preparation in several stages: (a) submitting a topic; (b) submitting a sentence outline; (c) submitting a rough draft (which is returned carefully marked by the teacher), and (d) submitting the final and error-proof draft. Class discussion preceding the exercise should deal with the use of reference materials, the card catalogue, footnotes, bibliography, and other mechanical details. It is recommended that the paper not be long (two thousand words are enough). If possible, teachers should insist on both primary and secondary source materials, but the paper should represent serious, personal effort on the part of the student. The ideas and organization should be his own, not those merely gleaned from a myriad of sources.

CHAPTER SEVEN

Verbal Dishonesty: Abuses of Language in Today's World

ONE OF THE CHIEF COMPLAINTS of teachers of English these days is that they are asked to do too much, by which they mean that in recent years more and more materials have been crowded into the English course, from how to order groceries on the telephone to how to conduct the monthly meeting of the Ladies' Auxiliary. The English classroom is thought of as the place where the student is to acquire not only facility in the use of communication but poise, social grace, and the principles of etiquette. The teacher generally does not quarrel with the legitimacy of these materials as part of the course, but there is real concern about the amount of time which they consume in proportion to the amount at the individual teacher's disposal. The plain truth is that the English teacher has less and less time to do more and more.

Prospective teachers of English need to be aware of these pressures and should be determined to scrutinize very carefully the new materials which are suggested to them as teachers. Increasingly, the teacher of English is asked to be another social scientist, and although this may, to many of us, seem a valid request, since language is man's chief instrument for social organization, we still have to insist on recognition of the basic axiom that no use of language can be socially responsible unless it is the product of well-developed skills.

The questionable uses and abuses of language in today's world and the need of the secondary school to make its students conscious of these questionable uses and abuses are fairly new materials in the English curriculum, but no one is likely to deny the necessity of handling the problem. S. I. Hayakawa in *Language in Action,* his well-known and tremendously useful book, comments on the amount of persuasive language encountered every day in the modern world.

We now have, as the result of modern means of communication, hundreds of thousands of words flung at us daily. We are constantly being talked at, by teachers, preachers, salesmen, public officials, and moving-picture sound tracks. The cries of the hawkers of soft drinks, soap chips, and laxatives pursue us into our very homes, thanks to the radio—and in some houses the radio is never turned off from morning to night. Daily the newsboy brings us in large cities from thirty to fifty enormous pages of print, and almost three times that amount on Sundays. The mailman brings magazines and direct-mail advertising. We go out and get more words at bookstores and libraries. Billboards confront us on the highways, and we even take portable radios with us to the seashore. Words fill our lives.

This word-deluge in which we live is by no means entirely to be regretted. It is to be expected that we should become more dependent on mutual intercommunications as civilization advanced. But, with words being flung about as heedlessly of social consequences as they now are, it is obvious that if we approach them with primitive habits of evaluation, or even with a tendency to revert occasionally to primitive habits of evaluation, we cannot do otherwise than run into error, confusion, and tragedy.

Young men and women in college who are planning to teach English generally have some experience with semantics in their undergraduate preparation, perhaps a bit too much. Students have been warned so frequently in recent years about easy generalizations, hasty value judgments, and vague abstractions that many of them have come to believe that *all* generalizations are wrong, *all* value judgments unreliable, and *all* abstractions meaningless. They have been made to fear slanting and loaded words so strongly that they are afraid to say anything at all, and they are so concerned to construct nothing less than an *operational* definition that the operation which demands an exigent definition often does not get done. In far too many cases experience with semantics has created so many new fears about language in the student that his language becomes a confused, self-conscious mumble.

Students of language are generally agreed now that the semanticists went too far in their enthusiasm for their new activities, and we are just beginning to restore the balance. (In this connection see John Carroll: *The Study of Language*, pp. 160–68.) For a while there was a tendency for the semanticists to take over the whole English course of study, though this was truer, perhaps, of college freshman English than of high school English. As Margaret Schlauch says, semantics was announced as a kind of universal panacea, the be-all, end-all, and cure-all of human existence. The claims made by the semanticists were extravagant; suddenly we were being told that all problems are merely verbal and that the conflicts between democracy, fascism, and communism could all be solved if men would just sit down together and analyze verbal connotations.

World War II and its aftermath made us properly skeptical of such mischievous claims, as we saw that there was much more agreement on and understanding of the abstractions of modern democracy than we would have imagined—agreement and understanding which could and did make resistance to a common evil forceful and effective. The man who says that he cannot be against fascism and communism because he cannot define them merits our suspicion, and we would be impatient with him today. But he once existed, and in comparatively large numbers.

Then along came George Orwell to point out to us that the persistent simplification of language in the direction of concreteness could have very hazardous implications. The Appendix to *1984*, titled "The Principles of Newspeak," is required reading for all who intend to teach English.

Newspeak was designed not to extend but to *diminish* the range of thought, and this purpose was indirectly assisted by cutting the choice of words down to a minimum. . . .

[The A vocabulary] was composed almost entirely of words that we already possess—words like *hit, run, dog, tree, sugar, house, field*— but in comparison with the present-day English vocabulary, their number was extremely small, while their meanings were far more rigidly defined. All ambiguities and shades of meaning had been purged out of them. So far as it could be achieved, a Newspeak word of this class was simply a staccato sound expressing *one* clearly understood concept. It would have been quite impossible to use the A vocabulary for literary purposes or for political or philosophical discussion. It was intended only to express simple, purposive thoughts, usually involving concrete objects or physical actions. . . .

The greatest difficulty facing the compilers of the Newspeak dictionary was not to invent new words, but, having invented them, to make sure what they meant: to make sure, that is to say, what ranges of words they canceled by their existence. . . .

Relative to our own, the Newspeak vocabulary was tiny, and new ways of reducing it were constantly being devised. Newspeak, indeed, differed from almost all other languages in that its vocabulary grew smaller instead of larger every year. Each reduction was a gain, since the smaller the area of choice, the smaller the temptation to take thought.

Orwell's point, of course, is that there is great danger in any attempt to reduce the number of words available for the expression of human thought. Thought is made more precise not by eliminating concepts but by clarifying them and making them capable of exact penetration.

This is surely what the more reliable semanticists have always aimed at; they have wanted to make us conscious that many people, wittingly or otherwise, use language irresponsibly and in doing so multiply and magnify the problems of human living. The semanticists turned their attention chiefly to advertising and political statements since these, as might be expected, contained the most glaring abuses. Wherever men are trying to persuade other men to a course of action, whether it be buying an automatic washer or supporting a new farm bill, there will be some calculation about devious means of persuasion. This practice is at least as old as fifth-century Athens and Aristotle's *Rhetoric*.

And the semanticists are right to insist that today's student be made aware of these pressures which are all about him. He must learn to see exactly what is going on in the appeals for his support (an excellent book for high school readers is *The Hidden Persuaders* by Vance Packard); he must be taught to analyze advertisements, political pamphlets, and speeches in a cool-headed, clear, scientific, neutral, objective way. Unfortunately, the analysis he has been exposed to in the classroom has not always been impartial and scientific. Some of our teachers of English have given the impression of using semantics for purposes of specific political identification. They have seemed like frustrated politicians who would much rather be running for Congress than running a class, and they have attempted to make a whole curriculum of the latest issue of Consumers' Guide and the speeches of demagogues. This is the kind of teacher who, perhaps, represents most graphically for our time the moral fervor of the old Puritan fathers. The habit of moral strenuousness persists even though the dogma is gone. The teacher regards himself as a kind of vestigial priest, and semantics is his new sacrament. The high school English class becomes a kind of puberty ritual in which students are initiated into the salmon-pink mysteries of Korzybski and Stuart Chase.

What should be done in the classroom to make students aware of language abuse?

First, we can give the student an introduction to logic. High school students have demonstrated that they can handle the syllogism, in very elementary fashion, and they are fascinated by it. Simple principles of both deductive and inductive logic can be presented to them, and they can thus be prepared to see that many of the abuses of language which we encounter daily are no more than flagrant violations of logic, particularly with the use of the enthymeme—the syllogism with one of its parts missing. Once students have had some practice with the syllogism and see the necessity for stating clearly each of the three parts, they will see the deception which develops when major premises are eliminated from advertising and political slogans. When we find ourselves confronted by such a statement as "Blinko's is Milwaukee's greatest beer; I ought to know, I lived there," accompanied by a picture of some sports or motion picture personality, we can test the validity of the statement by trying to give it a major premise, which would have to be "Everyone who has lived in Milwaukee knows what good beer is" or "Everyone who lives in Milwaukee knows that Blinko's is Milwaukee's greatest beer," and both of these are certainly questionable. In the political world, the student will see the doubtful reasoning in such a statement as "Send me to Congress; I am a veteran of three years' combat duty in World War II." Obviously the work with logic must be of an elementary variety, but students should know at least the difference between reasoning from particulars to the general, and from the general to the particulars. They should see that both kinds are useful to effective persuasion and that the nature of the argument rather decisively determines which of the two we will use. The classroom discussion of faulty syllogistic reasoning can be a particularly exciting activity. It will be something students have probably not encountered previously, and they will have a good time.

Second, we can make the student aware of denotation and connotation in words. Again, this should be little more than an introduction, but he can see how some words of our daily intercourse are "good" words and others are "bad." As Hayakawa says, there are "purr" words and there are "snarl" words—words that give pleasure and smooth our feelings, and those that upset us and make us want to fight. This kind of unit is already in a number of high school courses of study, as well as in a number of textbooks, and it has considerable meaning for students who are just beginning their work in critical thinking. Let them see the difference, for example, between what a word like "flag" *denotes* and what it *connotes*. Let them see how words are employed to convey attitudes, feelings, strong reactions, even though these conditions are not in the words themselves at all. Students respond to this exercise with warmth and bring to class many examples which they find in their daily experience—from television, radio, newspapers, magazines, and even car cards. One caution should be observed here, however: in many places students do work of this kind in social studies also, and there is danger that they might get too much of it, with the resulting development of a cynicism that would make them hostile to all public statement and argumentation. They would lose the natural enthusiasm of youth too soon and have a humorless and difficult time at college. I would be reluctant to introduce critical analysis of language to students unless I could show them that it operates both positively and negatively—in short, that language is employed for many purposes and by all kinds of men, the noble as well as the base.

Third, we can make the student aware of the persistent kinds of false argumentation. He should see, for example, how often all of us come into contact with *post hoc ergo propter hoc* reasoning, the "after this; therefore, because of this" fallacy. The use of this device can generally be found on both sides of a political argument, and it can be a very subtle and ingenious technique, giving off illusions of virtue. In two different communities I have seen it employed in public controversy over whether or not to retain a particular method of voting which had come into existence in connection with charter forms of government. As a result of a system whereby the affairs of the city were in the hands of a city manager appointed by duly elected councilmen, a great deal of the corruption which had existed when a political machine had controlled a mayor and the men he appointed to jobs had disappeared. The method of voting, however, had no explicit connection with the form of municipal government; another form of voting could have produced exactly the same kind of councilmanic-city manager administration. In the election campaign, however, the constant cry of the supporters of the unusual form of voting was that municipal graft had been eliminated *because of that particular form of voting*—"after this; therefore, because of this."

Similarly, students should see how often newspaper columnists use the device known as *begging the question*, that is, assuming as proved something yet to be demonstrated. The columnist begins, "The unconstitutional practice of building publicly owned dams for electric power should be abolished," thus announcing at the opening of his sentence that he has already reached the conclusion toward which his argument is supposed to move with logical precision. Student editorials often beg the question. One that I have in front of me begins, "The unfair practice of requiring all students to take a fourth year of high school English should be discontinued." Starting that way, the editorialist could only assume that his argument was already won, and the rest of his piece is, therefore, only a prolonged improvisation on this single theme.

History texts will show students how often and how recently the leaders of modern states have used the *faulty dilemma* to deceive their followers. This is the practice of presenting only two choices when more than two are possible. Hitler, before he came to power, told the German people that they must choose between National Socialism and Communism—that they had only these two choices. Near the end of the war the Nazi leaders told the people that they must fight on or be killed, that surrender meant death. In California and Ohio the supporters of "right to work" bills told the voters that failure to pass such legislation would result in the continued oppression and corruption of big labor bosses, completely ignoring the possibility of control by federal legislation; as a matter of fact, a labor control bill was already before the houses of Congress.

Ignoring the question can produce humorous results, and indeed it is probably the easiest form of faulty argumentation to recognize and identify, yet we never seem to have done with it. Technically, it is simply the use of a second accusation to blot out a first; generally the second has very little, if any, relevance to the first. This is actually no more sophisticated and responsible a form of arguing than the dialogue of two tots on the playground: "You hurt my arm." "Well, you kicked me." The story is told of two American engineers being entertained by two Russian engineers, who were showing the Americans a beautiful new subway in Moscow. "Isn't this superb?" they asked the Americans. "See those beautiful tile mosaics, those beautiful and modern aluminum rails, that beautiful fluorescent lighting. You don't have anything like that in America. You have to admit that the Soviet subway is far superior to the American." "It's very fine indeed," said one of the Americans. "But tell me, where are the trains? We've been down here about half an hour, and I haven't seen any subway cars. Where there's a subway shouldn't there be subway trains?" "How about all those lynchings in Mississippi?" asked the Russian.

The shoddiest form of false argumentation is probably the *argumentum ad hominem*, the argument addressed to the man rather than to the issue. This is where politics becomes really ugly: "Don't vote for that man. He's divorced," or "Don't give that guy your support; his mother was an alcoholic." The technique is often used positively as well, but is nonetheless offensive intellectually. Thus a candidate puts pictures of himself and his family in the newspaper, indicating that the number of children which he has is somehow a recommendation for office, as if he intended being used for breeding purposes. The number of his civic clubs, his church membership, military service, and humble origin are all offered as positive assets for every political job from county coroner to United States Senator. But this positive side of the coin is usually not harmful socially; the other, or negative, side shows the nastiness to which false argumentation can degenerate.

The truncated syllogism which we call the *sham enthymeme* has already been illustrated. It results from leaving off one part of the syllogism, usually the major premise, which, when supplied, shows how invalid the argument is. If I read "The TVA has been successful in controlling and using the Tennessee River; therefore, the TVA plan should be used for all other American rivers," I can see how doubtful the argument is if I supply the major premise, "Whatever is effective for the Tennessee River will be effective for all other American rivers."

Most of our high school textbooks now list, explain, and illustrate various propaganda devices—the "tricks of the trade," as they are sometimes called. The "band wagon" and "plain folks" appeals are always with us, as are the elaborate testimonials of the advertisements. For some curious reason, I am supposed to rush out and buy a Lincoln because Carlos Romulo drives one, or I am supposed to enjoy Crispies because that ubiquitous American family—father, mother, two children (one boy, one girl), the father in shirtsleeves, the mother in a gingham apron, all of them radiant and happy— keep themselves regular with the roughage which the body needs and Crispies contains.

The dangers of vague abstractions, hasty judgments, and quick generalizations, the real harm which these practices do in modern living, should be a vigorous part of the high school program in language. Again, Hayakawa can be useful to the teacher. Sections of *Language in Action*, particularly the famous Abstraction Ladder and the delightful "Cow$_1$ is not Cow$_2$" interlude can prove permanently instructive to our classes. The students will not forget and they will use what they acquire. Mr. Thomas Devine, of Winchester, Massachusetts, Junior High School, in a unit on critical thinking actually attempts with junior high school students some mastery of the following abilities and skills:

1. The ability to define a problem.
2. The ability to recognize unanswerable questions.
3. The ability to recognize "high-level" abstractions.
4. The ability to recognize "two-valued" orientations (the either-or dilemmas).
5. The ability to distinguish between the symbol and the thing for which it stands.
6. The ability to distinguish relevant from irrelevant information.
7. The ability to judge the reliability and accuracy of data.
8. The ability to detect bias in information.
9. The ability to determine representativeness of data (to detect errors in sampling).
10. The ability to distinguish fact from opinion.
11. The ability to distinguish between the affective and informative connotations of words (ability to detect "loaded" words).
12. The ability to recognize levels of abstraction.
13. The ability to detect propaganda devices.
14. The ability to recognize the inadequacy of definitions and the importance of context.
15. The ability to recognize insufficient evidence.
16. The ability to detect inconsistency of opinion.

This is a large and ambitious order, and I admire Mr. Devine's determination, to say nothing of his energy. Personally, I am not altogether sure that the eleven-, twelve-, or thirteen-year-old has a psychological readiness for quite all of this program, but Mr. Devine is right in his assumption that the child should be early aware of what happens in language when appeals are made for his support. It goes without saying that language exploration of this kind should never be practiced without constant reference to real examples. Techniques of language chicanery must always be illustrated, and not with manufactured materials. Our subject is verbal dishonesty in today's world, and we compromise the subject unless we can produce incontrovertible evidence that such dishonesty exists. We should have no difficulty finding abundant resources.

CHAPTER EIGHT

The Revival of Rhetoric

IN THE HISTORY OF WESTERN THOUGHT the term "rhetoric" has had various meanings. To Aristotle, as later to Cicero, it meant the art of persuasion. As Aristotle put it, rhetoric is the art of discovering in a particular case what the most effective means of argument are. In Greece and Rome rhetoric was a preparation for service to the state, the necessary equipment of legislators. Aristotle specified three kinds of rhetoric: deliberative, that which has to do with determining courses of action; forensic, that which has to do with defense and accusation; and epideictic, that which has to do with praise and blame. We can see at once the practical character of Aristotle's rhetoric and its relation to the duties of statecraft. For the Greek or Roman student, rhetoric was a large part of the curriculum—almost the whole course of study.

In the late Middle Ages and the Renaissance the term came to have a broader meaning. Rhetoric became a system of classifying and cataloguing devices of language used for particular effects, the tropes and figures. It became a means of exploring literature, of seeing how the special language effects of classical writers were accomplished. Schoolboys went through elaborate analyses of poems, orations, and epics, marking, naming, and listing the rhetorical devices to be found there. Under the late Michael Krouse, a Milton scholar, I once studied the poetry of Milton in the manner of the rhetorician, as the members of the seminar took special note of how thorough Milton's preparation was, both in classical rhetoric and the rhetorical principles of Ramus. The exercise was an extremely formidable one, and it is certainly not recommended for the secondary school, though students in advanced Latin courses are likely to get a touch of it. Once, however, it was the major part of the secondary school curriculum.

Partly as a result of this minute kind of cataloguing, "rhetoric" became for a time a bad word. It acquired the connotation of chicanery or deceit, fancy euphuistic prose designed to obscure meaning or hide motive. The adjective "rhetorical" became a term of contempt and is still so used occasionally. Recently, however, we began to change our views and to look again into the books of thirty-five or fifty years ago to see what rhetoric meant to the schools then. The only English book the schoolboy had was probably titled *Composition and Rhetoric*. What did it contain? What use, if any, can we make of it now?

Teachers of writing know that trenchant prose style in student papers is more than a matter of grammatical correctness and mechanical scrupulousness. Students turn up every year whose work is free from errors in usage, faulty sentence structure, and butchered syntax. Yet the papers are insufferably dull, and we put them to the bottom of the pile in favor of the papers of other students, who, though possibly markedly deficient in the mechanics, have nevertheless a sense of balance, of parallelism, of figurative language, and of prose rhythm. These are rhetorical accomplishments—this is the rhetoric we would revive—and we believe it can be taught. Donald Davidson makes clear the difference between merely writing grammatically and writing rhetorically.

> Grammar is the law of the language, considered as language; rhetoric is the art of language,* considered as thought. Grammar tells what is correct; rhetoric tells what is effective and pleasing—and often what is logical. From grammar you learn within what limits you must stay; from rhetoric you learn how to use limitations or even at times to transcend them. Grammar leads to good form; rhetoric, well practiced, leads to style.

On the most immediate level this means that the student must be trained to sense the effect of what he writes and then to revise and reconstruct at need, so that the final result is a thoroughly satisfactory representation not only of his meaning but also of his attitude toward the subject, his attitude toward the reader, his attitude toward himself. He must know how to be selective, how

---

* *My reason for including this chapter on rhetoric in the first part of the book is simply that I wanted to emphasize the relationship of rhetoric to composition and the student writing program in general. Furthermore, it can serve here somewhat as a transitional chapter, preparing the way for attention to the professionalism in the art of language which is literature.*

to substitute one sentence unit for another—a phrase rather than a word, or a clause rather than a phrase. He must know when to use long sentences and when to use short; when to put several ideas into a single construction and when to put only one; when to use complex sentences, and when compound, or even simple; when to use concrete language, and when abstract; when and how to employ figurative language gracefully. He must know the principles of coherence and emphasis, of position, order, and variety, of economy and tone.

For many of our students these finer points of style will be redundant; an appreciable number of youngsters will have neither the need nor the ability to do close work in rhetoric. But for the college-bound student the work will be highly beneficial, and the teacher of English will be wise not to rule out too easily the border-line cases. As with a number of other subjects of the English course of study, so with rhetoric: let us not give up too soon. A youngster's intention to go to college should not be the sole criterion of whether or not he is given training in rhetoric, and, by the same token, it is certainly conceivable that some who plan to go to college will be altogether insensitive to rhetoric, though it seems unreasonable that a college-bound student would want to avoid rhetorical training.

The place to begin, obviously, is with sentence variety. Students probably will have had practice in constructing simple, complex, compound, and compound-complex sentences, but one of the duties of the teacher of rhetoric will be to make classes alert to the advantages and disadvantages of each of the kinds, depending on what they want to say. The simple sentence is usually shorter than the other varieties and, for this reason, is used when we want our ideas or impressions to stand out boldly. A writer who wants sensory effect to register strongly with the reader likes simple sentences; D. H. Lawrence and Ernest Hemingway are masters of the simple sentence used for rhetorical effect. The idea set off from others in a terse sentence calls attention to itself and acquires greater emphasis. The reader notices and remembers.

The complex sentence appears more frequently in modern writing than the other kinds, and for good reasons. No one kind of sentence is better than any other kind, yet because it shows a relationship of ideas, the complex sentence has strong rhetorical force. It shows one idea subordinated to another, and thus a dramatic organization of thought occurs. Students need much training in the use of the subordinate conjunctions and the relative pronouns. A favorite exercise with teachers of English, and a very profitable one, is that in which students are asked to join pairs of single sentences indicating a variety of subordinate relationships through the use of conjunctions and pronouns. Professor Porter G. Perrin tells us that many of the sentence errors of the run-on, or comma-fault, variety result simply from the writer's failure to subordinate; ideas which are not equal are made to seem so. Professor Perrin recommends that the student have regular practice in seeing the relationship of ideas to one another, in both his reading and writing.

The conjunctions regularly used in compound sentences, *and*, *but*, *or*, *nor*, and so on, are called co-ordinate conjunctions, and the term has implications for rhetoric as well as grammar, for the ideas being connected must have not only grammatical equivalence —that is, must be expressed in independent clauses—but they must be related in thought as well. A student would readily see the absurdity of "Thomas Jefferson wrote the Declaration of Independence, and I like strawberry shortcake," but possibly not of "Baseball is America's favorite sport, and there are nine men on a team." The student should see that as his writing becomes more and more sophisticated, the relationship between the clauses of the compound sentence becomes tighter and tighter. Frequently the compound sentence is used to establish contrast, as when the topic sentence of a paragraph determines the whole structure of development, for example, "General Grant was practical, hard-headed, shrewd, willful; General Lee was quiet, reflective, theoretical-minded, imaginative." A paragraph following from this sentence could scarcely do anything but develop the contrast. Davidson says that "the pattern of the compound sentence is relaxed and easy; its structure is that of the simple sentence repeated and prolonged. It develops as if by addition, subtraction, alternation." A favorite rhetorical pattern for writers is the balanced sentence like the one above on Grant and Lee; the semicolon is a divider between two statements exactly similar in form. When more than two independent clauses are joined in the compound sentence, we often have parallelism, with some form of climactic order.

Compound and compound-complex sentences are generally longer than simple and complex sentences, and thus they are used in the kind of prose which attempts a dignity and reflectiveness corresponding to the subject. Ideas are brought together to show how they supplement one another and to lead the reader into contemplation and thoughtfulness. The predicates are vivid and persuasive; they hold the reader's attention long enough for him to respond thoughtfully to the passage. The long sentence is the instrument of reason and analysis.

Sentence length as well as sentence pattern should be determined by the writer's thought and by the way in which he wants his readers to react to his thought. Sentence length and structure can even be a means for him of getting to know his subject better: the rhetoric he uses is a means not only of refining but actually of clarifying what he wants to say. He will discover that for one kind of emphasis he wants a loosely organized sentence where the verb comes early and brings the reader to attention. For another kind of stress he wants to keep the meaning suspended to the end, where he finishes the subject-predicate arrangement. This is the periodic sentence, the kind which holds off the predicate almost until the period; indeed the verb is sometimes the last word in the sentence. Obviously, then, sentences become means of controlling the reader's reactions quite apart from what they say; the most desirable responses are those which are brought about by a fusion of subject and pattern to show that they are complementary and exhaustive. The periodic sentence shapes to a high spot; the loose sentence falls away from one; which of the two kinds we use ought to be determined both by what we wish to say and by what effect we want it to have.

Rhetoric has to do as well with such matters as prose rhythm, graphic vocabulary, unusual word combinations, stress, parentheses, words and phrases in a series, appositives, transitional devices, analogy, and illustration. Students can explore the rhetorical achievements of the masters of prose to see just exactly what a passage contains. For example, I have often had students work with one of Hamlet's prose utterances.

I have of late—but wherefore I know not—lost all my mirth, foregone all custom of exercises; and indeed it goes so heavily with my disposition that this goodly frame, the earth, seems to me a sterile promontory; this most excellent canopy, the air, look you, this brave o'erchanging firmament, this majestical roof fretted with golden fire, why, it appears no other thing to me than a foul and pestilent congregation of vapors. What a piece of work is a man! how noble in reason! how infinite in faculty! in form and moving how express and admirable! in action how like an angel! in apprehension how like a god! And yet, to me, what is this quintessence of dust? man delights not me: no, nor woman neither, though by your smiling you seem to say so.

The passage starts conventionally enough in a plain narrative tone, but at once we have the first of a number of rhythmical interruptions, the first one actually anticipating, as a modifier, the verb and its object that follows it. Verb and object are intensified by a similar appositivelike construction. The semicolon and "and" prevent a stop here, so the reader goes on into the momentum of a clause which looks back at the condition announced in the first clause, Hamlet's melancholy, while moving on at the same time to the central emphasis of the passage—that nothing in nature or man can relieve his dejection. The thought is completed ("This goodly frame, the earth, seems to me a sterile promontory"), but then begins a series of appositives with adjective modifiers which builds in a kind of spiral and a whirling tempo, the only interruption being the imperative "look you," which has the effect of focusing the reader's attention even more intently on what is being said and prepares for the contrast between the gloriousness of Hamlet's epithets and his assertion that these majestical natural surroundings are merely foul and pestilent to him. Immediately, however, he returns to sublimity with a series of apostrophes; the first is an exclamatory sentence, the next two are ellipses, both beginning with "how," but in the three that follow, though Shakespeare retains the "how"—ellipsis form, he begins each of the three with a prepositional phrase starting with "in." The first of these prepositions has a compound object, the other two a single object, as the whole passage begins to narrow its complexity. It is time then for the next contrast—just as the earth and sky were only foul and pestilent to him, so the godlike man is only a quintessence of dust in which Hamlet takes no delight.*

But this is a passage from a play, and at its end it must move us back into the dramatic action. The touch at the conclusion is superb. Noticing the surreptitious glances of Rosencrantz and Guildenstern, Hamlet turns upon them ("though by your smiling you seem to say so"). He has had his moment of rhetoric; he has shown us, somewhat self-indulgently, perhaps, what a prose stylist he is, but his tragedy must now move forward. Analysis of Hamlet's rhetoric is, for the student, a means of underscoring the tragic predicament of the Prince. Hamlet and his rhetoric are expertly attuned.

The rhythm of the passage, a slow, casual opening, then an acceleration mounting almost to frenzy, then a diminution back to colloquial plainness at the conclusion, is remarkable. Yet one

---

* *I am aware that there is disagreement about the punctuation of this passage from* Hamlet, *but rhetorical analysis of either version will be equally productive.*

doubts the ability of the high school student to go very far in the analysis of prose rhythm. It is one of the subtlest of stylistic considerations and, for many readers, an absolutely closed book. The introduction of the subject, even the slightest reference to the rhythm of a prose passage, is certain to produce puzzled expressions, even on the faces of some of the best students. Probably if the subject is to be brought up at all, it should be just mentioned and then dropped. Sir Herbert Read's comment, from his book *English Prose Style*, is about all that would be necessary.

Rhythm is not an *a priori* construction. It is not an ideal form to which we fit our words. Above all it is not a musical notation to which our words submit.

Rhythm is more profound than this. It is born, not with the words, but with the thought, and with whatever confluence of instincts and emotions the thought is accompanied. As the thought takes shape in the mind, it takes *a* shape. It has always been recognized that clear thinking precedes good writing. There is about good writing a visual actuality. It exactly reproduces what we should metaphorically call the contour of our thought. The metaphor is for once exact: thought has a contour or shape. The paragraph is the perception of this contour or shape.

The writer . . . has towards his material, words, the same relation that an artist, say a modeler, has towards his material, clay. The paragraph is a plastic mass, and it takes its shape from the thought it has to express; its shape *is* the thought.

And I think this is the distinction between a dead paragraph and a living paragraph: in the first case a writer's words flow until either a phrase of his logic is complete, or the simulated oratory of his periods demands a pause, or for no reason whatsoever; but in the second case the words rise like clay on the potter's wheel: the downward force of attention, or concentration, or intuition, and the driving force of emotion or feeling—between these forces the words rise up, take shape, become a complete pattern.

With figurative language teachers are on surer ground, and the discussion of it in connection with prose will make clear to students that figures of speech are not the sole province of poets and literary criticism. A consideration of figurative language in connection with rhetoric can demonstrate the frequency with which all of us use figurative language in regular communication. We are all of us constant makers of metaphors, for "speech is as inevitable as thought," said Alfred North Whitehead, "and metaphor is as inevitable as speech."

The figures of sound or tone are inescapably the purview of the verse writer, but figures of comparison (simile, metaphor, conceit, personification), figures of association (metonymy, synecdoche), figures of size and depth (hyperbole, litotes) are to be found quite as much in prose as in poetry, and their frequency in daily speech will be a revelation to students. The discussion can begin with the teacher's calling attention to the dead or buried metaphors which we take for granted: the *foot* of the bed, the *mouth* of the river, and so on. Striking metaphors from literature can then be introduced by way of illustration, but it will be wise to have ready a number of examples from present-day sources—from advertising, perhaps, or from journalism, where, on the sports pages particularly, metaphors abound. High school texts generally define metaphor as "an implied comparison," or "a comparison without the use of *like* or *as*," or "a comparison in which one object is given the properties of a different kind of object," and all of these are useful as far as they go. Personally, I have always used Aristotle's definition. It is difficult for students at first, but careful class analysis of it is a lesson in both rhetoric and vocabulary. Aristotle says in the *Poetics* that "a good metaphor implies the intuitive perception of the similarity in dissimilars." *Intuitive* is the key word. Metaphor is a matter of a brilliant, unforeseen illumination. We see in a flash how two fundamentally unlike objects can be made to seem alike, and language comes at once to crystallize the observation. Sir Herbert Read's definition is also more helpful than those in the textbooks. He calls metaphor "a synthesis of two or more units of observation in one commanding image." Here the importance of *synthesis* can be insisted upon: the two objects *merge* in the image; after the metaphor has been announced their properties are scarcely separable. The student who tells his friend on a cold morning, "The motor of my Chevy coughed and coughed before it started this morning," has made a good start along the paths of metaphor and should be able to make an easy transference of such stylistic vigor to his writing.

The term "metaphor" is often used generically to mean any kind of figurative language, but, in the interests of rhetoric, it is probably better for the student to see the degrees of stylistic refinement as we go from simile, through metaphor and conceit, to personification. All are comparisons, but they operate with varying effectiveness, depending on what we are trying to say. The simile, say the textbooks, is a comparison of two unlike objects with the explicit use of "like" or "as." The student will find the simile easy to manage, his only difficulty at the outset being that he may want to compare objects which are not sufficiently dissimilar. To say "Jane looks like her cousin" is not to speak figuratively.

The conceit, a bold comparison which shocks the imagination until we see its contextual aptness, is rare in prose. It was one of the favorite devices of the metaphysical poets, particularly of Donne, Herbert, and Crashaw. There are exciting conceits in T. S. Eliot, and students can be shown the wit and daring in some of the lines from "Prufrock," for example, "I have measured out my life with coffee spoons," or the opening, "Let us go then, you and I/ When the evening is spread out against the sky/Like a patient etherized upon a table," with its suggestions of the hygienic sterility of Prufrock's existence.

Personification is too easy—and too "corny"—and students should be warned against it. It became unfashionable right after the Romantic poets, and a good thing, too, but fledgling romantics in our classes seize upon it as though it were their own private discovery, and start apostrophizing everything they encounter.

I have often asked students to compose a paragraph in which they use the four figures of comparison to develop a statement of similarity. They begin with the simile and then develop the comparison through to personification. The exercise is an artificial one, and students are cautioned against anything so deliberately figurative in their normal work, but practice of this kind has the advantage of making them aware of the usefulness of imaginative comparison, and of the stylistic advantages of metaphor and conceit over simile and, especially, personification.

Metonymy and synecdoche are so common in everyday communication in America that the student will be amazed to discover how skillful he already is in the use of these figures of association. He uses metonymy (something associated with an idea is made to stand for the idea) when he says "This has been an exciting season on the gridiron," or "Dorothy Kilgallen is a columnist who writes about stage and screen," or "From the cradle to the grave, his life was an uneventful one," or "Elizabeth began to doubt that Essex was loyal to the throne." Synecdoche, a closely related figure (a part of a thing is made to serve for the expression of the whole, or the other way around) is equally familiar: "all hands on deck," "Einstein was one of the greatest minds of our century." Robert Frost, in one of the most accurate comments on his verse, says that he is a synecdochist—that is, that he regularly uses a single experience to stand for the general or universal plight—and all of us have a way of using the part and the whole synonymously. Again, our sports pages are filled with synecdoche, as individual players and teams come to stand for an entire sport or sports enthusiasm.

The American youngster who is not aware of our penchant for hyperbole in today's world has his eyes and ears closed. He uses it himself a dozen times a day. He says to a friend, "Thanks a million," or "I'm sick and tired of such stupid television shows," or "In the last analysis, these two stories are identical." It takes little effort on the teacher's part to show him hyperbole in the advertisements for motion pictures or, once more, in the sports pages.

The opposite of hyperbole—litotes, or deliberate understatement —has become one of our newest forms of slang. Legitimately, it is the use of a negative to make an affirmative assertion: "Tony Trabert was not a bad tennis player," but in recent years it has become an almost offensive kind of language casualness with the adverb "too." "When I got home at two o'clock this morning, my mother wasn't too happy." This is slang litotes, and students are at the moment using it too much.

But calling the attention of students to the frequency of figurative language in their daily language habits will certainly make them more receptive to figurative language everywhere and to the practical advantages of rhetoric generally. The gains for them are measurable and many. A rhetorical poise, controlled by taste and judgment, will open for them, at college and elsewhere, many doors that otherwise might remain closed. Rhetoric is more than the skill of saying something imaginatively; often it is the most skillful and the most economical means of realizing what we want to say.

Epilogue to Part I

I AM NOT INSENSITIVE TO THE FACT that the preceding chapters present a kind of rhapsodic tribute to the English language—the best of all possible languages. I have insisted on its virtues possibly to the point of reaction in the reader. Isn't there anything wrong with it? Has it no defects at all?

Unfortunately, it has, and the worst of these can be indicated if I ask you to pronounce a single word: *eight*. You will, of course, say āt, the accepted pronunciation, but how really absurd! How can that combination of letters possibly give āt? The human voice could never utter such a combination of sounds as would be produced by *e, i, g, h,* and *t*. Also, what are you going to do with *ough?* To begin with, you can't say this either, yet in English we say it in six different ways: *though, bough, through, rough, cough,* and *ought*. This inconsistency is our great defect, what Jespersen calls "the pseudo-historical and anti-educational abomination of English spelling." It is the result, partly, of the frequent lack of correlation between spelling and pronunciation, but also to blame is our fondness for bringing into English words from many languages, as well as our continued determination to make pronunciation of words easier for our vocal equipment.

Everyone knows George Bernard Shaw's little joke that, given the chaos of English orthography, we would be logical to spell "fish" *photi*—the *ph* is the *ph* of *photo*, the *o* is the *o* of *women*, and *ti* is the *ti* of nation. Shaw, you will recall, strove throughout his life, and even afterward, through the provisions of his estate, to effect spelling reform according to reasonable principles, but with very little success. Almost nothing is being done at present about such reform. A few intrepid souls and occasionally a stern organization or two make a feeble effort to use *tho* and *thru* and even *nite*, but no one seems to take them very seriously, and indeed this form of abbreviation seems doubtful practice. We are obliged to admit that, where orthography is concerned, we have a mess on our hands, and no one knows quite what to do about it. Furthermore, the felony is compounded by our eagerness to construct phonetic monstrosities which also do their share to confuse. If I drive my car no farther than three city blocks I can see *Kwik-chek* (the name of a supermarket), *Tru-blu* (the name of a laundry), *Pre-vue* (something the moving picture theater has in its display cases) and the *Finast* grocery (a combination of the first letters of First National Stores). Faced with these coinings and inconsistencies in addition to the incongruities which the legitimate vocabulary contains, what can the teacher do?

First of all, he can use the history of the English language. There was a time when many of the letters which we have by now made silent, as in *knight*, were pronounced. Show the student when this was and how this word and other words were said, and let him speculate on why the pronunciation changed—and why, furthermore, we retained the original spelling. Why don't we change the spelling of *eight* to *ate?* The student will see the answer at once. We already have such a word with a totally different meaning.

Second, make every spelling lesson a language lesson. The spelling lesson should include careful work in pronunciation, vocabulary, the use of the word in a variety of contexts, and brief attention to the derivation or etymology of the word. Students may begin then to see the evolutionary character of language and the unpredictability of its change. If they do, the battle is half won.

PART II

The Art of Language

CHAPTER NINE

The High School Literature Program Reconsidered

THE FIRST ASSERTION THAT MIGHT BE MADE about the teaching of literature in the high school is that there is probably too much of it. As Dr. James B. Conant says, skill in composition is surely our first need in today's world; training in the clear, orderly expression of thought should be, in my judgment, the first subject of the curriculum. But the excess of literature is easy to understand. Teachers of English prefer to teach literature rather than composition, sentence structure, and grammar. It's an esthetic activity and gives all of us a sense of nobility. We are convinced that we are saving civilization, perpetuating Western culture, preserving the human race. Ivanhoe, it could be, arriving, as once before, just in the nick of time, will save us from Sputnik.

It's a pleasant mythology, and, like all fiction, it has its element of truth. Symbolic illusion can be very useful; it tells us a great deal about the aspirations of a society—or a profession. There is no quarrel with the premises of the mythology, only with its materials, and with the amount of time which we seem to feel that attention to these materials demands. One hears of units on *A Tale of Two Cities* which last for six weeks, with all of the other language exercises suspended. Is the book worth it? No—quietly, monosyllabically, unequivocally—no! Why six weeks on a work for which the author spent part of his life apologizing? For any of the *greatest* works of Dickens—*Bleak House* or *Great Expectations* or *Hard Times* or *Martin Chuzzlewit* or *Our Mutual Friend*—a unit of two weeks' concentration can demonstrate the full power of substance and craft in the work. This is not disparagement of Dickens or of the novel, but only consideration of the amount of class time that ought to be devoted to any piece of fiction. It is difficult to think of any novel which would require more than ten discussion periods.

The fiction of the high school literature program can bear scrutiny of another kind also. Just how good are the novels which we go on teaching term after term? It has often seemed to me that we have all of the right authors and all of the wrong books. We are right to insist on the inclusion of Dickens no doubt, but is it possible that we could use with more effective results stories other than those to which we are accustomed? Take *Great Expectations*, for example. Here, said Dickens, is the novel he hoped to write when he started *David Copperfield*. It's a made-to-order tale for the senior high school, containing a teen-age narrator, a suspenseful plot which takes the boy through mystery, terror, crime, adolescent love, disappointment, humiliation, and charity; a plain-truth morality which is in no sense platitudinous or cliché-ridden; a surprise ending which, even when anticipated by the most astute student readers, has a necessity about it which gives it a compelling charm; an earnest tone which testifies to a secure moral persuasion in the author, equal to that which brought into being the greatest classics which preceded it; and a structure and form not to be found elsewhere in Dickens or in very many other novels of the period. And yet, in spite of half a dozen inexpensive editions of the story, where is *Great Expectations* in our curriculum? A major work of a major novelist is neglected while we go on reading the saccharine interludes of *A Christmas Carol*, the unfortunate judgments of *Oliver Twist*, or the commonplace truisms of *David Copperfield*.

As with Dickens, so with a dozen other writers. All of our youngsters are required to read *Silas Marner* and, indeed, as Dr. F. R. Leavis has pointed out, George Eliot is one of the chief figures in the Great Tradition of the English novel. But where in our curriculum is her best work? To say nothing of *Middlemarch*, *Felix Holt*, or *Daniel Deronda*, where is *Adam Bede*—a magnificent first performance, as well as a startlingly accurate prognostication of the future which is our present? Take Hawthorne. *The House of the Seven Gables* is, for many of us, an exciting work, yet the critical reader must admit that it is seriously flawed because of the confusing perplexities engendered by the joining of such contradictory approaches as melodrama and irony, an incongruity central to an understanding of the deficiencies of all the novels of Hawthorne except *The Scarlet Letter*, which the high school is rapidly abandoning. To move outside fiction for a moment, take Walt Whitman. What do the students know? Only "O Captain, My Captain," a very inferior piece of verse, which is in no way representative of the distinctions for which we honor Whitman. And take Shakespeare. Our classes have put numberless garlands of flowers on the head of Queen Titania, and they have romped endlessly through the forest of Arden with that girl in boy's clothes, activities which presumably will not do them any harm, but how many of them have been in the Rome of Coriolanus to see conflicts exactly like those of this morning's newspaper, a kind of civil turmoil which produced its own Jimmy Hoffa and its own Governor Faubus?

The question here is not the tedious and largely pointless one of whether or not to teach the classics but, rather, what classics? There is in some quarters today a move to withdraw from the high school curriculum any piece of literature written before 1920 on the grounds that the students just do not care about the past. *When* a book was written is one of the least relevant considerations for the high school teacher; I have seen students tense with excitement as they discussed the *Antigone* of Sophocles, a play which ought to be part of every high school curriculum, and I have seen the same students bored by Carl Sandburg, about the high school use of whose work—his poetry at least—I have very serious doubts. This effort to withdraw older works seems unfortunate to me for several reasons. For one thing, some of us are much less sure than we used to be that we know what today's student cares about or can be helped to care about. Furthermore, we don't know how we can go about forming his taste, his perception, and his curiosity unless we are able to place before him the literary records of the experience of the human race. There is room in the curriculum for both *Pride and Prejudice* and *The Great Gatsby;* as a matter of fact, they can be used to complement one another, for both are novels of manners, each in its way a brilliantly cogent reading of the values of the society which it mirrors. There is room for both Wordsworth and Robert Frost; the step from the Lake Country to the New Hampshire woods is a very easy one. There is room for both Shakespeare and Arthur Miller; let students see Miller's skillful reversal of the pattern of Renaissance tragedy; Macbeth is a noble man who brings about his downfall through serving an inferior master, his own ambition; Willie Loman is a man whose culture has taught him to regard himself as inferior and to serve the imagined superiority of material success, a service which brings about *his* downfall. The *age*

of a literary work is of little consequence in determining its suitability for high school use; what counts is its power to affect us, its
authority to convince us that its author has brought strikingly to
our vision the reality of man's condition, the esthetic shaping of
human truth.

High school teachers who want to use an appreciable amount of
modern American literature are likely to feel that their success will
be in exact proportion to the wisdom of their choice. Not all modern works, not even all of the most celebrated, are for the high
school. This is not a matter merely of the degree of sensationalism
which a book contains but also the degree of maturity required in
the reader. A favorite modern novel of mine is *The Middle of the
Journey* by Lionel Trilling, yet I have never been able to interest
a teenager in it, not even a college undergraduate. The reason is
quite obvious: this is a novel about the turning point in a man's life
when he has reached middle age—when, that is, all of his previous
experience has come together to give him a breadth of outlook
which is denied the very young. The very young simply do not
care. I saw recently a disastrous use of the wrong modern materials.
A number of very able students had read in their English classes *No
Exit* by Sartre, *The Plague* by Camus, *Cat on a Hot Tin Roof* by
Tennessee Williams, and *The Castle* by Kafka, and I saw the results
of the test in which they were asked to write on these works. The
papers bordered on illiteracy, yet these were very able youngsters.
The point is, of course, that in terms of the simple cumulative acqui-
sitions of the psyche and the biological organism, the students were
just not ready for the books. Even, therefore, when a book is "safe,"
when, that is, it is not likely to meet the community objections to
its sensationalism, we must be sure that it is within the range of the
student's maturity, that his own experience makes it possible for
him to become *engaged* in the work.

Two other considerations, it seems to me, are fundamental in
choosing from modern American literature. We must ask always
whether or not the work is *literature*, whether, that is, it demonstrates serious intent on the part of the author. I do not mean, of
course, to rule out humor; funny books can be very serious indeed.
Take *Pickwick Papers*. This is a hilarious work, yet it is serious in
that it decries the inhumanity of certain forms of seriousness. What
I refer to is the feeling we have in reading a work of literature that
the author is up to something; we can abstract from the narrative
detail; in short, we can say, or attempt to say, what the story *means*.

In questioning students about their reading, whether in oral or written quizzes, I always ask them to try to estimate the author's purpose in writing the work. They must see that men write books for reasons, that the author has an idea which he wants us to entertain or accept, depending on the vigor of his temperament. Many of our difficulties with modern American literature vanish if we can be fairly certain that we know what the author intended a particular piece to accomplish. Knowing that Erskine Caldwell intended *Tobacco Road* to be a serious sociological study will make it possible for us to eliminate this book at once by virtue of the fact that he did not succeed. Jeeter Lester is a clown; we don't take him seriously; we laugh at him. It is unlikely that he ever moved anyone to social action or reform, as his author intended he should.

It stands to reason, of course, that when we have chosen one work by a particular modern American author we will not go on automatically to include everything that he wrote. We do not do this with the authors of the past; why should we do it with those of the present? *Guard of Honor* by James Gould Cozzens can certainly be read by many senior high school students; it is very possibly the best novel of World War II; but I would be very doubtful about *By Love Possessed*. Because of their importance in the literary picture, we must give attention to a number of modern writers, but we must be highly selective in choosing from their total output.

The extent to which we will use some of these works and reject others will probably be determined by the degree of sophistication in the community which we serve. Some places are definitely more liberal than others, and a book can be used in one town but seriously frowned upon in another. Teachers and administrators are usually quite sensitive to the tone of the community in which they work, but surely the question of whether or not particular books can be used might be made a matter of consultation with parent groups, community librarians, and members of the Board of Education. When *strong* resistance is offered, the teacher, in my judgment, should yield and select something else. There are many, many modern American works, and no one is under compulsion to read them all. There is some vestige of Puritan moral strenuousness in the American cultural experience which makes us feel that we must read *every* book, hear *every* symphonic work, and see *every* painting. This is a patently absurd compulsion; obviously we have to compromise somewhere. If a teacher wants to use Hemingway and the community shies away from *A Farewell to Arms,* there is always *The Old Man and the Sea.* The English teacher can anticipate rather well what the community reaction to a particular book is likely to be and should try to avoid embarrassment for everyone. Always it should be stressed that the teacher is trying to help the youngsters approach modern literature in the proper frame of mind, for certainly the readers of the community cannot deny that ours is a highly realistic literature.

The classroom itself must reflect this purpose of the teacher, for when modern realistic literature is being discussed there must be a serious, adult attitude about the activity. A titter in the back of the room when a frank passage is reached will spoil everything. The students must be appealed to as adults. The best way of doing this, in my judgment, is to help them to see what the literary works reflect, to see books as a record of ideas, of social values, of historic conflict. This means of procedure is best prepared for by handling traditional literature in the same way. Books, our students must always see, are about something, something real and important.

In seeking to bring a greater amount of modern American literature into the high school classroom, I think we should, above all, not be too intense about it. We will win few friends for materials not previously tried if we attempt to proselyte or convince with too apparent a missionary zeal. The teaching of literature is largely a matter of quiet common sense, and we can accomplish most by knowing modern American literature well, believing in its values, and quietly asserting its meaningfulness. There is no literature anywhere in the world today which is superior to American literature; we have reached that point in our cultural history where we need no longer apologize for the condition of our literary art. The foremost novelists, playwrights, and poets of our time are ours, and we would be failing one of our major national achievements if we were to deny this literary art to the American high school student. A list of selections from American literature written since 1920 will be found on page 240.

A basic obstacle to the admission of modern writings to the classroom is that to many of our teachers twentieth-century literature, or at least a great deal of it, is still suspect. What's clear is not clean, and what's clean is not clear. The world is past the half-way mark in the twentieth century, and some of the literary reputations are pretty firmly established, but three of the six American writers who have won the Nobel prize, the highest distinction our age provides, are still largely outside the classroom. The student who wants to know something about Ernest Hemingway, T. S. Eliot, or William Faulkner will generally have to learn it on his own. The picture magazines and the news weeklies are filled with articles about these people, and some of our youngsters are sure to be curious, but so far about all we've said to them is Hands off! Don't touch! You're not old enough yet! If the youngster is genuinely interested, these answers do not satisfy him, and he goes on to read the authors for himself, without the guidance and instruction which they require. The English teacher must not overlook the fact that literature of a mature and highly sophisticated nature is more accessible to our youngsters than ever before. The teenager can and does buy for half a dollar at the corner drug store the most sensational books of the last few decades. Make no mistake about it: he has read *From Here to Eternity*, *Studs Lonigan*, and *God's Little Acre*. His favorite book right now is *The Catcher in the Rye*, by J. D. Salinger, which he reads somewhat sheepishly at the same time that he knows the truth of Salinger's work and its astonishing capacity to move and frighten him. He might not want his English teacher to know he's reading the book, but, on the other hand, he might change his mind if he knew that in two recent critical studies of the American novel the book is highly praised as an original and even profound interpretation of modern anxiety and moral confusion. Actually the book is a deeply religious one, the story of a boy's fumbling quest for spiritual values as he sees the shams of modern society and learns to value only innocence and self-sacrifice.

As teachers of literature we must not run away from modern literature; in a world of unanimously realistic works the English teacher has a new obligation: helping students to approach the realism in the proper frame of mind. In this regard, perhaps above all others, we must not underestimate our students. They are likely to be most knowing about the very matters which both we and their parents wish they could postpone for a few years. Where the circulation of information is concerned, taboos have all but vanished in today's world. We have no choice but to accept modern literature; we must, first of all, *know* it and then be ready to talk with our students about it. Today's high school student will meet as an affectionate equal the teacher, parent, or friend who can talk with him about the anguish and distress of a novel like *Light in August* or a play like *A Streetcar Named Desire* without making him feel shy or apologetic about having read it. What he says about such works will be worth hearing, and parents and teachers may delightedly discover in the youth the taste, judgment, and discrimination which they hoped would be the product of their instruction and loving care.

Dealing with obscurity in modern literature requires a greater diligence. If we have failed so far to make sufficient use of our modern poets, the neglect is understandable: we are not always sure what they are up to, and until an informed criticism can help us, we prefer to avoid the risk of misreading and misinforming. And yet so much is this an age of criticism that a poet of reputation can scarcely publish a new work before explications of it are available in the critical journals and the little magazines. Most of the works we once thought quite obscure are no longer difficult; the obvious example is *The Wasteland*, which, with the help supplied by critics like Cleanth Brooks, F. O. Matthiessen, Kimon Friar, and John Malcolm Brinnin, has become wholly meaningful and clear, to the point of being suitable for high school reading. Studies in interpretation have helped us with difficult modern fiction, too, and the teacher who works with the superior student and wants to explore Joyce or Virginia Woolf or Mann or Kafka or Faulkner will find a copious literature of critical aids. There are, to be sure, some dangers here. Many of our younger English teachers are coming now from colleges and universities where the New Criticism is rather firmly entrenched, and their reading of literary texts has been limited to the kind of writer who best rewards the careful textual analysis which the New Criticism favors and to the kind of reading which keeps the attention focused on problems of form and technique. The teacher of high school English has in the past given inadequate attention to the craft of literature, and certainly the New Criticism can be highly instructive and salutary. But it is easy for preciosity to set in here, with the high school becoming the last frontier of the avant-garde. Nothing is quite so benumbing as an arty high school senior, whose chief claim to esthetic distinction is that he has just read *Nightwood* by Djuna Barnes. Better a healthy enthusiasm for Byron at age sixteen than an effete preoccupation with John Donne!

An important thing to know, of course, is what the youngsters themselves are reading outside their English classes. In this connection a revealing document was prepared in 1956 by Professor Albert Friedman of Harvard and Mr. R. S. Peterson, head of the English Department of New Trier Township High School. This is "A Report on the Literature Examination, 1955, of the School and College Study of Admission with Advanced Standing"; in other words, a study of the works of literature cited by students in answering the questions on the Advanced Placement Literature examination for that year. It is tremendously revealing of the range, the seriousness, and the complexity of what high school students have read well enough to be able to write about authoritatively.

True, these are superior students, but even so, the record of their reading is impressive. Here is a document to use in answering the critics of today's schools who charge that we are failing to instill the desire and the capacity to read. Obviously quite a few of today's boys and girls are not only reading much but reading deeply and well—both the classics *and* modern works. As a matter of fact, the amount of modern literature cited is one of the principal revelations of the report. In the papers of one school the authors most frequently cited were Joyce, Eliot, Faulkner, Kafka, D. H. Lawrence, Scott Fitzgerald, and Joseph Conrad. In the papers of this school *Hamlet* was referred to three times and *Macbeth* six times, but Eliot was cited fourteen times and Joyce seventeen.

The Friedman-Peterson Report is revealing in another direction also—the large number of foreign works cited. Today's student may be considerably less provincial than his teachers; he wants to know not only English and American literature, but French, Russian, Spanish, Italian, and other literatures as well. Stendhal, Flaubert, Tolstoi, Dostoevsky, Lorca, and Silone are names that he is beginning to know. True, with a very few exceptions, he is reading the work in translation, but certainly it is better for the student to know *The Red and the Black* in translation than not to know it at all. Croce was undoubtedly right when he said that the work of literary art is never really translatable, that the translation is a new entity altogether; but our reasons for reading are various, not the least of which is our desire to expose ourselves to ideas; and in reproducing the ideas of a foreign work, today's translators are extremely scrupulous. Publishers at present choose translators with great care, and it is not uncommon to see a reviewer of a translation remark that it captures faithfully not only the meaning but also the spirit and tone of the original. In recent years we have had some remarkable collaborations of author and translator—that of Thomas Mann and Mrs. H. T. Lowe-Porter is perhaps the most felicitous example. Here the translation of virtually every phrase was a matter of conference and consultation, with both author and translator working to make the transference into the new language wholly exact and artistic. Constance Garnett's Modern Library translation of *Crime and Punishment* may not have the full cataclysmic intensity of the original, but today's student cannot afford not to know Dostoevsky in one form or another.

Furthermore, this is the age of One World—of the United Nations and international cooperation. We have imbued our people with the feeling that peace and international good will are possible only when a full understanding of the characteristics, habits, and customs of foreign people exists, and surely the most rewarding source of this information is the literature of other lands. Balzac and Turgenev, Goethe and Cervantes, Ibsen and Aeschylus—these are the storehouses we must visit if we are to know the shaping of the continental mind and the development of national attitudes and conventions. One of the aims of the English teacher in today's world ought to be to instill in his students a desire to know other languages and other literatures. It seems to be nothing less than an abdication of public responsibility for most of our people to be monolingual and to know none of the literary treasures which have been produced outside the confines of a single language. The high school literature program is definitely out of step with what we have come to regard as the major necessity of modern political organization if it ignores Continental and even Asian literature. The English-speaking people do not have a monopoly on the production of literary classics, though many high school anthologies would lead us to think so.

Yet the anthology makers are scarcely at fault. Anthologists will put into books exactly what we want them to, and publishers will bring these books out if they can be guaranteed sales. The trouble is that whenever a publisher tries something experimental in the way of a literature text, when he tries to incorporate new material into the collection, he meets with a wall of resistance and hears the same tiresome chorus, "Where are the good old reliables? Where are *Evangeline* and *Treasure Island* and *The Lady of the Lake?*" Publishers are business men and want to make a profit. The first step in getting exciting books with world literature orientation is up to the teachers. Let us applaud the efforts of editors and publishers whenever they decide to do something different and to include numerous selections which haven't been in the books previously. They take big risks here; publishing such books is a very expensive operation. But the teacher who uses them will have the opportunity to bring some fresh air into the high school literature course and to prepare for establishment of a world view because of sections which indicate through literature the ties Americans have with the rest of the world.

There is a danger here, in that literature may come to seem nothing more than an adjunct to the social sciences. Committed to the democratic ideal as we are, we make the teaching of literature part of our humanitarian liberalism; we tend to see the uses of literature only in a social context. The essay, the story, even the poem or play, becomes our means of instruction in racial equality, social justice, international brotherhood and good will. These, to be sure, are legitimate and even desirable uses of the literary work, but unfortunately some of our teachers have come to see them as the only uses. Literature does indeed serve the social side of man—throughout history it has been one of his most effective means of ordering society—but it serves also that part of him which is individual, distinctive, and alone. Literature helps form the community, but it speaks also to the man who from time to time must stand apart and wrestle in solitude with his soul. When we make literature subservient to social science, we tend to see man only in terms of the social unit, or, even more disastrously, in terms of a limited segment of it, and thus we dishonor the only element of man which establishes his communion with others, namely, his individuality.

"Poetry," said Shelley, "is *connate* with the origin of man"; that is, it is part of the biological organism; he could not escape it if he wanted to, just as he could not escape music or painting. Our anthropologists have never found a society without its drawings, its dances, its chants, and its stories. "Man is man by virtue of language," said the German philologist Von Humboldt, and the corollary is that man is civilized man by virtue of the esthetic shaping of that language which goes into his literature. In our zeal to make the good democratic society, let us remember that it can be nothing more than barbarous unless the esthetic impulses of man are known, honored, and satisfied. That means, for you and me, remembering that whatever else literature can be and do, it is first of all an art, having almost its own autonomy, and that it is older than any human institution of social organization. As long as man *is*, his art will be with him. Some of the new literature textbooks seem to forget this and to involve the reader only in that kind of literature designed to create certain attractive social attitudes and to bring forth approved social responses. This is the same spirit which motivated the New York City Board of Education recently in its removal of *Huckleberry Finn* from the high school curriculum on the grounds that Twain's book is offensive to the Negro race. Fortunately for our sanity the action was vigorously opposed by a Negro member of the Board who could see (1) that the book is not offensive to the Negro race—Jim is by far its noblest character, (2) that Twain's use of the word "nigger" is a matter of historical accuracy, and (3) most important of all, that whatever it may contain, it is perhaps the greatest work of the creative imagination yet to come out of America—nothing less than a magnificent heroic poem about man in timeless struggle to find direction in his life on this physical earth. If *this* book can turn us away from the democratic ideal, we are already lost.

Perhaps literature does most for society when it performs its oldest function, that of enriching personality, of extending the boundaries of individual vision, of giving new dimension to human sensibility, in short, of developing that combination of virtues and talents which for both ancient Greece and Renaissance Europe made the complete man. Perhaps the state is served best when its education seems to serve it least, when, that is, the man rather than the state is the center of the focus. Perhaps wholesale or large-scale reform is never possible, only the remolding of the hearts of individual men, with literature used as an instrument through which man learns to investigate himself, study his own motivation, and come to self-identity.

Yet here, too, in a clinical age like our own, caution must be observed, lest literature be thought of only as a means of psychotherapy. There are movements in this direction also in today's public school, efforts to use literature as a branch of guidance counseling, one of the materials by means of which deviation of whatever variety is corrected and the youngster's personality brought back to a psychological norm. The great word in this undertaking is "adjustment," and teachers of English who subscribe to the view adopt for use only those stories, essays, poems, and plays which vicariously do the operations of the analyst. "Literature as psychiatry" is a very real design in many of our secondary schools, and though no one would deny the power of literature to force upon us a penetrating scrutiny of ourselves, something like the law of diminishing returns begins to set in when we will admit to the curriculum only those literary works which our psychology assures us are sufficiently innocuous. I have heard teachers with this psychiatric point of view object strenuously to any fixed curriculum in literature, arguing that a reading program must never be imposed from without, lest it block the free development of personality according to a standard determined by an educational psychology. One may legitimately wonder, it seems to me, which is the more hazardous imposition here—that of the literature or that of the psychology. I know of one public school system which now employs "personality adjustment coordinators," and the images invoked by this term are very painful for me. I keep seeing little boys and girls come down a conveyor belt, with a personality adjustment coordinator standing at the end of the line holding some horrible metallic gadget, ready to adjust the personalities. And then

I see all the little children marching away, every one alike, every one anonymous, every one adjusted to the cold grim reality of Mr. Orwell's 1984.

The horrors of the world of Orwell's imagining are made possible, you will remember, because of the corruption of man's language, the organization of patterns of communication according to the linguistic aberrations of Newspeak and Doublethink. Orwell correctly understood that no enslavement of man is possible without a corresponding, and usually preliminary, interference with the expression of thought. Precision, honesty, concreteness are the qualities which distinguish man's use of language when he is free; and the powers that want to manipulate man and force him into darkness and bewilderment or into an inhuman automation know that they must, first of all, tamper with the instruments which he uses for communicating with others.

Teachers of literature should realize that there is much which they cannot accomplish even though they feel that they should attempt it. Because literature is an art, the results of many of our dealings with it can never be prescribed, either educationally or otherwise. Our results with it will always be, in a very real sense, unpredictable. The Committee on Curriculum of the National Council of Teachers of English puts the matter very sensibly: "Neither teachers nor the public can grasp the full significance of the intellectual and emotional experience that may come from the penetration of the ideas and feelings of human beings, recorded—whether in prose or poetry—with what may be called poetic truth. Poetic truth is the truth which is not factual, but that is true to the actions and aspirations of mankind."

As with literature, so with all the other arts; educationally, we must not be too knowing about them. Many teachers who can spell out in minutest detail their reasons for teaching a particular story or a poem are ones to whom I would have some doubts about entrusting the task. The teacher of literature needs to start with a very large supply of intellectual humility and to be very willing to consider that the tasks of a piece of literature are never done, and that we had better be prepared to accept the fact that we can never anticipate fully what it can do *to* and *for* students.

First of all, literature ought to provide students with pleasure. In our present academic hyperseriousness, we are likely to forget occasionally that the first end of literature, as of any art, is to provide pleasure. It is encouraging to see this point insisted upon by the Curriculum Committee of the National Council; the Committee says, quite succinctly, "If the study of literature does not provide enjoyment, the teaching has been a failure." To be sure, literature can be a source of moral, political, and psychological instruction—a great work like *The Divine Comedy* actually contains all three—but *before* this instruction must come the directness of the pure esthetic delight which we take in the poem. This pleasure is, to be sure, not exclusively of one kind; there are infinite possibilities. But certainly we want our students to come out of the schools with the ability to take real enjoyment from reading of various kinds, as well as to have more socially productive lives as a result of reading experience.

How many of our youngsters are coming out of the high school today with this sense of enjoyment? How many learn to like what they read—to the point at which they talk about it among themselves with affection and go on remembering it significantly after the classroom has finished with it? If each of us attempted to construct a list of the books which he really enjoyed in his high school reading, how many would we come up with? For many readers, the list would be depressingly brief.

There are some teachers of English who think we have recently made too much of this matter of getting the student to like a piece of literature; they deride our going so far as to allow him to read only what he wants to read, putting very popular materials into his hands, being willing to accept book reports on *Joe Anderson, First Baseman* rather than insisting that he stay with the more or less standard works of the traditional curriculum. These teachers argue that there are times when the materials must be brought in without too meticulous a regard for student likes and dislikes. They insist that there are times when the student simply must be told what is good, and good for him; that his taste for something better can be formed only if we expose him to materials which at the outset are so challenging that the question of whether he likes or dislikes them is largely irrelevant. In other words, we often discover that the very novel which he begins by resisting and even disliking, *Pride and Prejudice*, for example, comes to mean the most to him, as a source of both instruction *and* enjoyment. A teacher of my acquaintance once used this analogy: would the school cafeteria serve the students only what they like? Hot dogs and ice cream, probably? How would the kids ever get a balanced diet?

Can the two points of view be reconciled? Can we somehow combine what a student likes with what he ought to read?

The beginning teacher of English can feel certain that he is going to meet with some resistance as he offers various books to students, even in programs where he has almost unlimited freedom in setting up the curriculum and where the reading course is very liberal. What should he do when this resistance manifests itself?

First, he should not be too worried or distressed. Some teachers who see their students resisting a book get desperate and panicky; one sees accounts of what they do written up for the publications of state and local teachers' organizations: "How We Made a Football Game of *Julius Caesar*," or "How We Turned Our Discussion of *The Scarlet Letter* into a Panel on Teenage Dating." These are the practices in which we start "conning" students again—forcing them into false positions which both they and we know are absurd. The teacher who has to construct these "cute" teaching devices— "What Does Drag-Strip Racing Tell Us about *Ivanhoe*?"—generally has a very limited understanding of the values of the work itself. The first thing he ought to do is to reread it, or read a few first-rate pieces of criticism about it.

Certainly a first obligation of the teacher of literature is to *know* his material, to know it in full dimension, to know it critically and imaginatively, to know it in the way that causes him to be forever asking questions about it, to know it in ways that never fully satisfy him. To know *Huckleberry Finn* not only as the record of a boy's growing up but also as a great lyric poem about the mysteries of life and death. To know *The Scarlet Letter* not only as a critical comment on the moral rigors of Puritanism but also as an intricate symbolic arrangement partly accepting and partly denying the advanced thought of Emerson. To know *Green Mansions* not only as an assertion of the values of nature against those of the commercialized city but also as an ingenious and perhaps even blasphemous travesty on the story of the Christian redemption. To know *The Return of the Native* not only as a story of how a man cannot go home again but also as a story of its author's resistance to the whole doctrine of nineteenth-century romanticism, so that nature becomes a frightening antagonist which destroys with equal casualness those who accept and those who reject it. To know what he teaches, in short, in terms of the capacity of the literary work to talk to man about what must forever concern him because he is man: family, love, money, war, and death—and to talk to him on an adult level, or at least on a level which will seem adult to the teenager.

Second, the teacher of literature can do much to prepare in the student a receptive frame of mind. With introductory materials about the author, the subject of the book, the times in which the book was written, the teacher can usually stir up a little enthusiasm or expectancy about it. I have heard students make such remarks as, "I can't wait to read *The Ancient Mariner* in Miss So-and-So's class. Everybody says she makes it so interesting." If the teacher can develop this kind of reputation or this brand of expectancy, the job is half done. A very major part of the preparation for the reading of any work is the teacher's own enthusiasm and his ability to project this enthusiasm and pass it on to others. The teacher should have a large stock of anecdotes, biographical data, historical incidents, and so on, to clarify points of the introduction. The good teacher will like the material he is presenting so much that he will make his own interest in it catching, to the point that students will look up in surprise when the bell rings at the end of the class because the time has passed so fast.

Third, the teacher can ask the students to give the book a fair trial, not to form their judgments too soon. He can, for example, help them to see that it may have values not immediately apparent, values which will be brought out through discussion and closer acquaintance. Confronted with lack of interest or inattention, the teacher should face these attitudes head on and talk about them with the students. Generally the teacher finds that the lack of interest stems from a few misconceptions which can be easily cleared up. But he must be careful here; there should be no preaching or condescension. He must, above all else, be fair, giving credit for interesting views and listening to all honest views with respect.

Fourth, in every way possible, the teacher should help relate the book to the experience of his students. We have heard this so often in recent years that it has become a cliché, but it remains sound advice. Particularly, teachers should relate the book to student experience with language. We should help our students to see the work as *achievement*, to see the literary problem as the author faced it. Having come to the realization that most royal honors in eighteenth-century England were farcical, how did Swift, in the first book of Gulliver, go about getting this into words? What kind of structural conflict did he set up to make his meaning stand out with unusual strength? Students can be asked to place themselves in the position of the writer wanting to get an audience for his work and testing various methods for doing so. Here the possibilities for language instruction are tremendous—language instruction which should be reflected in both the students' understanding and future composition work. Some authors can be used specifically for language values. Here are a few examples: In "The Pit and the Pendulum," Edgar Allan Poe says of his protagonist lying on the floor of the pit that he "unclosed" his eyes. Why *unclosed* rather than *opened?* In an exciting poem like Gerard Manley Hopkins' "God's Grandeur," why the repetition in such a line as "Generations have trod, have trod, have trod"? Why does Shakespeare call it a "primrose" path to the everlasting bonfire? The possibilities are endless.

Fifth, students should be encouraged to give their own honest reactions to the work. Students are flattered when the teacher says, "Give your own opinion," but they have to be helped to see that indiscriminate opinion-giving is treacherous and not always productive; in short, they have to be helped to see the difference between informed opinion and careless opinion. The values in this kind of exercise are salutary even beyond the literature class.

Sixth, individual pieces of literature can be related to other works. An interesting way of handling this is to demonstrate that certain themes are persistent through literary history. Without going into the advanced modern theories of myth and archetypal patterns, the teacher can demonstrate recurrent situations in stories, poems, and plays. Some of these would be (1) the return of the hero, as it is found in the *Odyssey, Agamemnon, Ulysses,* and *Mourning Becomes Electra;* (2) the quest for the Holy Grail, in *Idylls of the King,* and in all works where some great ideal is pursued, as in *Arrowsmith;* (3) the defiance by a minor deity or spirit, the Lucifer or Prometheus theme, as it can be found in *Moby Dick* and *Jude the Obscure;* (4) enchantment by *la belle dame sans merci,* as in *Of Human Bondage* and, to change the sex, *Death in Venice;* (5) the idyllic bliss of a Golden Age, as in the Leatherstocking Tales and Melville's South Sea romances; (6) the theme of Christian atonement, as in *Lord Jim* and *Light in August;* (7) the experience of being alone on a desert island, as in *Robinson Crusoe, Swiss Family Robinson,* and *The Admirable Crichton;* (8) the picture of the "other society," either as Utopia in *Utopia, The New Atlantis,* and *Erewhon,* or as the world of horrors, *Brave New World, 1984,* and parts of *Gulliver's Travels;* (9) the hunt as ritual, as in *Moby Dick,* the Leatherstocking Tales, and *The Bear,* and (10) the return of the man given up for dead, as in *Enoch Arden* and a number of recent works. Suggestions of this kind can often send the student to other books which he will read on his own and report on, even, at times, with his enthusiasm sending other students to the books.

One question which the teacher of English has to resolve at the outset of his career is how much outside reading he will require of his students and how many book reports, if any, he will ask them to submit. For many beginning teachers the question is already settled by the department of which he becomes a member. Department committees at many schools have worked out book report plans which require a definite number of books each semester from a department list, reported on in department-prescribed forms. Other teachers, however, will find that the matter is left entirely up to them and that their solution will have to be personal and individual.

There are excellent book lists which can easily be secured. *Good Reading,* a paperback prepared by The Committee on College Reading and published as a Mentor Book, is revised fairly often and offers numerous suggestions. Books are listed in various ways, and the student will find the lists easy to use. Two reading lists appear as appendices to this book, though they are somewhat specialized. Teachers who want a first-rate precollege list should see "What Have You Read?" prepared for the students at Phillips Exeter Academy. Indispensable are the lists in *Literature Study in the High School* by Dwight L. Burton, published by Holt, Rinehart and Winston, 1959.

The traditional book report, with its list of important characters, summary of the plot, and brief sketch of the author's life, has fortunately just about disappeared. Indeed, some teachers have abandoned the written book report altogether in favor of individual conferences with the students, or oral reports before the class, or the recording of titles on three-by-five cards which are handed in occasionally, or just free discussion periods in which students talk about their reading with their classmates. My personal preference is for some kind of written work—a composition, ideally, developing the thought of the book. Often I have asked students merely to answer two questions, "Why do you think the author wrote the book?" and "Why do you think he wrote it as he did?" The results are not always satisfactory, but they have the advantage of being the work of the students.

The teacher who wants students to read should, above everything else, make books easily accessible to students. The English classroom should be filled with books—in shelves, on tables, on the window sills. A room library is imperative. The books should be of many kinds, and they should be attractive. Keep the jackets on them if you can. Room displays can feature books in the news, one from which a current motion picture has been made, or a Pulitzer prize winner, or one dealing with a current national problem. From this experience of being surrounded by books students will take the impression that books are a necessary and inescapable part of life, with much to say about what matters most.

CHAPTER TEN

The Teacher
and the Art of Fiction

THOUGH THEIR STUDENTS SEEM TO ENJOY fiction more than any other kind of literature in the secondary school course of study, teachers of English often feel when they come to the end of a novel that the class has profited very little from the experience. No matter how diligently they read the book and no matter how eagerly they participate in discussions of it, students often give the impression that they consider the whole exercise of novel reading in the school frivolous and of little value to their future lives. What they seem to want is some *practical* motivation for reading stories, since story reading for them still has associations of childhood; a story is something which was read by Mommy or Daddy at the end of the day, if you were good. They are not moved by arguments that the school must instruct in the wise use of leisure time or that one of the marks of a civilized man is the high quality of his amusements. Students in America do not like to feel that they are wasting time. It is not unusual for a teacher to hear a tenth-grade boy say, "Sure, I enjoyed *A Tale of Two Cities,* but what good is that stuff? What's it all for?"

The complaint is not hard to understand. American youngsters are the product of two dominant points of view, the Puritan and the pragmatic, both hostile to frivolity and time-wasting, both suspicious of the indolence of fantasy and make-believe, both uncertain about the claims of the imagination. In America novels were once sermonized against from the pulpits of New England; in some communities they were banned by zealous pastors. Part of the frontier culture was the resistance to books other than the Bible, religious tracts, and practical studies of husbandry. Our Midwestern and Western writers have left us abundant evidence of their struggles to convince parents and elders of the values of reading literature. Abraham Lincoln reading by firelight is an important part of the American mythos. Men of practical affairs in America take pride in their ignorance of the arts; they never quite accept as one of themselves the man who knows music, or painting, or literature. We have made a great comic situation of the plight of the successful businessman who discovers that his son wants to be a poet. American men for the most part read novels with a guilty conscience. With leisure time on their hands they are more comfortable working in the yard or improving their bodies on the golf course or talking with friends. When men read for pleasure they are happier with nonfiction: books of travel, adventure, science, biography. It is their wives who bring home the new novels from the lending libraries. Though they may have enjoyed fiction very much in college courses, the reading of novels is an activity which they seem to put away with the things of their youth when they go out to make a living. In my teaching experience I have known two ultra-serious-minded fathers who asked that their sons be permitted in high school to read something other than novels. "I don't want my boy to waste his time," said one of these parents. "Please let him read a book on science instead."

Naturally this attitude filters down to the students, and the teacher detects, particularly in the boys of the class, a certain uneasiness or discomfort when class time is being spent on novels. Painful as they are likely to find the experience, the students would prefer to be at work on grammar—or "English," as they significantly put it. I have known teachers who preferred heavy concentration on literature in high school years to receive complaints from their students. "We're not getting enough *English*," the young people said.

Faced with this resistance to the novel on the grounds of its impracticality, teachers have quite frequently done the obvious thing—they have tried to make the novel very practical indeed. They have told their students that novels are great repositories of moral truth, that we read them in order to acquire moral and civic virtue, that there are lessons to be learned and great messages to be apprehended in novels, that novels (only certain good ones, mind you) are a guide to the better life, the richness of personality, the happiness of earthly existence, and the eternal rewards of the life to come. The discussion of novels in the classroom had a homiletic rather than an esthetic air, as the teacher worked doggedly to extract the last ounce of inspiration from the book. At the end of the hour everyone in the room was radiant with the glow of having known the finer things in life. (And then on the way home the boys bought *Peyton Place* at the corner drug store.)

But the teacher is not altogether wrong in this approach. Men write novels for reasons—very good reasons usually. The most responsible novelists of literary history have been men and women with observations to make about life, and these reflections were always moral in the sense that they attempted to illumine human behavior. Even the extreme naturalists—Zola, Dreiser, Farrell—have had instruction to offer. Studs Lonigan is, perhaps, the most unfortunate character in American fiction, for he is damned in two worlds, this one and the next, and the book is plainly intended as a warning. Surely no reader coming to the end of *An American Tragedy* ever supposed that Dreiser is saying of Clyde Griffiths, "Go thou, dear reader, and do likewise." As in the Bible, moral instruction in fiction is often a matter of being told what *not* to do.

So the teacher who wants students to see the moral profit that can be gained from reading fiction is very much on the right track. The difficulty is likely to be that what the teacher understands as morality is too limited, too unimaginatively prescribed by the standards of middle-class gentility. The morality of a great novel will often *not* be that of the Sunday morning ten o'clock service. To be sure, it very well may be. But the teacher of fiction had better be prepared to accept the fact that our novelists have generally taken a somewhat unorthodox view of human affairs, even those, like George Eliot, for example, who now seem so "safe," and that the teacher is consequently obliged to consider and clarify for students points of view which the teacher may be entirely unwilling to accept. Few of us today would accept the world view of Thomas Hardy, yet the high school curriculum would be much poorer without *The Mayor of Casterbridge* and *The Return of the Native*.

Seeing the full scope of the morality with which a novel is qualified to deal makes necessary some knowledge of how the novel came into being in the first place. We sometimes forget that, in its present form at least, it is the youngest of all our literary forms, only a little more than two hundred years old. Literary scholars are generally unwilling to say what the first English novel was, *Moll Flanders* or *Pamela* or *Clarissa*, but most would agree that the middle of the eighteenth century is the starting point. Similarly, they are cautious about saying a great deal on the subject of how the novel came into being. Two explanations are offered, one esthetic, the other social.

The first explanation, of limited utility in the high school classroom unless the students are following a survey program in English literature, says that some form of prose narrative was in existence almost from the beginning of our literature, and that this form of fiction developed through the centuries, appropriating unto itself more and more advantages, until the novel as we know it became a reality. The greatest impetus to this development was the varied literary activity of the seventeenth century, including such literary exercises as the essay, the character sketch, the religious meditation, the literary sermon, the vogue of literary letter writing, journalism (particularly journalistic character studies like the Sir Roger de Coverley papers). This explanation says that there was a gradual fusion or amalgamation of these kinds of writing with the narrative art of the prose romances which had been popular in the sixteenth century, works like Sidney's *Arcadia*, Lyly's *Euphues*, Nashe's *The Unfortunate Traveler*, and others, and that the coalescence resulted in *Moll Flanders*, *Pamela*, and *Tom Jones*. This explanation also, naturally, takes note of the influence of foreign narratives, for example, of such works as *Don Quixote* and *Gil Blas*, on the English literature of roguery.

Obviously this explanation has much to recommend it, and it is probably the more conventional and generally accepted one. Some scholars and critics, however, have felt that several objections might be raised, the first one being that the explanation is too simple and too easy. A work like Richardson's *Clarissa* has so little in common not only with the prose romances of the sixteenth century but also with the literary exercises of the seventeenth century (with the exception of literary letter writing, of course) that some students of the novel have questioned the fact of coalescence. Or, better, perhaps, the most distinguishing features of *Clarissa*, namely, coherent moral and social commentary in relation to character delineation and thematic organization, are so totally alien to the earlier works as to cause us to wonder how attention to these earlier works can show the way in which *Clarissa* came into being. There are, of course, in the late seventeenth and early eighteenth centuries, some narratives in which we see the various literary conventions merging; the writings of Mrs. Aphra Behn would be cases in point. At any rate, this is one way in which the origin of the novel is explained.

The other explanation is a social one; it insists that the development of the form of the novel cannot be separated from the rise of the middle class; the development must be seen in terms of the contrast in the literary preparations of the nobility and the *bourgeoisie*. The nobility had traditionally been educated to both appreciation of and even sometimes proficiency in the poetic arts; according to the Continental tradition, to which English nobility generally subscribed, the noble young man was expected to be an amateur poet as well as the patron of poets and poetic dramatists. With the decline of the nobility, especially after the Glorious Revolution, the practice of patronage began to disappear; poetry, too, went into a partial decline, from which it was rescued by poets like Dryden and Pope, who learned to use it for political and satirical purposes. Members of the middle class now found themselves in positions of wealth, power, and authority, without the cultural preparation for such positions. Whether vocally or otherwise, they demanded an art form which would serve their needs, which would dramatize the acquisition of social and cultural graces, and which would instruct in a practical morality commensurate with etiquette and prestige. Many of the middle class were dissenters and thus were accustomed to reading religious narrative, for example, Bunyan or Puritan moral parables. The novel, then, came into being to serve the middle class and to give its members the social and moral instruction they wanted in the artistic form most palatable to them. Men who in a time of patronage might have written poems dedicated to noblemen now turned to the writing of fiction to please a middle-class audience.

The first novels themselves would seem to support this explanation, since it describes them very well. The fiction of Richardson, Fielding, Smollett, Fanny Burney is that in which we see, above everything else, class relationships, with shifting cultural, social, and moral values. The characters of the novel frequent the centers of activity of the time: the fashionable resorts like Bath; the theater, opera, and stylish balls in London; the country houses of the gentry or upper middle-class. And all of these novels contain some form of moral instruction in terms of judgment made on the behavior of the characters who have not yet made the proper adjustments to the approved standards of the day.

Both explanations are valuable to the teacher of English; they are not, in any sense, competitive. But the second is probably the more dramatic for secondary school youngsters, and it has the advantage of helping both teacher and students to see that a discussion of the form of a novel is inseparable from a consideration of its social and moral attachments. The form of a novel is not solely a matter of esthetics. As Professor Mark Schorer, of the University of California at Berkeley, has said, "The novel, written in prose, bears a closer resemblance to discursive forms than it does to poetry, thus easily opening itself to first questions about philosophy or politics, and, since it is traditionally a middle-class vehicle with a reflective social function, it bears an apparently more immediate relation to life than it does to art, thus easily opening itself to first questions about conduct." In other words, the form of the novel begins in idea and the thematic treatment of idea in terms of human relationships. The two explanations of the origin of the novel might be brought together if we say that the novel is a coalescence of simple narrative art with a variety of the literary exercises of the seventeenth century, resulting from a social exigency and middle-class demand which caused individual writers to engage in the practice of working out with these materials a new art form. Or, in still other words, if we want the most nearly accurate explanation of the origin of the novel, we will probably be wise to accept *both* explanations, allowing each to elucidate the other. In this connection a number of studies are helpful to the teacher of English, but the standard work is Ernest Baker's *The History of the English Novel.*

Either of these historical approaches should provide teachers with some substance for discussion of the *art* of the novel. Teachers and prospective teachers of English have regularly indicated their need for help in this matter. Lacking the considerably more precise formal outlines of the poem or play, the novel spreads, often at great length, over the whole of human experience, and the shaping hand of the author behind the work is sometimes difficult to see. The teacher, understandably, falls back on a discussion of content alone, a consideration of the values and attitudes which the book seems to promote, while trying, sometimes desperately, to elicit student evaluation of these attitudes and points of view. Rather soon the teacher realizes that this kind of attention is in no sense a discussion of literature but of religion, philosophy, social science, or psychology. Teachers are now eager to pattern lessons so that the *whole* piece of fiction can be seen, the craftsmanship as well as the content, the form as much as the matter.

Suggestions can be drawn from various critical studies of the novel, and in recent years these have been greatly increasing. The close textual analysis which was once given only to poetry and poetic drama is now being applied to novels, particularly to those which give evidence of careful planning and construction; and the teacher of English on the secondary level must be aware of a new critical and scholarly seriousness about *how* fiction is written—in other words, about the novel as a work of art.

For if our students are to have adequate awareness of a writer's accomplishments, if, that is, they are to respect a work and see reasons for inclusion of it in a course of study or on a reading list, then they should be helped to see the full formal nature of the achievement. The teacher must show the problems raised by the writing of a particular work and the strategies applied by the author. How the teacher will do this is a matter of the most careful methodology; usually, of course, generalization and definition will grow inductively out of discovery and illustration, as the teacher and students compare and contrast various narratives of their experience, and as the teacher makes a working synthesis of various critical points of view.

Thus any scheme for handling the form of fiction is almost certain to be highly speculative and eclectic—at the present time, at least. But it should provide the security of using such words as "theme," "tone," and that great old *bête noire* of student book reports, "style," with some degree of particularity and exactness.

The first decision for the teacher of a particular novel is the amount of time to be spent on it. This will vary from novel to novel, but it can safely be said that teachers usually spend more time than necessary on a full-length piece of fiction. In teaching a novel, the instructor should be constantly asking various questions of himself: Am I inclined to be too meticulous, to insist on the retention of picayune detail? In asking myself whether or not the students are getting the meaning of the book, am I taking sufficient time to evaluate the material itself? Am I asking for a kind of reading inappropriate to the high school, a mere cataloguing of names, places, dates, and objects? Am I distinguishing between *essential* plot detail, necessary to an understanding of the author's purpose, and that which is mere embellishment and decoration? Are there some sections of the book through which students can move more rapidly than through others? Should I select several scenes of major importance, work with these in class carefully, and then loosely relate the rest of the book to them?

Through the whole unit the teacher must constantly ask this

question: What am I doing this for? Am I going to ask for a complete reading of the book within, perhaps, a week before we begin our discussion of it, or shall we read a few chapters at a time, a certain number of pages each night? Answers to these questions are likely to be determined by the special objectives implicit in the nature of the material. Obviously the procedure with *Robinson Crusoe*, a narrative which has little formal order, will be quite different from that with *Pride and Prejudice*. In the first case, there would seem to be no special reason why the book in its entirety should be seen before discussion of it begins in class. Besides, it is quite long, and since it is generally used in junior high school, youngsters of that age can hardly be expected to retain an over-all picture of it. For *Pride and Prejudice*, however, there are marked advantages to seeing the book as a structural whole before any discussion of its meaning begins. With books of high literary distinction, a suggested procedure is that the teacher, in distributing the books, assign the reading to be accomplished during a two-week period while the class is working on some other language activity. At the end of that time, a one-week intensified discussion of the book begins. During this week students will be taking notes and organizing their ideas about the book so that they will be prepared to write a careful paper of analysis when the week's discussion is over. Obviously, under this plan, some of the daily discussion time can be used to clarify misunderstood points, but this can be done without breaking the pattern or scheme of discussion which the teacher decides upon in order to deal adequately with the work. The important thing is that there be in the teacher's mind a certainty about the purposes for asking students to read the book in the first place.

With fiction especially the question, "What are we doing this for?" must be repeatedly faced, and the answers must direct the nature of class activities, the length of assignments, the kinds of testing, the extent to which supplementary activities will be used: writing, word study, further reading on a similar theme. The class discussion itself can be a means of clarifying the detail of the story. Students should certainly take notes as they read, in order to keep the large perspective of the novel in mind. The teacher will want to make constant associations of the material with what students already know, with other stories, motion pictures, television programs, plays.

Throughout the discussion, reference must be made to the text. Students should not be permitted to make assertions about idea, theme, or character unless they can support what they say with specific passages in the book. Furthermore, close attention to the text makes possible a constant analysis of the art of its language. Students should realize that the novelist works *only* with language; he does not have the advantage of stage presentation, which the dramatist has, or of meter, rhyme, and the order of words on a page, which the poet has. He must explore every possibility which language offers his story, and of course this is going to mean that he will, from time to time, take chances with language and use it in unfamiliar ways. Syntax in a novel can be a highly creative matter; length of the sentences and word order can actually be part of the subject. It is inconceivable that Ernest Hemingway's stories could say what they say if they were written with any other kind of sentence structure. Also, novelists occasionally apply special meanings to words, and the reader must be alert to unique semantic considerations. Sentences of structural complexity should be analyzed; passages of strong sensory appeal should be singled out for observation and comment; the effects of irony, wit, satire, and parody should not be missed. Tone, too, should receive its share of attention, for it is tone very frequently which reveals the author's attitude—toward his subject, toward us, his audience, and even toward himself. The teacher of fiction never forgets for a moment that his subject is language, language shaped as story.

With this kind of critical analysis in the classroom, students should see that the principle of form in a novel is chiefly a matter of coherence, of the way in which all parts of the novel work together toward a successful whole, so that, in a very real sense, they are not even separable—each part complements every other part.

Teachers, like critics, will differ in what they call the various parts of a novel, but the instruction should, of course, be consistent. Once specific meanings have been established in a class, they should be followed throughout the discussion, and students should learn to use them responsibly. To demonstrate what discoveries about a book might be made during careful discussion of a work, I have chosen to do here a formal analysis of William Faulkner's short novel *The Bear*. This piece is infrequently used at present in the high school, but if we omit the long fourth part, with its involved stream-of-consciousness (as several anthology reprints of the story do), then it becomes, in my judgment, a first-rate story for the upper levels of senior high school, particularly in classes of better-than-average ability. And it is time that American students should know the major contemporary writers, of whom no one, at the moment, has a higher literary reputation than William Faulkner.

Any discussion of the importance of Faulkner would certainly have to deal at length with this story, for it represents his most extensive use of primitive myth, legend, and ritual. It is a story of consecration and dedication, as well as an explicit statement of Faulkner's view that the South was corrupted and the seeds of its destruction sown by the institution of slavery. Critical readers of Faulkner are certain that whenever Ike McCaslin appears in a Faulkner story, he speaks for his creator; so in the long and difficult fourth section of this work, we are presented with the most sustained development in all of Faulkner of the qualities in men which he admires and respects. And looking about him at the encroaching materialism of modern industrial society and its betrayal of the old primitive impulses, Ike comes to a deep admiration for the Negro, of whom he speaks an eloquent tribute. (Though the class would not be reading this fourth section, Ike's tribute should be presented by the teacher.) "They will endure. They are better than we are. Stronger than we are. They have the lasting virtues—endurance, and pity and tolerance and forbearance and fidelity and love of children. Because they had it already from the old free fathers a longer time free than us because we have never been free."

As Harry Modean Campbell and Ruel E. Foster say in their book on Faulkner, *The Bear* is the best example of Faulkner's "overt use of Nature as norm and the noble savage motifs." In the mixed blood of Sam Fathers (notice his name), half Indian and half Negro, are combined two things Faulkner greatly admires—the primitive stoicism of the Negro and the Indian's physical contact with nature.

The idea of the story is that man realizes the full dimension of his being only when he is in close alliance with nature and when he has learned the ritual, in this case the hunt, by which man discovers how to be at home in the natural world; and that when man has acquired that knowledge he is no longer fitted for the artifice and the greed and the inhumanity of the money-grubbers and the exploiters who enslave their fellow men either through the actual institution of slavery or through the economic slavery produced by factories and railroads and banks.

The theme is established in terms of a conflict between two worlds: the world of the wilderness and animals (that is, the world of the old free fathers) and the civilized world of contemporary man who has set up barricades between himself and nature in the form of houses, manufacturing plants, and material values. The conflict is resolved in the story with the defeat of the first world, the destruction of the wilderness, as the saw mill buys the hunting lands and sends its train into the forest with men who will cut down the trees.

The plot of the story, insofar as we mean only the hunting story—that is, exclusive of part four—is clear, simple, and interesting. Malcolm Cowley says that it is unquestionably one of the greatest hunting stories in any language. The necessary background is as follows: Major de Spain was a leading citizen of Jefferson, Mississippi, a descendant of one of the old aristocratic families. As a result of tax sales and foreclosures, he acquired most of the one hundred square miles that Thomas Sutpen once owned. He remodeled the shack where Wash Jones had died (in Faulkner's *Absalom, Absalom*), and there, late every fall, he used to entertain a group of his friends, including General Compson, McCaslin Edmonds, and young Isaac McCaslin. Sam Fathers was their guide through the wild lands in the Tallahatchie River bottom. Also included in the party were a white man of Indian ancestry, Boon Hogganbeck, and various other Negroes, particularly Uncle Ash, the cook. Briefly the story is this: Ike McCaslin, a boy of ten, is initiated by Sam Fathers into the ritual of the yearly hunt for Old Ben, a huge legendary bear marauding the wilderness some forty miles from Jefferson. For six years the hunt proceeds: the men see the bear regularly and the dogs chase it, but they never bring it down. Ike feels that they probably do not want to, that they are comfortable in knowing that the bear will always be there to talk about and return to. Sam Fathers says that their pursuit is only half-hearted because they know that they do not have a dog fierce enough to lead the attack. At last Sam acquires such a dog, a great wild hunting dog, Lion. Old Ben is then brought to bay and killed. In the struggle Lion, too, is killed and a few days later Sam Fathers, as if he has nothing to live for now, also dies. This is of course symbolically the last of the wilderness, for the bear, dog, and the old man were its bravest and freest specimens. The story resumes when Ike is twenty-one, when he has given up the land which he inherited because he believes that the land has been cursed by slavery and that the only way to escape the curse is to relinquish the land. He has been married, but his wife has repudiated him because of his willingness to surrender the land and practice the trade of carpenter. Part Five of the novel shows us the autumn when Ike was eighteen and we see him making his last visit to the woods, paying a call to the graves of Lion and Sam, and there finding Boon beating one part of his dismembered gun against another—the final symbol of the end of the hunt.

Again, as Campbell and Foster point out in their somewhat detailed analysis of the story, the hunt portion of the tale shows many parallels to the motifs of primitive religion. As they say, Old Ben assumes the character of a fetish-figure in the primitive cult and Sam Fathers that of the high priest, with Boon Hoggan-beck the acolyte, and Ike McCaslin the novice. There are other interesting parallels: when Ike is twelve years old, he kills his first buck, and after he cuts its throat, Sam Fathers, acting as high priest, dips his hands in the blood and wipes them back and forth across Ike's face. Thus Ike is forever committed to the communion of man and nature.

The story is divided into five sections, each section having its high spot, which usually comes near the end. For example, Section I ends with Ike as a boy of ten seeing the bear for the first time. Section II ends with Lion's first encounter with the bear. Section III ends with the deaths of Old Ben, Lion, and Sam. Section IV ends with Ike's discovery of the truth about his own ancestry—that his grandfather sired a line of mixed blood; and Section V ends with Boon's symbolic gesture of destroying his gun to indicate that the world of the wilderness is no more.

All characters of the story are presented sympathetically. This is a story of love, of the brotherhood of men when they work together in a cooperative project. Each of the men is distinctly and separately characterized, yet all are the objects of the author's affection. Perhaps the most outstanding are Sam Fathers and Boon Hogganbeck. With these two figures character delineation is managed through language; Faulkner's handling of dialect is masterly. He has listened to people speak, to colloquial phrasing and idiomatic patterns. Here are two short passages:

"Just like a man," Sam said. "Just like folks. Put off as long as she could having to be brave, knowing all the time that sooner or later she would have to be brave once so she could keep on calling herself a dog, and knowing beforehand what was going to happen when she done it."

Sam didn't seem to have heard. He put out his hand and touched the little dog in the boy's arms which still yapped and strained even though the two hounds were out of hearing now. "He's done gone," Sam said. "You can slack off and rest now, until next time." He stroked the little dog until it began to grow quiet under his hand. "You's almost the one we wants," he said. "You just ain't big enough. We ain't got that one yet. He will need to be just a little bigger than smart, and a little braver than either."

The point of view throughout the story is Ike's; everything is seen through his eyes, and this is all the more an accomplishment since *The Bear* is a story of Ike's coming to maturity. We see the central intelligence develop in understanding right before our eyes. There is a marked difference in the emotional and intellectual quality of Ike's point of view from section to section of the narrative. The story belongs to Ike in every way.

In spite of its tremendous action, the story manages to maintain an elegiac tone; from the very beginning there is sounded a note of farewell, which grows in volume until the end of the story. Tenderness, love, human sympathy are the means of sustaining this atmosphere of valedictory, growing out of a dedication which modern society has made obsolete. A story like *The Bear* attests the deep moral seriousness of its author—not, perhaps, the kind of moral seriousness teachers of the novel once insisted upon finding in fiction, but a positive moral commitment nonetheless. It should be enough to satisfy students that they do not waste their time when they read novels.

Work with the short story should follow the same general pattern of discussion; the art of fiction does not differ significantly because of the length of the narrative. As the short story is now written, authors generally try to accomplish only a single dominant effect, for example, a major change in a major character, a change brought about by what James Joyce called an "epiphany," a revelation, or showing-forth, a moment of understanding beyond which the central character can never again be what he was before the epiphany took place. This kind of story is very popular now, and first experiences with it may prove puzzling to students, since they may not be aware that anything has really happened. Often the revelation is led up to by means of a clever planting of key symbols in the story, and when these are added together, the reader sees an underlining of the meaning of the tale.

For every short story read for purposes of class discussion, high school students should be required to read at least another one entirely on their own, and to do a written exercise suggested by the story. They should be allowed a good deal of freedom in the assignment, but two requirements should be specified: they should limit their interpretations to a single insight, and they should indicate their understanding of how the art of the story is served by language.

CHAPTER ELEVEN

Language
and the Art of Poetry

THOUGH THERE ARE NUMEROUS DEFINITIONS of poetry, ranging in time from that of Aristotle down to that of T. S. Eliot, no single definition, or even all of them put together, ever seems entirely satisfactory, particularly not when we attempt to introduce poetry to students. Is it perhaps true, as poets and literary critics have often asserted, that poetry is essentially undefinable, that its true character can never be known, that to try to specify exactly and finally the attributes of any one poem is automatically to damage or even demolish the poem? Is poetry something which we merely hold our breath in front of, enjoying its essence but prevented from systematic and rational analysis of the poetic experience simply by the nature of the art itself?

In an age of science and skepticism we naturally distrust such a statement. It seems an evasion. As teachers of English, we especially distrust it, for we have seen in action large numbers of teachers who subscribe to this view, and we know the incalculable and the irreparable harm that they have done not only to poetry but to the whole cause of literary art. We suspect that when they say that the nature of poetry cannot be known, we should really understand them to mean that their disordered sensibilities make *any* kind of difficult definition impossible. If poetry is part of man's endeavor, a significant element in his experience, then of course it *can* be known. Impatiently we come to feel that any insistence on the so-called mystery of poetry is but the poet's device for placing himself above the men who, for one reason or another in our civilization, scorn him. His mastery of the unknown sets him apart, the poet implies. He is the seer, the mystic, the prophet, or, as Shelley called him, the unacknowledged legislator, formulating man's decisions a quarter of a century before man is ready for them. He is, then, the voice of man's esthetic duty, the conscience which provokes man's service to beauty.

This species of apotheosis is probably all right; at least it seems to do poets very little harm. It is probably as innocuous as most fictions and not too dangerously untrue. There are almost certainly large elements of truth in it. The Romans, as Sir Philip Sidney tells us in his "Defense of Poesy," called the poet *vates*, which means "seer," or "prophet," and even so exasperating a poet as Miss Gertrude Stein can make us aware of the close relation between poetry and incantation, between the poetry and the spell. Possibly that is all she makes us aware of, but here is one of her efforts:

Stanzas in Meditation VI (1940)

Why am I if I am uncertain reasons may inclose.
Remain remain propose repose chose.
I call carelessly that the door is open
Which if they can refuse to open
No one can rush to close.
Let them be mine therefor.
Everybody knows that I chose.
Therefor if therefor before I close.
I will therefor offer therefor I offer this.
Which if I refuse to miss can be miss is mine.
I will be well welcome when I come.
Because I am coming.
Certainly I come having come.

These stanzas are done.

That the experience of poetry borders on the experience of religion is a truism too firmly established to have to be labored. Meditative verse abounds, and much religious writing has a poetic cast. The Psalms of David, like many other sections of the Bible, are poems, as are the mystical studies of St. John of the Cross and St. Teresa. When we study the lives of the poets, we see an unwavering preoccupation with the spiritual. If there is a denial of what is spiritual in the traditional sense, there is a frenzy to construct *new* spiritual dimensions. Shelley again is a case in point.

The line which leads from the agnostic bitterness of his early *Queen Mab* to the triumphant and ecstatic measure of *Prometheus Unbound* is a straight line, determined by his need to serve that side of man which has its origin, as the poet probably knows best, outside the physical part of his being.

> Our birth is but a sleep and a forgetting:
> The Soul that rises with us, our life's Star,
> > Hath had elsewhere its setting,
> > And cometh from afar:
> Not in entire forgetfulness,
> And not in utter nakedness,
> But trailing clouds of glory do we come
> > From God, who is our home:
> Heaven lies about us in our infancy!
> Shades of the prison-house begin to close
> > Upon the growing Boy,
> But He beholds the light, and whence it flows,
> > He sees it in his joy;
> The Youth, who daily farther from the east
> > Must travel, still is Nature's priest,
> > And by the vision splendid
> > Is on his way attended;
> At length the Man perceives it die away,
> And fade into the light of common day.

It is Plato's old fancy about a pre-existence, and modern man would be absurd to scorn it. For neither the fifth-century Greek nor the nineteenth-century Englishman is entirely wrong in thus allying poetry with divinity. When we truly *realize* the poem, our souls speak, and if not to a precisely recognizable god, at least to the most currently fashionable approximation of him.

So if the poet wants to think of himself as saint or holy man, probably we'll just have to let him do so, while we struggle more painfully in the abysses of the study, or the classroom—or, more often nowadays, the clinical laboratory—to say what he's really doing. Not that all definitions of poetry by poets and philosophers are untrustworthy. Here are a few which, so far as they go, are very useful.

Aristotle says that poetry is the art of imitation, that is to say, a representing, counterfeiting, or figuring forth—to define metaphorically, a speaking picture—with this end, to teach and delight. This art of poetry Aristotle called mimesis, and the notion of the poet as counterfeiter of the processes of life is an engaging one, though we must not be misled here into seeing the poem

only as a vicarious effervescence, like the drabness of Emily
Dickinson's

> I never saw a moor;
> I never saw the sea.
> Yet know I how the heather looks
> And what a wave must be.

Aristotle's mimesis is life lived through the poem, not the poem
substituting for life.

The definitions of both Wordsworth and Coleridge are famous,
and both are frequently used in the secondary school. Wordsworth said that poetry is "the spontaneous overflow of powerful
feelings," and that it "takes its origin from emotion recollected
in tranquillity." Coleridge made the distinction between poetry
and works of science, and he added a statement about organic
order. "A poem is that species of composition which is opposed
to works of science by proposing for its immediate object pleasure,
not truth. The whole of the poem is not separable from its parts.
The poet brings the whole soul of man into activity with the
subordination of its faculties to each other according to their
relative worth or dignity."

But it is the second part of a statement by Shelley which teachers
are likely to find most helpful. "Poetry is the expression of the
'imagination' *and connate with the origin of man.*" In other words,
poetry is congenital; it is instinctive and intuitive. We are poets,
all of us, because we can't help it. Rhythmical fancy is part of
our being, and it must and does find expression, from the nursery
rhymes of our infancy to the sentimental ballads of our maturity
and old age. Alexander Pope said that he "lisped in numbers for
the numbers came," but so in a sense do we all. The teacher of
high school English must first show to students the impulse to
rhyming that is all around them. It is on the radio and television
in the singing jingle which advertises soap or a soft drink; it is
in the little girl's chant which accompanies her rope skipping:
"Whistle while you work/Teacher is a jerk."

We are all poets and share the poetic experience. Whatever the
attractions of prose, of drama, of painting, of sculpture, and even
of music, it is finally the art of poetry that we come back to, for
it is always moving in us, like spirit, and confirming our dedication
to the delight in beauty which is our common heritage. It *is*
connate with the origin of man. It is the index of civilization.
Benedetto Croce wrote,

If . . . poetry is intuition and expression, the fusion of sound and imagery, what is the material which takes on the form of sound and imagery? It is the whole man: the man who thinks and wills, and loves, and hates; who is strong and weak, sublime and pathetic, good and wicked; man in the exultation and agony of living; and together with the man, integral with him, it is all nature in its perpetual labour of evolution. But the thoughts and actions and emotions of life, when sublimated to the subject-matter of poetry, are no longer the thought that judges, the action effectually carried out, the good and evil, or the joy and pain actually done or suffered. They are all now simply passions and feelings immediately assuaged and calmed, and transfigured in imagery. That is the magic of poetry: the union of calm and tumult, of passionate impulse with the controlling mind which controls by contemplating. It is the triumph of contemplation, but a triumph still shaken by past battle, with its foot upon a living though vanquished foe. Poetic genius chooses a straight path in which passion is calmed and calm is passionate; a path that has on one side merely natural feeling, and on the other the reflection and criticism which is twice removed from nature. . . . The man of poetic taste treads this narrow path, in which he is permitted to share the delights of poetry. He knows how that delight is compounded: it is shot with pain; permeated by a strange sweetness and tenderness; torn between alternate impulses and revulsions, desire and renunciations, between the zest of life and the desire of death; yet always delight: the delight of perfect form and of beauty.

Teachers in the secondary school often approach poetry through attempting to instil in students a delight in language, to help students to see that, in addition to the work which he makes his language do, man has also used it for purposes of enjoyment and delight. He likes to experiment with its sounds, to see what unusual tonal effects he can get while expressing his meanings. We enjoy the sounds produced by certain words and combinations of words, sometimes quite apart from any meaning which they may have. This is true both of nonsense verse and "pure" poetry. So for a verbal picture of something he had seen, man fitted his words to rhythm; his first poems, like his first drawings, were probably nothing more than simple descriptions. After that, he learned the wonder of narrative and story-telling, and he composed ballads, sagas, and the long hero poems. There was an early association with music; elements of rhythm and cadence joined with the rhyming of word sounds.

The teacher of poetry will want to emphasize that poetry is language at its point of highest intensification, its most imaginative—not the conventional or expected way of phrasing a thought but a highly inventive, compact, vivid manner. A favorite method of my own has been to take common ideas and to put them at the blackboard in simple prose and then to show how poets have expressed their ideas in brilliantly imaginative ways. For example, "I'm always conscious of the swift passage of time" becomes the great couplet of "To His Coy Mistress":

> But at my back I always hear
> Time's winged chariot hurrying near.

Amusing to youngsters is the prosaic question of a girl addressed to her sweetheart, "Why don't you put down that book about all the great women of the past and pay a little attention to me instead?" This becomes a sonnet by Edna St. Vincent Millay in which they take much delight.

> Since I cannot persuade you from this mood
> Of pale preoccupation with the dead;
> Not for my comfort or your own good
> Shift your concern to living bones instead;
> Since that which Helen did, and ended Troy,
> Is more than I can do though I be warm,
> Have up your buried girls, egregious boy,
> And stand with them against the unburied storm.
> When you lie wasted and your blood runs thin,
> And what's to do must with dispatch be done,
> Call Cressid, call Elaine, call Iseult in.
> More bland the ichor of a ghost should run
> Along your dubious veins than the rude sea
> Of passion pounding all day long in me.

A thought which occurs to all adolescent girls and boys is the one that they may die before being able to accomplish all they hope to do in life. We discuss how terrifying this thought can be, and then I distribute to them duplicated copies of Keats's famous sonnet.

> When I have fears that I may cease to be
>   Before my pen has glean'd my teeming brain,
> Before high-piled books, in charact'ry,
>   Hold like rich garners the full-ripen'd grain;
> When I behold, up on the night's starr'd face,
>   Huge cloudy symbols of a high romance,
> And think that I may never live to trace
>   Their shadows, with the magic hand of chance;
> And when I feel, fair creature of an hour,
>   That I shall never look upon thee more,
> Never have relish in the faery power
>   Of unreflecting love!—then on the shore
> Of the wide world I stand alone, and think
> Till Love and Fame to nothingness do sink.

Students must see that poetry is the enhanced way of making an observation. Sometimes it is an observation of a very simple kind, the simplest picture of everyday life, as often in the Imagists or Emily Dickinson. At other times the thought itself is difficult, part of detailed reflection, analysis, and argument. Here I use carefully selected examples, and after we read the poem together, usually more than once, I have students try paraphrase. In doing this, I generally use a poem with some syntactic problems, something, perhaps, from Milton, Wordsworth, or Browning.

Also, we see that the poet frequently uses the poem as a more distinctive way of commenting on individual people. Using poetry for the character sketch makes the person stand out more sharply than in prose. We look at such poems as "Richard Cory," "Miniver Cheevy," "Bewick Finzer," by Edwin Arlington Robinson; "The Death of the Hired Man," by Robert Frost, and, in upper-level classes of able students, "The Love Song of J. Alfred Prufrock," by T. S. Eliot.

A fairly large amount of time is given to the poem as interior monologue, the poem in which the poet is talking aloud or arguing a matter out with himself. We see the excitement of his trying to come to some conclusion about a matter of importance to him. It is essential with this kind of poem to help the youngsters see the relevance of the idea to their own interests, and of why it would seem worthwhile to someone to express the thought under consideration in a form of greater lyrical intensity than prose, for example, Yeats's fears, as he walks along a troubled sea, for the future of his child in a time of war, anguish, and distress, and the magnificent poem they became in "A Prayer for My Daughter."

Students can respond well to the poem as an outburst of impatience: the poet is angered or irritated by something which he sees, something which he feels is very wrong or out of place; he wants to express himself in strong, bold fashion so that others will share his distress. And so Wordsworth, seeing the materialism of his time, writes,

> The world is too much with us; late and soon,
> Getting and spending, we lay waste our powers:
> Little we see in Nature that is ours;
> We have given our hearts away, a sordid boon!
> This Sea that bares her bosom to the moon;
> The winds that will be howling at all hours,
> And are up-gathered now like sleeping flowers;
> For this, for everything, we are out of tune;
> It moves us not.—Great God! I'd rather be

A Pagan suckled in a creed outworn;
So might I, standing on this pleasant lea,
Have glimpses that would make me less forlorn;
Have sight of Proteus rising from the sea;
Or hear old Triton blow his wreathed horn.

Having come to a full understanding of this statement, I often
then ask students to turn to another poet's version of practically
the same idea, except that the second poet draws quite a different
conclusion. "God's Grandeur" by Gerard Manley Hopkins is, for
students of any poetic sensitivity whatsoever, one of the literary
high spots of the year. They react almost with glee to the excitement of the special effects, the devious, intricate, and sensitive
uses of language, above all, the skillful placing of *words*.

The world is charged with the grandeur of God.
  It will flame out, like shining from shook foil;
  It gathers to a greatness, like the ooze of oil
Crushed. Why do men then now not reck his rod?
Generations have trod, have trod, have trod;
  And all is seared with trade; bleared, smeared with toil;
  And wears man's smudge and shares man's smell: the soil
Is bare now, nor can foot feel, being shod.
And, for all this, nature is never spent;
  There lives the dearest freshness deep down things;
And though the last lights off the black West went
  Oh, morning, at the brown brink eastward, springs—
Because the Holy Ghost over the bent
  World broods with warm breast and with ah! bright wings.

A poem like Hopkins's raises the question of whether or not to
teach the technique of poetry: versification, prosody, stanza
forms, figures of speech and thought, tonal effects. My answer is
an unqualified *yes*, and for the most obvious reason of all: they
are part of the poem. How can a youngster be aware of the poet's
achievements unless he sees them? Certainly a senior high school
student, in any but the most limited classes, should know and be
able to identify the five common meters: iambic, trochaic, an-
apaestic, dactyllic, and spondaic. He should have a few exercises
in scansion, if only in order that he may see how poets and literary
traditions differ on metrical regularity. Fixed firmly in his mind
should be the distinctions between rhymed verse (meter and
rhyme), blank verse (meter but no rhyme), free verse (neither
meter nor rhyme, but an underlying sense of rhythm which makes
the work clearly distinguishable from prose). Similarly, he should
know the words used for standard line lengths: dimeter, trimeter,
tetrameter, pentameter, and hexameter.

Students should know the stanza patterns which have served English poets most faithfully: quatrain, couplet, sonnet, Spenserian stanza, and a few others. They should know such tonal effects as alliteration, assonance, consonance, and onomatopoeia, as well as such assorted poetic terms as caesura, enjambment, foot, verse, rhyme scheme, and so on. To see the full pyrotechnical display of a poem like "God's Grandeur" or even of so homely a work as Poe's "The Raven" is impossible without this equipment. Poetry is an art; the art, therefore, must be known.

The alternative is an awkward struggle with words like "rhythm," "sound," "accents," and "form." Perhaps no word is used more loosely in the high school classroom than "rhythm," and all because teachers are resisting too hard the use of the terminology of poetry. If the word must be used, teachers should make it mean something definite, as Professor Louis Martz of Yale does.

Rhythm ties the common words of the poem more closely together than they usually are found in common speech; rhythm helps the words to cohere in a special form that gradually lifts these words out of the flux and routine of the ordinary. Thus both the versification and the rhyming are here essential in making this poem an artifact, an object created in words, set apart, firmly and finally organized, for our contemplation. By rhythm I do not mean simply meter—iambic tetrameter; by rhythm I mean that continuous excitement that always occurs in a good poem when we feel the tension between the basic pattern of the verse and our actual timing, accent, and tone of voice as we read it. Our natural emphases, our natural pauses, guided by meaning, are continually straining away from the struck pattern, but never far away. The good poet too has promises to keep—promises that he makes in adopting a certain stanza-structure; we expect him to keep it, and he does. But at the same time both poet and reader have a large measure of freedom; no two readers will ever read this poem in precisely the same way, nor will the same reader ever read this poem twice in the same way, for the simple reason that, by the time he has got around to reading it the second time, he is no longer quite the same as he was . . . thus every reading of a poem is a unique experience, both in rhythm and in total meaning, despite the "sameness" of the stanza-form. Stanza-forms are only the bones of a poem—upon which our reading puts the flesh.

The statement makes clear the advantage of *hearing* the poem, and, for this reason, it seems to me that most of the reading of poetry in the classroom should be done by the teacher or by particularly able youngsters who have had a chance to prepare the reading of a particular poem. Impromptu reading by tone-deaf students will destroy a poem and lose the patience of the class. A great boon to teachers of poetry in recent years has been the recording of poems, in most cases read by the poets themselves. A number of high schools now have fairly comprehensive collections of poetry records, in the same way that they have films and film strips. If the school has not yet made such an investment, the teacher should try the local public libraries, or nearby college and university libraries. The teacher may be able to interest the PTA in a record-purchasing project or convince a departing senior class that records would make an excellent class gift. When the money is appropriated, the teacher and a committee should select the records carefully, *purchasing only after listening*. Some poets are not the best readers of their poetry, and some read much too dramatically, so that students have a tendency to laugh.

At the end of a poetry unit, students may be encouraged to write a piece of verse. I know of one school, for example, where seniors, after reading a number of sonnets of Shakespeare, are asked to try a sonnet. They actually look forward to the effort and learn a great deal about the difficulties of successful verse writing. Again, as with all creative efforts, this should not be a matter of grade-taking compulsion. Most teachers make it a voluntary rather than an obligatory exercise. Those who do not want to try verse can be asked to do some other kind of composition. The verse produced by such efforts is generally not very respectable (the student verse submitted in national writing contests is always inferior to the essays and the stories), but once in a while a gem appears. Here is a poem written by a senior girl.

Condemned

He might as well
Just go to hell,
As far as I'm concerned.
When I get there,
I shall take care
To see
If he
Is rare,
Well-done,
Or burned.
—Jane Hastings

This is facetious, even insouciant, but certainly preferable to the imagistic, self-pitying exercises which flood into student poetry contests.

At best, however, the teaching of poetry is difficult in the American secondary school. In some places only the most courageous teachers are willing to attempt it. And, even where the teacher can count at least on tolerance, he is likely to stay with "safe" poets and the good old reliable poems. In modern poetry this means usually nothing more than a rather haphazard excursion through Edwin Arlington Robinson, Carl Sandburg, and Robert Frost. Students first become acquainted with "Stopping by Woods on a Snowy Evening" in the elementary grades, and they go on reading it annually until they graduate. And if there is any youngster in any American high school who has not heard at least three times before his junior year that "the fog comes in on little cat feet," he must be in a remote area indeed. John Ciardi's minutely detailed analysis of "Stopping by Woods" in *The Saturday Review* of several years ago was intended, I take it, to be of assistance to teachers of high school English, but I could not help wondering about Mr. Frost's reaction to the article, if he saw it. I have imagined that he might have wished that the analysis would lay the poem to rest and that maybe readers would forget it for a while. It would be unfortunate for American students to miss Robinson and Frost, but it is equally unfortunate for them to get the impression that modern poetry contains little more than "Miniver Cheevy" and "Mending Wall." As far as Sandburg is concerned, I've never understood just what the students are supposed to take from a discussion of his work; I have never been able to discover any advantage in Sandburg's setting up observations in poetic form. They would go just as well in prose paragraphs. I can appreciate only too well the Sandburgesque effort of a student of mine several years ago after he had just been through a unit on these poems:

Carl Sandburg

The people,
yes.
The poetry,
no.

But if teachers rely on a few good old favorites in teaching modern poetry, their attachment is not hard to understand. The obscurity of many modern poets has had the effect of denying these poets access to the high school classroom, and certainly there is much in the past to which we can turn for curriculum materials. But the teacher of English cannot help wishing that students might see that poetry is not only of old, far-off, forgotten things and battles long ago. The good teacher will want students to see that poetic statement is possible for our time, that we have quite able poets at present, most of whom deal directly with contemporary experience. Diligent teachers, partly because of their own interest and partly because they are always on the alert for fresh, new materials, read as many new volumes of verse each year as they can acquire, but they find very little they can use. The verse is highly distinguished, for the most part—our young poets are able and accomplished—but the high school teacher of English has to pass up most of the poems. Often the poems are exceptionally difficult *for the teacher*, and they are not presented to classes because of the teacher's own uncertainty about meaning and interpretation.

This is not a plea for poets to return to plain statement. The poet is under no obligation to provide new material for the high school. If modern poetry is obscure, there are reasons in the literary history and the esthetic *Zeitgeist* why it probably cannot be otherwise. Yet the implications for the cause of poetry are serious, it seems to me, if poetry is not to become the dead art which some critics friendly to the cause of poetry are already claiming that it is. Teachers greet with enthusiasm these days any body of work which is both distinguished and, for their students, comprehensible, and we see some younger poets slowly making their appearance in the textbooks, poets like Karl Shapiro, Peter Viereck, and Randall Jarrell. But the poems are few, and, for the most part, are used only with advanced classes.

The general obscurity of modern poetry has had another unfortunate effect, also. It has caused teachers to feel that some of the rather securely established modern poets are more difficult than they really are. Furthermore, teachers are likely to forget that time has a curious way of making clear to one generation what was baffling to its parents. I have noticed, for example, that high school students now read Eliot with much greater ease than I first read him, and I see no reason why a number of poems by people like Eliot, Yeats, Pound, Cummings, Ransom, and others cannot be used in the high school, provided the teacher is willing to make the extra effort required for handling them. Teachers of Advanced Placement English *must* make the effort, for the Advanced Placement Examination has made a point each year of demanding of the student an exegesis of a modern poem. The examiners have often based on the student performance their estimation of what the student could be permitted to bypass in subsequent literary study.

From time to time I have tried to demonstrate to prospective teachers of English what might be done in the classroom with distinguished pieces of modern verse formerly thought too difficult for high school study. One of these—a poem I regularly used with high school seniors—is "Sailing to Byzantium," by William Butler Yeats. This is a poem of great richness and compression, of fine texture and intricate symbolic structure. No analysis of it is ever likely to exhaust the possibilities of discovery. It is a superb poem with which to teach the fusion of subject and form in a completely successful piece of verse.

Sailing to Byzantium

That is no country for old men. The young
In one another's arms, birds in the trees
(Those dying generations) at their song,
The salmon-falls, the mackerel-crowded seas,
Fish, flesh, or fowl, commend all summer long
Whatever is begotten, born, and dies.
Caught in that sensual music, all neglect
Monuments of unaging intellect.

An aged man is but a paltry thing,
A tattered coat upon a stick, unless
Soul clap its hands and sing, and louder sing
For every tatter in its mortal dress;
Nor is there singing school but studying
Monuments of its own magnificence;
And therefore I have sailed the seas and come
To the holy city of Byzantium.

O sages, standing in God's holy fire
As in the gold mosaic of a wall,
Come from the holy fire, perne in a gyre,
And be the singing masters of my soul.
Consume my heart away—sick with desire
And fastened to a dying animal
It knows not what it is—and gather me
Into the artifice of eternity.

Once out of nature I shall never take
My bodily form from any natural thing,
But such a form as Grecian goldsmiths make
Of hammered gold and gold enameling
To keep a drowsy emperor awake;
Or set upon a golden bough to sing
To lords and ladies of Byzantium
Of what is past, or passing, or to come.

Analysis of poetry can, of course, take many forms. In the high school class, first attention should always be given to what the poem says. Students want meaning first. What is the idea that the poet wants them to think about?

The discussion of the meaning of a poem should begin with its title, and students should learn the importance of studying titles carefully, no matter what type of literary work they approach. What does "Sailing to Byzantium" suggest? Obviously, *movement* —going from one place to another. Through adroit questioning the teacher can help the students to see that the whole poem is actually one of movement: from one geographical location to another; from youth to age; from physical experience to intellectual experience; from the life of the body to the life of the soul; from the warmth of animal sensuality to the stylized austerity of gold enameling.

To Byzantium implies sailing *from* somewhere. Where? What is the antecedent of "that" in the first line? What does the first stanza suggest about the climate and geography of the country which the speaker is leaving? Obviously that it is a place of warmth, of rich vegetation, of long summers, and excessive physical life. A Mediterranean country is suggested, possibly Italy or southern France.

What kind of place, on the other hand, was Byzantium? Do students know anything about it? Probably not, though an interested history scholar can have been alerted to look it up, or for that matter may even know its importance. Byzantium was, of course, the holy city of the Eastern Empire in the early Middle Ages. What, then, does the poet tell the reader about the place? What kind of esthetic activity was celebrated there?

Students should be aware that this poem, like many others of our time, is what we call "an interior monologue." The poetic situation is that a speaker—the protagonist—is going over something in his own mind. The poem is actually somewhat like a play—"an interior drama of the mind," Allen Tate has called it.

As we listen to what the protagonist is thinking, what do we notice? We see at once that he feels out of place; he is impatient and dissatisfied with where he is and wants to be somewhere else. How does Yeats begin the man's complaint?

We notice the bluntness of the opening, "*That* is no country for old men," as if to renounce the land completely and forever. The opening of the poem is almost unpoetic, or, as we would say, ametrical. A strong dactyl sets the tone of exasperation, impatience, weariness, a casting-off: "Let me get out of here."

The first stanza is crammed with *physical* life—the young are in one another's arms, the fish are spawning. The processes of life surround the speaker; everyone and everything is aware of birth and death, and in this preoccupation with the quality of physical existence, all persons neglect those kinds of effort and creativity which have a permanent and lasting value, "monuments of unaging intellect." The last line of stanza one announces the first of the contrasts on which the poem is built, and brings the stanza to a conclusion in a refrainlike couplet, the heavy rhyming of which is a preparation for the introduction of the song of the next stanza.

Stanza two is richly figurative. The conceit "soul clap its hands and sing" is especially effective; the soul has been made childlike in its purity and simplicity in contrast to the physical decay of the old man's body, "the tatters in the mortal dress." Students might look for comparison at Shakespeare's sonnet beginning "Poor soul, the center of my sinful earth." Lines five and six may require special attention; it should be rewarding for students to work out the syntax carefully. The lines are not really difficult, but they are typical of the kind of poetic grammar which often causes confusion. What Yeats is saying, of course, is that there is no school in which the soul can study how to sing except that in which it will study "the monuments of its own magnificence."

The union of the esthetic and ascetic toward which the poem has been moving is crystallized in the image of the gold mosaic; the image of the holy fire should be clarified. This, it would seem, is the Pentecostal flame, the tongues of fire. The obsolescent "perne in a gyre," or move upward in a spiral, need not disturb students if they are reminded that "gyre" is a word still used fairly often, as in "gyrate" or "gyroscope." It is important to make clear why the protagonist asks that his *heart* be consumed. The heart is the center of physical passion, the seat of his attachment to all that is ephemeral and mortal, to all that will die. Line seven, "It knows not what it is," returns to the kind of impatience with which the poem opened and has a similar ametrical quality, strongly and forcefully monosyllabic. The last line of the third stanza is one of the most memorable lines of modern poetry. Like some of the great phrases of the metaphysical poets, it conveys meaning both backwards and forwards, at the same time. It means both the artifice of eternity and the eternity of artifice, the workmanship and craft which endures and thus makes a mockery of time.

Stanza four opens with the reinforcement of the ascetic principle, and the meaning of the first four lines, the break with natural, or physical, existence, should be related to the beginning of the poem. Again in this stanza we see the passage of time: the drowsy emperor and the lords and ladies are like the people of the first stanza, and the protagonist of the poem will differ from them in having given his allegiance to that which, like the gold enameled bird, is above them and above their passing. Though he is above the lords and ladies, like the golden bird, he can sing to them *of* time.

The reintroduction of song should serve to show the extraordinary intertwining of the images of the poem: singing has been in the poem from the beginning—at first it was the physical song of the birds, then the spiritual song of the soul, then the arrested or immobilized singing of the mosaic, and now the mute transcendent song of the golden bird. Words constantly reappear, for example, "monument," "gold," and "holy," all suggestive of what will endure and hold. On a more mechanical level, students can notice the interplay of vowels in the poem, the brilliant use of assonance. This is essentially an "o" poem, the "o's" richly contrasted with sharp "a's."

By way of conclusion the teacher might return to the lines at the end of the second and fourth stanzas that act as a sort of modified refrain. They are most effective in what one might think of as the rhetorical pageantry of the poem, where movement, eloquence, and sound join in a near refrain which keeps us attentive to a rare performance: the poet moving through the ritual of his art to a successful poem about the art of his subject.

Poetry of such textural richness belongs in the secondary school, particularly in the upper grades. Analysis such as that performed here will not be, in any sense, a full and final treatment; it should not even attempt to be. Students must learn that analysis can be of various kinds providing various revelations. They can, to be sure, learn that some poets—modern poets, in particular—have felt that a too-explicit statement of meaning damages the poem and that a poem, in some cases, can get along very well without meaning, at least in the conventional sense of meaning. But it would be very easy to confuse students here, to the point of their resistance or even antagonism to the poem, and the teacher would be wise, after the first careful readings of the poem (once aloud by the teacher; once silently by the students) simply to ask what the poet seems to be saying. After arriving at some agreement—it does not have to be unanimous—the class can then go on to consider the diction, figures of speech, versification, stanza form, rhyme scheme, and stanza arrangement. These matters should *not* be discussed in isolation from one another or from meaning. The teacher's first responsibility is to help the class see how each of these parts supports, and is actually an inextricable part of, the others, how meter and rhyme and diction are appropriate to what the poet is saying. This is to underscore Coleridge's emphasis: the whole of the poem is not separable from its parts, and we must see how each part helps to control each other part. If students do not see what the teacher has in mind, the teacher might assign the reading of some analyses of poetry in *Understanding Poetry* by Brooks and Warren, or any one of a number of other similar books. Introductions to literary criticism must be handled skillfully in the classroom, lest students get the impression that we can never understand a piece of literature unless we go to a secondary source and read something about it. The technique of analysis is new to them, and a few examples or illustrations will make the introductory work easier. An exercise like that given above should make them conscious of how much work goes into the writing of a successful poem, and they should emerge from studying a unit of poetry with a great deal more respect for the art of poetry than they had at the beginning.

CHAPTER TWELVE

Society and the Art of Drama

FOR THE MOST PART, drama in the secondary school means Shakespeare. Other plays are read—nearly all schools now attempt to do something with contemporary drama—but one of the most important of the year's activities is the reading of a Shakespearean classic. Usually this begins in the ninth grade, and one play is read in each succeeding year. A typical but by no means universal program would be Ninth Grade: *Julius Caesar* or *A Midsummer Night's Dream;* Tenth Grade: *As You Like It;* Eleventh Grade: *Macbeth;* Twelfth Grade: *Hamlet.* Schools with a strong academic and precollege tradition would probably do more, and the private schools generally read two or three plays on each grade level. A few schools begin the reading of Shakespeare below the ninth grade.

Many teachers feel that the work in Shakespeare must be led up to, that it should be preceded by careful preparation. The school texts of the plays usually have elaborate introductory materials which try to facilitate the teacher's task of establishing a proper reception for the play. Almost always in the classroom, teacher and students spend some time "getting ready" to read Shakespeare, and the kinds of preparation are fairly conventional.

One of these is to give students some knowledge of the history of drama from its origin to the time of Elizabeth. Students see how drama came into being in the religious ritual of the Greeks, as narrators gave accounts of the deeds of the gods, particularly of

Dionysos. Classes learn how, through a gradual evolutionary process, the stories became secular, the narrators telling of great ancient families, like the House of Atreus. The story telling soon became a dialogue between the narrator and a chorus, then a dialogue between the narrator and another man, with comments by the chorus, and, finally, actors began taking the parts of the characters of the narratives. Eventually costumes and scenery were added; students learn about the masks and the sandals, the design of the amphitheater, the nature of the audience. They see the emergence of a "professional" drama, the competition among the poet-playwrights, and the development of tragedy. They learn the important names: Aeschylus, Sophocles, Euripides, and possibly Aristophanes. They become acquainted with the titles of a number of the plays, especially *Oedipus Rex*, *Antigone*, and *Medea*. It has become more and more the practice to read one of the plays, since excellent translations are now available in inexpensive editions. Some attention is given to the Roman theater; because this is part of the introduction to Shakespeare, students should certainly hear the names of Seneca, Plautus, and Terence, but they should know also that the Romans were not the theater-goers that the Greeks were; the Romans preferred spectacular diversions, chariot racing and gladiatorial combats.

Then, with the barbarian invasion and the Christianizing of Europe, drama completely disappeared. The Northern tribes had no sophisticated literary interests, and the early Church considered both the plays and the actors immoral, as, by our standards, we very probably would consider them. Through the Dark Ages there was no drama in England, and when it began again, the process was not unlike that in which Greek drama developed; that is, it had its origin in religious ritual and the gradual extension of the religious stories. Students learn of the "quem queritas" interlude at Easter and of the other brief scenes at Christmas, performed first inside the church at the side altar and then eventually, as elements of humor and realism entered the episodes, outside in the church yard.

The drama of the Middle Ages is chiefly found in the cycle plays, sometimes called the mystery and sometimes the miracle plays because they dealt with the mysteries and miracles of the Bible. Students are generally fascinated by accounts of how, when, and where these plays were given and what they were like. Quite good drawings are available now of the wagons, the scenery, and the costuming which were used, and there are many colorful details about the plays themselves—the way in which the guilds chose to enact scenes appropriate to their craft, the butchers doing The Slaughter of the Innocents, the fishermen the Flood, the bakers the Last Supper; the way in which certain characters became stereotypes, Herod, the wild, raving madman, Noah's wife a shrew, and Noah, the henpecked husband, Lot's wife, the woman of eternal curiosity; and the way in which the guilds competed in presenting the character of the Devil. Students are sometimes given an opportunity to act out one or two of the miracle plays. These can be easily located, and are so brief and easy to read and interpret that they can be done on the spot in the classroom with no previous preparation; the parts can be read from duplicated sheets. Students become aware of how the plays grew and expanded, with, as in the case of the Greeks, the addition of secular elements. Eventually the guilds abandoned them, but by this time an audience for theater had been created, and troops of actors formed and went through the towns and villages performing—anywhere they could, sometimes in the village square, sometimes in the inn yard. There are vivid accounts of what this life was like; and a knowledge of how the wagons were placed in the octagonal inn yard, with the guests of the inn seated on the porches and the villagers standing in the yard, is helpful in showing students where the theater builders afterward got their notion of what a theater should be like.

The later and more sophisticated developments of the morality play and the masque are discussed (in a few schools *Everyman* is read) and thus students are brought up to the period of the Renaissance and the rediscovery of the Latin playwrights. Classical plays were read in the colleges, then acted, and, finally, as might be expected, the students were writing their own plays, comedies at first. An accumulation of forces in the sixteenth century—drama at Court, the formation of players' companies, more leisure time, and finally the building of the theaters—brought about an intense interest in drama in England, and by 1580 the Golden Age of English drama was under way. Shakespeare is, of course, the most glorious product of the age.

The advantages of this method of introduction are obvious. The background material is rich and colorful, and students acquire a sense of how a literary form is shaped through long periods of growth. There are some disadvantages, however, and the principal of these is that there are few ways in which the students can help themselves. The teacher who uses this method of preparation will probably have to do too much lecturing; almost the only alternative is the presentation of student reports, which can be equally dull and often duller. Students can read some of this material on their own, and discussions then can be arranged around this reading; and, as has already been suggested, there are possibilities of dramatization with the miracle plays, even, possibly, with brief scenes from the Greek plays, but the dangers of insufficient classroom activity remain. The teacher wants to avoid a situation in which the students merely sit and take notes.

Another kind of preparation for Shakespeare is a study of the shaping of dramatic form; students learn how the basic types of tragedy and comedy came into being. They see different concepts of the tragic hero; to the Greeks he was often a great man who, in some way, willingly or otherwise, had committed an act of *hubris*, or offense against the gods. For this offense, a tragic catastrophe was visited upon him. Often, however, he had done nothing and was merely a victim of divine whimsey. This is what Gloucester has in mind in *King Lear* when he says, "As flies to wanton boys are we to the gods/They kill us for their sport."

In the Renaissance the tragic hero became a man of will who, because of a flaw in an otherwise noble nature, willingly chooses to do evil. He is generally the very noblest man in his milieu, but service to the tragic disorder in his being brings about his destruction. There is, in short, a temporary disruption of the order and harmony of the universe. Because of its importance in a number of the plays of Shakespeare—*Julius Caesar, Macbeth, King Lear, Richard II*—many teachers now give their students some notion of the poetic fancy of the Great Chain of Being, and of how the balance and order of the whole scheme of organization could be upset because of acts which interfered with the hierarchical positions. The murder of the rightful king, or any threat to his authority, produces disturbances in nature—fires fall from the heavens, sparrows attack owls, and lions whelp in the streets.

Moving into the drama of modern times, students see additional views of the tragic hero. In the social plays of Ibsen, a new dimension is added; we see the individual in conflict with his environment, which is usually bad. A popular play in many schools is *An Enemy Of The People*. Dr. Stockman is indeed a tragic hero, but his tragedy is not really a matter of his own doing. (A careful reading of Ibsen's play with the orientation of modern psychology may lead one to conclude that Stockman suffers from an acute persecution complex, that he actually seeks his own destruction. At times he seems in a frenzy to develop hostility against himself, and we feel that all of his aims might have been accomplished if he had only been somewhat less hysterical.) The tragic hero in social drama is a good man in bad surroundings, and the playwright's lesson for us is that there can be only a compounding of tragedies until the social evils are corrected. Man has lost his free will; individuals are victimized through no fault of their own; the tragedy is generally provided by the failure of men to see values in their proper perspective. Thus Willy Loman in *Death of a Salesman*, an excellent modern play for the high school, gives his energy and devotion to the wrong things and even takes his own life so that his son Biff will have the same values of materialistic success. Biff, however, wants a different kind of life. He is saved from tragedy by seeing the unworthiness of what his father had championed.

Material of this sort can provoke many exciting class discussions, but only if students have done much previous reading. The chief disadvantage of this preparation is the limitation of the students' experience. They are not familiar enough with a variety of plays to be able to offer valuable and useful comments in class discussion. Development of concepts of the tragic hero would seem to be more fitting as the outcome of a whole unit on drama, rather than preparation for one kind of play. However, I have seen teachers who prefer a thematic approach to literature use this method in getting ready for Shakespeare, and with considerable success. Of course, they had very small classes of excellent students.

A third approach, one which I particularly favor, attempts to make students aware of how the theater building and its audiences had a shaping effect on the plays. The problems which were raised by the design of the building and the kind of people who came to watch the drama had much to do with what the playwright could put into his plays. Students will see the necessity for the introduction of supernatural characters (what better way of quieting an audience?), fighting, rowdy humor, royalty and pageantry, murder and sword play. Teenagers having their difficulties with Shakespeare's blank verse always ask how the poetry was received by Shakespeare's audience. Did they understand it? Did they like it? What special interests in language did the audience have? Students can be helped to see that the novelty of the plays probably made the audiences patient with speeches they found difficult, but the age was one which took delight in language ornamentation and verbal display.

Students will want to know when the theater in its present

physical form came into being, and the story of the innovations after the Restoration can be presented to them—the proscenium arch, the backdrops, lighting, scenery, elaborate costuming, the introduction of women on the stage.

The teacher can present to the class for discussion the question of why in recent years, at least, in the presentation of serious drama, we seem to be returning to the Elizabethan methods of production; we are cutting down on the amount of scenery, even, as in many theater-in-the-round productions, doing away with it altogether. Why have we come to feel that we can dispense with it? What, if any, is the advantage to the audience, and what does this tell us about the power of Shakespeare's language? The emphasis in Shakespeare is on the play, not on artificial and extra-literary forms of presentation.

Just as they differ in the ways of introducing Shakespeare, so teachers differ in their ways of handling the text. Some feel that every word of the play should be read in class, with careful explication of the lines so that all problems of meaning, versification, metaphor, and even staging will be settled and the full dramatic activity clarified. In the classes of such a teacher the reading is often done exclusively by the teacher, or by the teacher and a few very good student readers who have had a chance to prepare in advance some of the less difficult scenes. In either case, however, there is frequent stopping for clarification.

One can certainly understand the reasons for use of this method. The most frequent student complaint against Shakespeare is, "I can't understand it," and teachers who read all of the text in class can feel certain that students will at least know what is going on in the play. Furthermore, if the teacher is a good reader—and this method should certainly not be attempted otherwise—there is a chance to show the dramatic power in individual scenes and speeches. A bit of the "ham" in the teacher can come out. Interpolations of various kinds can keep the class active, and students should especially be asked to work out the meaning of tricky passages, once the teacher has read them. Furthermore, the reading of the play by someone who knows what he's about will make many lines vivid without further discussion. The consideration of stress and emphasis serve to clarify what students would probably find difficult.

There is a major disadvantage to this method, though, in that students get no practice in reading Shakespeare for themselves, and thus are not encouraged to read other plays on their own.

They are likely to feel that reading Shakespeare requires too much outside assistance, to feel that they are incapable of getting anything out of the play for themselves. The method of exclusive teacher reading limits their own discovery of literary excellence and beauty. To offset these disadvantages, teachers often select certain scenes from the play which they know students can handle successfully and have these read outside class as assignment work, with careful discussion of the scene or scenes the next day, before the teacher-reading begins again. Or, better still, teachers who favor the teacher-reading method may assign the outside reading of another play by Shakespeare, which is made the basis for the writing of a paper of analysis and criticism. This work is going on simultaneously with the class reading and thus constitutes the assignment activity. Generally the teacher limits the selection to two or three plays which are related either in theme or in time of composition to the play being read in class.

In nearly all English classrooms now some effort is made to get the students to "see" the play, to visualize it in performance. The teacher discusses with students such matters as how they think particular scenes could most effectively be presented. How, in other words, would *they*, the students, stage strongly dramatic scenes? What kind of set, lighting, and costuming would they use? What colors would they emphasize, what stage pictures would they arrange? This kind of class work is particularly effective with plays of dramatic intensity, like *Macbeth*, where the problems of the three witches, the ghost of Banquo, the apparition, and the battle sequences have to be worked out. Class work emphasizes the advantages for the students of seeing the play on their own terms, of highlighting the graphic elements, just as it also gives classes some sense of theater craft, the problems of producer and director.

Because of recent television and motion picture productions of Shakespeare, as well as revivals at such places as Stratford, Ontario, Stratford, Connecticut, Antioch College, and Central Park in New York, many students now have opportunities to see Shakespeare performed. Teachers should see these plays whenever possible and talk with students about unusual details of production. There have been many creative treatments of Shakespeare in recent years, starting, probably, with the famous Mercury Theater production of *Julius Caesar* as a modern-dress, anti-fascist play. We have seen an all-Negro *Macbeth*, with its emphasis on voodoo, and Sir Laurence Olivier's motion picture version of *Henry V*, which started within the Globe Theater and then moved out as the preparations for the battle of Agincourt began. All of these modern experimentations have given new meaning and life to classical drama.

Many teachers are somewhat hesitant about arranging student theater parties to see productions of Shakespeare. Near a large city or university, there are opportunities practically every year to see one of the plays, done either professionally or by a student group. Experiences in getting large numbers of students to see these performances, however, have often been unfortunate, particularly if the play was not prepared for by careful advance reading and discussion. Certainly students should be encouraged to see Shakespeare, but the necessity of getting ready for what they see should be insisted upon. If the teacher wants to accompany the group in order to assist them with problems of interpretation, very well.

Class dramatization of some scenes persists as a favorite method of making the play more interesting. Students who have prepared to do so act out various scenes before the class, or even before the whole school at assemblies. Class dramatization can lead to a consideration of the possibilities of interpretation, showing the importance of key words in various lines. The teacher can demonstrate that a single word often shapes the entire metaphor in a passage and that this word, therefore, must receive a major emphasis. Class acting can make possible an appreciation of the problems of the actor: the difficulties of memory work, analysis, gestures, action suited to speeches, and so forth. Most teachers now take advantage of the excellent recordings of Shakespeare by people like Maurice Evans, Sir Laurence Olivier, the Old Vic Company, and others. Teachers may play two different recordings of the same scene to show the different effects achieved by shifts in emphasis, tone, and tempo.

Though they may groan about it, high school students are likely to feel cheated if they are not required to do some memory work with Shakespeare. They have been led by their parents or older brothers and sisters to expect this—it is one of the misfortunes of growing up—and they will be somewhat let-down if they don't do it, also. Personally, I favor it very much. For about a week students will be a chore and a burden to their parents and to you as they go around seeing daggers before them or reciting Hamlet's soliloquy, but they will not really regret the experience. Even the slow students have fun with it.

Throughout the Shakespeare unit, however, the teacher must

constantly be thinking of the objectives in teaching the play. Why is it being done? What benefit to the students will study of the play promote? The answers to these questions will have the greatest determining effect on the way in which the play is studied, whether or not, for example, it should have a line-by-line treatment which exhausts every speech of meaning and all metaphorical content. Almost certainly methods of procedure will vary from class to class; some students will gain from concentration on certain small areas of meaning, the repetition of key words, symbols, and images. For other classes, a preferable procedure will be to locate a scene central to the meaning of the play, work carefully with it at the outset of the unit, and then see all other scenes in relation to it. This is the only possible means of handling the material for some groups, who would otherwise fail to see the forest because of the trees; if there is heavy concentration for them on small details, the larger meanings of the play will be obscured. Here, again, it will be wise for the teacher to remember always that the college classroom and the high school classroom are different. The way the teacher was taught Shakespeare by a distinguished scholar at college is not the way to teach it in the secondary school. Similarly some of the plays read in college are not really adaptable to the high school. Of the plays of Shakespeare I would almost certainly not use the following, for either intensive or extensive reading: *Henry VI, Titus Andronicus, Love's Labor's Lost, Troilus and Cressida, All's Well That Ends Well, Measure for Measure, Timon of Athens, Pericles, Prince of Tyre,* and *Cymbeline.* I would have serious doubts about *The Merchant of Venice, The Merry Wives of Windsor, Twelfth Night, King Lear, Antony and Cleopatra,* and *A Winter's Tale,* for various reasons: personally, I find the anti-Semitism of *The Merchant of Venice* offensive. True, there is Shylock's famous speech, which seems to intend to produce a sympathetic reaction in the audience, but the play is filled with the Renaissance cruelty toward Jews, and its plot forces the conversion of Shylock. Of course, I would not forbid the play or deny to any youngster the opportunity to read it if he wanted to do so. *The Merry Wives of Windsor* is inconsequential; *Twelfth Night* and *King Lear* are far too difficult for high school— surely *Twelfth Night* is one of the subtlest of all the plays; *Antony and Cleopatra* deals with the sophistications of middle age in a way which can hardly be meaningful to adolescents, though I have taught the play, with some success, to Advanced Placement seniors; *A Winter's Tale* requires an act of faith which students in the space age are likely to find difficult, but otherwise it is a pleasant fantasy. Time spent on it however could be better spent on something else, *The Tempest*, for example.

Is Shakespeare to be the whole program in drama for secondary school? Is no attention to be given to other drama, particularly that of our own day? Is the study of drama to be a matter of one or two plays a year, all of them from a single illustrious playwright? Of the types of literature, surely there is less drama in the classroom than anything else. At the Yale Conference of 1957 Professor Maynard Mack of Yale commented on this situation.

I want to preface my remarks . . . this morning with one expression of wonderment. Wonderment that there is not more use made of plays —plays of all shapes, sizes and periods, including Shakespeare's—in our schools. I know that usage in this matter varies somewhat from system to system, state to state, public to independent school, but in general I believe it is fair to say that if drama appears at all in our scholastic English programs outside of the college preparatory course, it runs a poor third or fourth to novels, short stories, poems, and discursive prose. This is an odd state of affairs, I think, not only because drama is far the easiest of all the literary forms to make exciting in the classroom, but because, all things considered, it is also the most effective introduction to the pleasure of reading literature and the skills involved in enjoying it.

. . . It has been my observation that when the public experience of a great play is brought into the right kind of relation with the private experience of the individual student, there comes a flash of illumination into the classroom that nearly crumbles the plaster, as the student contemplates his own image in the play and the play's image in himself. At this moment, what we like to call 'education,' the 'leading out' of the intelligence and human spirit, takes place. No one will have to tell that student that reading is a key to understanding, that knowledge gives self-knowledge, that literature has much to say to him about life. He knows.

Drama, that is, enforces more vigorously than either poetry or the novel the relation of the student's life to the lives of others, in short, to society. The play is an acting out of private emotions and beliefs, but the dramatization is possible only because other people are involved—other people are affected by what a character in a play does. Throughout its history, drama has been a mirror in which the society which came to the theater could see itself. The spirit of Shakespeare's plays, no matter where they are placed in time or space, is the spirit of the time of Elizabeth: Hamlet is a Renaissance prince, though he lived in eleventh-century Denmark. Restoration comedy is what it is because it was the product of a frivolous age; Chekhov's dramas tell us much about the ambivalence of late-nineteenth-century Russia. The plays of Clifford Odets came out of the depression era; and Arthur Miller's tragedies are close to today's headlines. The art of drama, because it is visualization, gives us a picture of ourselves; to trace the history of drama by reading representative plays from various times of the past is to see the changing pattern of man's conception of himself. For this reason the American high school should give more attention to drama. Before he leaves high school, today's student ought, in addition to his study of Shakespeare (at least six plays), to have read one of the Greek tragedies, a play by one of Shakespeare's contemporaries, preferably Kyd, Marlowe, or Ben Jonson, one comedy of the Restoration or eighteenth century, a play by Ibsen, one by Shaw, and one by a contemporary American playwright. This I would think of as the minimum; much more might be required of the student who plans to be an English major in college.

Whatever he reads—*Everyman* or *Volpone* or *The Beaux' Strategem* or *The Beggars' Opera* or *The Cherry Orchard* or *The Doctor's Dilemma* or *Desire under the Elms*—the student will make an identification with characters caught, like him, in the conditions of shared life. For most of us the willing suspension of disbelief is easy; we are up there on stage, and the *art* of drama is lost in the reality of life.

CHAPTER THIRTEEN

Men and Ideas:
The Essay and Biography

ESSAYS ARE NOT SO POPULAR in the high school curriculum as they used to be. The essay is thought by some curriculum planners to be old-fashioned and out of date. It has been crowded out of the course of study by novels, short stories, and, to a lesser extent, drama. Some of the novelists of today, E. M. Forster and George Orwell, for example, tell us that they would much rather have been essayists but realized the limited audience for discursive prose and turned to fiction instead. Indeed, the stories of Forster were once described as essays in motion.

If we are thinking only of the consciously literary essay, the essay as an exploration of the devices of rhetoric applied to a subject of great charm but limited utility, then possibly the essay has disappeared; certainly the audience for Lamb, De Quincey, Hazlitt, Carlyle, Ruskin, Macaulay, and Arnold is not what it used to be. Unless they attend a school which continues to offer a chronological survey of English literature, high school students will probably not even encounter these names. The reflections of the great Victorians, once so staple a part of high school study, have been slipping out of the program very noticeably. This, for many teachers, is a cause for regret; students are no longer exposed to the beauty of the prose styles which the nineteenth-century essays contain.

But if the disappearance of the highly literary essay is unfortunate, it is hardly unexpected. Perhaps above all other kinds of literature, the reflective and the personal essay require leisure, ease, and extensive periods of contemplation, and modern man no longer allows himself many of these.

But there is a kind of essay for which modern man does have time—the essay which is to be found in popular magazines and better newspapers. Usually we call it an article, but it is, in reality, an expository essay, distinguished for clarity, order, and effective organization. This form of writing has been sorely neglected by the secondary school. There are, for example, almost no collections of these pieces designed for high school use, yet the expository periodical essay has a great deal to offer both the teacher and the student of English. So popular is this kind of reading with the general public that magazines have, for the most part, reversed their previous publication patterns. Where once a magazine printed more fiction than nonfiction, it now does just the opposite; the table of contents will show about two-thirds nonfiction and one-third fiction.

The kind of article I have particularly in mind is that which appears in *Harper's*, *The Atlantic Monthly*, *Commentary*, *The Nation*, *The New Republic*, *The Reporter*, *The Saturday Review*, *The Saturday Evening Post*, even in picture magazines like *Life* and *Look*. The pieces deal regularly with timely problems, providing an analysis of the issues and often making suggestions for solution. A number of the essays are directly persuasive and even indicated as such in their titles, which are attention-getting to the point of causing people to buy the magazines. Classroom discussion of the content and the technique of such articles can assist in every form of language instruction—composition, literature, and sentence structure.

Questions addressed to students after they have read such pieces should deal chiefly with content. What are the ideas of the piece? What is the problem being discussed? What are the author's recommendations? What data has the author assembled to support his contentions? To whom particularly does the article seem to be addressed? Is it of greater significance to one kind of reader than another?

But students can also notice the way in which the article is put together. What principles of coherence have been followed? What techniques of subordination? How has the writer accomplished his effects? What were his methods of organization, of transition, of paragraph structure? Especially enlightening for students can be the matter of transition, which, in popular writing of this sort, has to be quite skillful. Some investigation might even be made of the author's style, though style, as such, is not one of the first editorial demands of this kind of writing.

In other words, the study of the popular essay should be a demonstration of how language serves the clarification and orderly arrangement of contemporary thought—the ideas which are of paramount interest in today's world, the ideas which are essential to the solution of many modern conflicts. The reading of these pieces can furthermore serve as an introduction to areas of interest which the student has not previously known; the articles may get him excited about achievements, plans, and ambitions which he has never heard about.

The teacher should be familiar with magazines which publish special student issues, for example, *The Atlantic Monthly*, *Reader's Digest*, and *Scholastic*. *The Atlantic Monthly* student issue is an especially useful publication for the classroom, since it provides thoughtful exercises for dealing with essay material in class. These exercises are chiefly in reading practice, including vocabulary drill. Special subscription rates for students can be arranged. This is true, too, for the student editions of *Reader's Digest* and *Scholastic*, which also offer exercises for the improvement of comprehension and reading skill.

Anthologies of pieces of this nature are very few; there are excellent ones on the college level but almost none for high school. By writing to publishers, English teachers might very well make their need for this material felt. Existing collections of essays lean toward the traditional literary essay, but there are not many of these either. The ideal anthology would probably combine a number of recent pieces of magazine nonfiction with outstanding literary essays of past and present so that students could see, in an ascending order of expository and persuasive difficulty, the attributes of discursive writing. Certainly the essay of the past should not be abandoned or neglected, but room must be made for a kind of writing which is all about us at the present and to which we are going more and more for direction about modern affairs. Many of the magazine pieces are too good to be lost or overlooked, and the English class can do much to preserve the pieces of greatest distinction and utility. Obviously these essays can do much to stimulate the writing program as well.

Classroom work with the essay offers many opportunities for student leadership. Individual students can be charged with the responsibility of leading an entire class period if they are told sufficiently in advance that they will be called upon, and thus have enough time for preparation. The teacher can assist with the preparation so that the student comes to realize that directing a discussion is a matter of some skill, of phrasing questions in such a way as to bring forth rewarding responses, of keeping the discussion on the subject, of involving as many members of the class as possible, of keeping a few students from monopolizing the hour. The profit to the student in this kind of activity hardly needs to be mentioned.

Teachers can also arrange exercises in précis writing and outlining. Both offer practice in picking out the main parts of a piece of writing, in addition to showing the value of economy and the advantages of logical arrangement. Teachers should be cautious here, however, and not overdo either précis writing or outlining. Neither is a very exciting activity, and too much of either can produce tedium. Outlining is more profitable when applied to the organization of one's own thought before writing than to another's thought in something published.

The reading of nonfiction should, of course, extend to book-length works, and the student reading list ought to contain the titles of outstanding recent works of this kind. Many of our students resist novel reading but are eager to get their hands on good books about medicine, science, engineering, sociology, and the various other interests of modern man. Books on animals, birds, insects, reptiles, flowers, and trees are very attractive now—superbly written and illustrated. A book store for young people nowadays is a delight, particularly in the kind of offering discussed here. In addition there are the challenging sociological studies of recent years—the books of Vance Packard, John Keats, and, for more advanced students, Erich Fromm and David Riesman; in other words, books to make our youngsters think. Students should realize that not all of our reading is of a distinctly or exclusively literary nature, and that modern life requires communication on levels of practical immediacy. Training in this kind of reading is essential.

In a way, there is no such thing as the *teaching* of biography. We read biographies and share our pleasure with others as we relay exciting stories about the people of whose lives we read accounts, but there is very little that the teacher of English can do in the way of instruction in biographical reading. Biography is not a literary type. Actually it is a form of history made somewhat literary by the author's selection and interpretation of the events he includes in his work and, in the case of some biographers, by the manner of his writing style.

In recent years, however, biography has been so popular in general that teachers of English have felt that some attention to it should be paid in the secondary school. Reading lists include biographies, and in many schools a biography or a group of biographical selections is read in each of the grades. Classroom work with this material is limited generally to a discussion of the outstanding events of the subject's life, the inspirational qualities which the life contains, and possibly to some comments on the way in which the biography is written.

In introducing the work in biography, teachers might indicate that biographies are usually prepared according to one of a number of patterns, though sometimes several of the patterns are combined. There is, first of all, what we might call the "official" biography. This is biography as tribute; often it is commissioned after an outstanding man has died. American industries frequently commission the writing of biographies of their founders and leaders, and publication of the book is limited to as many copies as will be distributed to the man's family and business associates. This kind of biography is frankly laudatory and inspirational. It exists only to celebrate the outstanding achievements of the subject. Campaign biographies of presidential candidates are of the "official" variety, and we have in America the long tradition of the official biographer who is rewarded with some form of public office by the victorious candidate. There was a time, of course, when virtually all biography writing was at least partly inspirational, but that was before Freud taught us about the mysteries of personality.

Second, there is "romantic" biography, the life of an outstanding figure, someone unusual, exciting, glamorous, romantic. This is the kind of life which emphasizes temperament and the unpredictable. Painters, poets, composers, revolutionary leaders, actors and actresses, singers, explorers—these are the people who generally afford material to the writer of romantic biography. The reader takes satisfaction in learning about a way of life entirely different from his own and that of the people with whom he is in regular contact. Romantic biography is truly a means of escape; it carries the reader away from the commonplace and the ordinary. Byron, Van Gogh, John Barrymore, Mazzini—their unconventional behavior, their passions and vicissitudes, their effects on other men and women are detailed for us excitingly. We read the books not in order to see ourselves, but to see a way of life which attracts us by virtue of its being so different from our own.

Biographies written by scholars, historians, and professors are likely to be what we think of as "social" biographies; the person about whose life we read is seen as a manifestation of his age, a representative of the times in which he lived. Quite often this fact is indicated in a subtitle of the work: *John Milton: His Life and Times*, or *Franklin D. Roosevelt: The Coming of the New Deal*. The man is seen not only as a personality but as one influencing his age or, conversely, being influenced by it. If he is a writer, the biography becomes one in which what he wrote is seen as being indicative of what was going on in the world of literature. This is a very popular kind of biography, it is likely to be the most carefully prepared. It is usually the product of exhaustive research and gives rise to our concept of the "definitive" biography—the one which has final scholarly authority. Social biography makes its appearance in the secondary school but not often in the definitive variety. Definitive biographies are usually of several volumes and detailed beyond the interests of high school students. Still I have known a number of youngsters to read with much enjoyment Douglas Southall Freeman's *Robert E. Lee*—all four hefty volumes of it.

Fourth, we have "psychological" biography, or biography as analysis of one man in order to know all men better. This is, in some respects, the newest of the kinds of biographical writing, and the kind which upset a number of people when it began to appear. It came as a shock to many of our patriots that some of our heroes of the past had human failings; in any case, many readers could see no reason why these failings should be brought to light. Our concern with psychiatry and psychoanalysis has made the popularity of this kind of biography inevitable, and it is certainly unfair to the biographers to imply that they are concerned only with the sordid and the seamy side of life. They are interested in seeing the *whole* person, not just the side which he showed publicly and their right to do this, they feel, originates in the conviction that they are thus serving the cause of the better understanding of all men. True, there have been some violations of good taste in recent biographies of this nature, and we have now the phenomenon of the biography of scandal or sensation, the public confessions of a former alcoholic or narcotics addict or playgirl, written generally by someone with a talent for getting the book on the best-seller lists. Actresses and singers, all presumably cured, have confessed to everything from too much gin to too many husbands, and the vogue is not yet diminishing. It is to be hoped that these books have not invaded the school or been added to the reading lists.

Many biographies, of course, are a combination of two or more of these types, particularly of the romantic and the psychological, or of the romantic and social. A man is quite often unusual and fascinating because of psychological disturbances in his personality, and sometimes a man's romantic nature has wide social repercussions. A rather special and very popular type of biography is the work which combines biographical and critical elements; the book is a study of both the life and the work. This is a particularly appropriate kind of treatment for writers, painters, and composers.

Teachers of English should know examples of all kinds and be eager to suggest them to students according to what seems appropriate to the individual reader. Personally, however, I would never serve biography at the expense of other types of literature. Biography, as literary form, is not so important as poetry, drama, the novel, or the essay. Individual biographies can provide very exciting and informative reading, but the literature course will find its greater satisfactions in those writings where man has worked to shape his language to the esthetic demands of literary form.

CHAPTER FOURTEEN

Teaching the Gifted Child in English

In our zeal to serve the gifted child we tend to assume his existence in large numbers without giving sufficient thought to the problem of identifying him. All God's chillun are gifted, if we accept their parents' views, and, perhaps, to paraphrase Will Rogers' famous remark about ignorance, we are all gifted, but in different subjects. If we are to do anything genuinely meaningful for the able or superior youngster in a particular subject, we had better start by learning to recognize him. This will be easier in some fields than in others, and certainly any sets of criteria which we establish will be partly inadequate; but we ought to be able to set down some marks of identification. We need, in short, to know what special abilities the gifted child displays and the definite methods by means of which these abilities can be sustained and developed.

The gifted child in English is one about whom the following assertions can be made:

1. He (or, of course, she) is able to deal with ideas. Of an independent turn of mind, he likes to talk about what he's been thinking. He demonstrates a genuine capacity for that ambivalent thing we call intellectual growth, and he wants to get the adult reaction to what he says. He will probably be a little cocky about this—and he will sometimes be more than a little absurd, in an engaging sort of way—but he will be deadly serious in his painful efforts to organize his reflections of life and human experience.

2. He is able to read perceptively. For example (and here is one of the most valid tests I know), he will know irony when he sees it, and he will be sensitive to style and tone. To try him out, I have given him a book a bit too difficult for him and asked him to answer two questions about it: why the author wrote it and why he wrote it as he did. I make it a book like *All the King's Men* by Robert Penn Warren or *The Big Rock Candy Mountain* by Wallace Stegner—not too tough, just something that will examine his understanding of human motivation and simple literary craft.

3. He is able to write a paragraph. This, to be sure, sounds modest enough, but what I have in mind is that he will have a secure sense of a paragraph as the rounded development of an idea. He will know that a paragraph is a coherent pattern of sentences which exhaust the potential of a single idea. He will be aware, that is, of the paragraph as a *constructed* unit, something that has been *shaped* or *designed*.

4. He has an intellectual interest or two outside the field of literature. Maybe it's progressive jazz or abstract art or Yogi or herpetology or playing the clarinet in the school band, but he is excited about *something* which can bring greater enrichment to his life as he learns how to ally it with skill in language. There are likely to be some surprises when we start to inquire into these special interests. Last summer, in writing to a bright youngster whom I had once taught, I happened casually to ask whether or not he ever listens to symphonic music. Here is his seventeen-year-old answer: "You may rest assured that I know the greatest music; since 1955 I have been regularly taking records from the library. In childhood I always preferred Tschaikovsky, Dvorak, and the like, but in my first year on library records I well-nigh exhausted all the famous symphonies and had to search for something new. I tried Mozart and Haydn and had many exciting hours but was not fully satisfied—then listened to all sorts of things until the summer of '56 when I tried the chamber music of Brahms. I cleaned out the shelves, and Brahms is still my favorite. However, in October of '57 I received an album of the Beethoven Quartets and studied each one with the score. Since then I have been on the cello and the piano sonatas. I bought a record of the last three, but of course the Opus III is the best, in my opinion."

5. He has a sense of the *fun* of words. Language sounds, as such, intrigue him. Give a good English teacher a boy or girl who has a feeling for intonation and onomatopoeia and the power of stress,

and the teacher can lead the youngster into literary judgment and compositional skill without distress for either teacher or child.

Discovery commits one to action, which, in this case, means immediate attention to curriculum and methods. What, in English, do we do for the able youngster? What special materials do we put into his hands? What particular techniques of presentation do we employ in guiding his learning?

The suggestions which follow were tested with twelfth grade Advanced Placement classes at Walnut Hills High School, a public classical high school in Cincinnati, Ohio, and Newton School in Newtonville, Massachusetts. There were approximately twenty students in each class, all of whom had been selected on the basis of a number of tests, teacher recommendations, and both student and parental approval of participation in the plan. At both Walnut Hills and Newton, Advanced Placement has been in operation since the inception of the national program, and though no formal attempt at evaluation has been made in either place (indeed it is difficult to imagine what form the evaluation of such a program would take), both communities support enthusiastically the idea of special classes for the able student in various subjects. In Cincinnati, as a matter of fact, Advanced Placement has been adopted on a city-wide basis, and special classes for the gifted can now be found in all comprehensive high schools.

For these youngsters the first subject of the English curriculum ought especially to be composition. The development of compositional skill must begin as early as possible. Before he gets to high school, the able youngster ought to have had many exercises in writing, proceeding in sequential fashion from the sentence as a unit of organization to the coherent, carefully organized composition of perhaps five hundred words. But in English classes set up for gifted students in the senior high school the writing should be particularly frequent. In a term or semester of twenty weeks, the teacher might certainly ask for fifteen themes, of varying word length, of course, some to be prepared as outside assignments and some written extemporaneously during class periods.

What the student writes about is of major importance, and it is hard to imagine a successful writing program which would not proceed in systematic order from one kind of writing activity to another. Probably no kind of writing should be disapproved, but surely the student will profit most from the composition of straight expository prose. Exercises in organization, interpretation, and analysis are especially rewarding here, as students learn how to bring related ideas together in well-shaped paragraphs, or apply themselves to selected quotations and passages from literature in order to demonstrate their understanding of the selection and the extent to which they are able to adjust it to experience. An excellent device in this connection is to ask the student to give a careful account of some event he witnessed which had special meaning for him, an event which could be thought of as having effected some change in his attitude toward life and other people. The idea here is not simply to write a narrative but rather to show how an incident or chain of events brought about a new understanding of the self and of its relation to the community. Before the writing of the paper, students may be asked to read several such pieces of writing, for example, "The Hickman Story," by John Bartlow Martin and "Hiroshima" by John Hersey. The results are usually surprisingly good, the students learning the importance of both logical and chronological order as well as developing the capacity to examine their beliefs and processes of thought. Character sketches in which students must rely entirely on the speech and actions of the person being described—no adjectives of judgment—are also quite productive, as are later persuasive themes in which students are required to argue for important changes in school and community policy.

Student papers should be marked carefully, with attention given to grammar, logic, and rhetoric. In the test program, the assertions of the paper were constantly questioned; marginal comments attempted to establish a kind of dialogue between the student-writer and the teacher-reader. The student was being asked to re-examine his thought, to rephrase it for clarity or fluency, or to substantiate more fully his assertions and conclusions. Revision of every paper was required, and students met the teacher in regularly scheduled conferences to discuss the themes. Thus a careful check was made on the progress in composition of each student, the conference serving also to show the student how to help himself.

High school youngsters able in English are generally somewhat proficient in the fundamentals of grammar, sentence structure, and usage, and for this reason it seems wise to let this part of the course of study be determined by their weaknesses as demonstrated in their writing. Faulty sentences used for classroom analysis might very well be taken exclusively from their own work. The gain in immediacy, as youngsters see the urgency of improving *their own* constructions and not the manufactured ones of the author of a textbook, will have a lasting effect. Occasional concentrated reviews of language conventions may be necessary as preparation for College Boards or other regional tests, but the able youngster ought above everything else in an English class to acquire a positive and constructive attitude toward language. His orientation to grammar must not be, as it so often has been in the past, negative and analytic. He should learn that we honor the conventions of grammar because they facilitate social communication and esthetic discovery.

The student gifted in English will generally need no stimulation to read, but his teacher will want to provide him with some direction and guidance. The youngster is likely to think of himself as particularly alert in this respect and will want to tackle some of the big names he has heard about. He is more likely to want to read Joyce's *Ulysses* than Emily Brontë's *Wuthering Heights*, and he must not be altogether squelched in these ambitions. He may not be ready for *Ulysses*, but he can read some of the stories of *Dubliners* and possibly *A Portrait of the Artist as a Young Man*, and through these experiences he can be helped to see the necessity for preparation to read advanced and difficult work.

Guidance of student reading, however, should not be too rigid. Beyond the number of texts which the class necessarily reads and discusses in common, the student should be provided with an extensive reading list and then be encouraged to go ahead on his own. Every bright student ought to have the chance to make some mistakes and to read some inferior books. The path that leads eventually to Aeschylus often starts with *Tom Swift*, and this, I believe, is as it should be. Let us not insist on cultural maturity too soon. College teachers will say that some of our youngsters are coming to the university now too well prepared in advanced literature. They have read too much too soon—too much, that is, of the esoteric and the *avant-garde*. They know Kafka but not Scott; they can trace patterns of myth and symbol in Faulkner, but they do not know the narrative power of Fielding and Smollett; they can apply depth psychology to the characters of Camus and even Sartre, but they have never learned the simple fun of character dimension in Dickens and Mark Twain.

I served for a season as consultant to a junior high school project which in some homogeneous groupings above the regular English classes was attempting to give additional instruction, according to the youngster's needs and abilities, in advanced literature, composition, or remedial reading. Thinking of the activities of each group, I asked myself in which of the first two I would want a bright youngster of my own to be (granted, that is, that he would not have to be in remedial reading), and I felt certain that I would want him in the composition class. The process of discovering the big names and the most exciting books in literature should be partly a private thing. One's first meeting with Paul Morel or Emma Bovary or J. Alfred Prufrock ought to be accomplished in secret so that the full impact of the meeting will not be lost. The tragedy of Holden Caulfield in J. D. Salinger's remarkable book *The Catcher in the Rye* is that his "learning" and "sophistication" have advanced far beyond the natural needs and demands of his biological organism. At a time when his reading and experience have taught him much about the sordidness of life, he is not yet sufficiently removed from the world of cowboys and Indians. He is a boy with a Scotch and soda in one hand and a teddy bear in the other. Advanced literature used injudiciously with gifted children can easily produce Holden Caulfields by the score. Let us not underestimate the able student and let us by all means bring fresh and exciting material into the curriculum, but this is not the place for careless choices. Far too much is at stake.

The literature program for gifted students in the senior high school might strive for a thorough and secure knowledge of literary types. The discussion would start with the working out of a careful definition, the reading procedure and discussion following a chronological pattern so that some attention is given to the developments which shaped the type. Thus, for example, the study of the novel might begin with an account of its origin, then proceed to a tracing of its history through the outstanding novelists of English, American, and Continental literature down to our own day. Students would be reading at this time a number of short stories, two or three novelettes, and at least two major novels. A similar procedure might be used for poetry, drama, and, to a lesser degree, the essay.

Many teachers of able students prefer a thematic organization of the literature program: students consider such a subject as "The Nature of Tragedy" or "Conformity versus Nonconformity," and the pieces of literature studied are used to illumine the topic. This can be a very successful method of arrangement, and bright youngsters will have many exciting ideas to contribute to discussions of this nature. One difficulty presents itself, however —the possibility of losing sight of the story, poem, or play as a work of art with a specific history of esthetic growth. That is, the work of literature is seen in isolation from other works which may have done much to shape both its content and form; the literary work is seen only in a social or psychological context. If a thematic approach is used, it must be supplemented from time to time with attention to problems of form and structure and to patterns of chronology.

The organic theory of literary excellence is one which cannot be impressed on the youngsters' minds too soon; they should see that subject and form are finally one and the same thing; that what an author says is not really separable from the manner in which he says it.

Literature as a history or record of ideas can also provide larger dimensions of understanding for the superior student. Let him see that stories, poems, and plays are a manifestation of intellectual currents and social tensions in the period when the work was composed. Let him see *Pride and Prejudice* not simply as a whimsical little exercise in depicting a gallery of eccentrics but rather as the record of economic desperation in which a ruling class, the landed gentry, saw its traditional eminence threatened by the parvenu industrialists moving from the cities into the English countryside. The old bogeyman of whether or not the students like a piece of literature will disappear as they see that liking or disliking is largely irrelevant once the book is *understood*.

Obviously the gifted student can be relied upon to contribute to lively classroom discussion. As a matter of fact, he is likely to be greatly disappointed if he is not given frequent opportunity to lead and direct such activity. The teacher of superior students in English ought to be reluctant to maintain a constant position in front of the class. The classroom atmosphere should be especially relaxed and informal; a free interchange of literate expression should prevail as standard operating procedure. Students themselves can occasionally perform in the role of teacher, provided of course that they have had opportunity to prepare the lesson and set up definite steps for leading the individual class session to desired objectives. Such student-taught lessons can result from a cooperative exchange of ideas several days in advance.

Yet the academically superior student must be able once in a while to listen well, also, for, being college-bound, he must be prepared to hear many lectures and to take notes. In areas where their preparation is negligible, good students like the authority and dynamics of good lecturing, and their teacher, especially in English or history, ought to be himself gifted in the vitality and energy of effective speaking. This requires that the teacher have many interests outside the subject; a lesson on a writer, Scott Fitzgerald, for example, can move across the whole range of social, cultural, and intellectual fashions which give the author identity and significance. No anecdote is too trivial, no story too apocryphal when it leads to student understanding and appreciation. What Fitzgerald said to Gertrude Stein and Edith Wharton and Thomas Wolfe is central to good lecture performance, not tangential and frivolous. Pleasure is the end of literature, and there is nothing illegitimate about promoting that pleasure through lively and discriminating lecture reference to the biographies of writers.

Teaching the gifted child in high school English will often continue beyond the classroom. There will be plays to see, concerts to hear, museums to visit—all of these activities supplementary to the explorations of language and literature. The teacher of the gifted child in English must be prepared for inordinate demands on his time and energy; he may have to be available for consultation at strange hours and in strange circumstances, and for this reason, among others, the job is certainly not for all teachers, not even for all good teachers. It is a job for the ultra-dedicated, the over-imaginative, and the extra-eager. It has its headaches, but it also has its joys, and the greatest of these is that moment when the bright youngster discovers through the experience of his study that his gift is both privilege and responsibility, that, being academically able, he will be humanly fulfilled only when he learns to put his gift at the service of others.

ADVANCED PLACEMENT ENGLISH AT WALNUT HILLS HIGH SCHOOL, CINCINNATI, OHIO, 1954–1957

General

The Advanced Placement Course in English at Walnut Hills High School was offered only to twelfth-grade students. Although the Committees on both Composition and Literature of the College Entrance Examination Board recommended that the English program begin in the tenth grade, as is customary, for example, in mathematics, we at Walnut Hills felt that this was not necessary, since the student body there is a select one, with only a precollege curriculum offered. Consequently all of the students by the time they become seniors have had adequate preparation for the kind of course outlined below.

The course at Walnut Hills was designed as the equivalent of a college freshman course. We were aware, to be sure, that these courses differ widely from college to college, some of them, as in most state colleges and universities, being highly functional courses planned to serve all departments of the school, and some, chiefly in smaller liberal arts colleges, being courses devoted exclusively to the examination and analysis of literary classics. Using our advantage of having the students five class periods each week, for one hour each period, for forty weeks, we tried to set up a syllabus which would incorporate the major features of both types of course, so that a student from Walnut Hills who won either exemption from freshman English or assignment to an advanced section would have fulfilled, no matter where he went, all requirements for further academic success.

Thus we felt justified in combining composition and literature. No attempt was made to specify the number of hours that should be spent on each, though a heavy emphasis on the techniques of composition occurred early in the first semester. We were aware of the dangers in combining composition and literature—that a curious kind of academic schizophrenia might result, with students never genuinely aware of how the two exercises complement one another. Our precedent, however, was firmly established. Of the many college freshman English courses we examined in constructing the Walnut Hills syllabus, the great majority instruct in both composition and literature. Furthermore, the writing in most of these courses is not limited to the critical examination of literary texts. From its origin the Advanced Placement Program has insisted that writing in the English course must be of a general nature, with principal emphasis on exposition. The Advanced Placement English course has never been thought of as a pre-professional arrangement designed to turn out English majors or literary critics. Various kinds of writing, from the process theme and the scientific report to the exegesis and short story, must be attempted.

Obviously this kind of work cannot be accomplished in large classes. Private preparatory schools have the advantage here, but we found at Walnut Hills that we could work effectively with a group of twenty-five students, and, conditions being what they are in public schools today, we were obliged to handle this number.

The paper work for the teacher was difficult but not impossible, and class discussion was not hampered by this number.

Students were chosen for the class on the basis of a number of considerations: the process began with the recommendations of eleventh-grade English teachers. The records of students chosen were then consulted (percentile ranks, ACE scores, tenth-year English grades, and so on), with a final decision on the membership of the class made by the principal of the school. Both students and parents were given careful explanation of what membership in the course involved so that entrance into it was a voluntary matter. Both students and parents also understood that students who performed adequately in the course were never graded below "B"; if the student's work did not warrant either "A" or "B," he was returned at once to one of the regular sections of twelfth-grade English.

Literature

1. *Intensive reading*. We tried to do a very minute analysis of a number of literary works, studying not only what the book said but also its form and structure. We approached every piece of literature in terms of the organic theory of literary art, that is, that subject and form are finally one and the same thing; that what an author says is not really separable from the manner in which he says it.

2. *Extensive reading*. Students were provided with a teacher-prepared reading list, which was discussed in detail in class early in the year. They were then instructed to go ahead on their own, being responsible for four critical reports on their reading each semester. Books on the list were for adult readers and were of all literary types: fiction, nonfiction, poetry, drama, and so on.

3. We strove for a thorough and secure knowledge of literary types. The discussion of each type started with careful definition, and our reading procedure and discussion followed a chronological pattern so that we could give attention to the developments important to the shaping of the type. Thus, for example, we started with an account of the origin of the novel and traced its history—briefly, to be sure—through the outstanding novelists of English, American, and Continental literature down to our own day. We did the same thing—again, briefly—with poetry, drama, and, to a lesser degree, the essay.

4. We gave some attention to contemporary literature. We read many more pieces of modern literature than are commonly read in

the high school: short stories by Hemingway, Faulkner, D. H. Lawrence, James Joyce, and others; poetry by T. S. Eliot, Yeats, Wallace Stevens, W. H. Auden, and others; drama by Chekhov, Shaw, O'Neill, and Arthur Miller. This does not mean that we slighted the classics; it does mean that today's able student wants to talk about modern ideas as they are expressed in our literature, and the English program should give him a chance to do so. Furthermore, as mentioned before, in a world of unanimously realistic literature the English teacher has a new obligation: helping students to approach the realism in the proper frame of mind.

5. We read literature, partly at least, as a history or record of important ideas. We tried to see a selection as an indication of intellectual changes and social currents in the period of its composition. Through our reading of the important classics of the past we got an introduction, even though superficial, to the philosophical movements and the changes and conflicts in man's thinking through the centuries. We became aware of "influence" and the ways in which nonwriters have had an effect on the writing of their time. Able students liked this exercise especially, and it created splendid opportunities for class reports and outside reading.

Composition

1. First—and most important—we did a great deal of writing. In a semester of twenty weeks, we did *at least* ten themes, ranging in length from 500 to 1000 words. Every fourth theme was written in class, but the impromptu or extemporaneous exercise was not so long as those prepared outside.

2. The study of composition was systematized: first semester, expository writing; second semester, persuasive writing and a research paper. An exact syllabus was set up: so many pieces of process writing, so many of analysis, so many of definition, so many pieces of straight reporting, so many character sketches, so many critical projects. Particularly effective was the kind of writing exercise which started with a springboard quotation demanding explication and analysis. We did not do any juvenile themes on "My Favorite Pet" or "What I Did Last Summer Vacation" or "The Relative I Like Best." In persuasive writing, students composed their first two arguments on subjects of school interest, the next on a community problem, the next on a national or international issue, and a final one on a subject specifically of their own choice.

3. Each student had regular conferences on his writing. The teacher always returned papers with *all* errors marked. Themes had to be corrected and returned to the teacher. In the conferences teacher and student went over all errors fully, the teacher pointing out weak points and suggesting means of improvement. Students here had a chance to raise any questions about their composition work which seemed relevant to them. Generally these conferences were held after school.

4. The teaching of grammar, sentence structure, the mechanics of English in general, was determined entirely by weaknesses demonstrated by the composition work. There was no drill in textbook exercises or memorization of "rules." In the early theme assignments the teacher selected various kinds of errors from student papers, and these were discussed together in class.

5. There was no narrative or description writing as such, though students did have two opportunities to do creative or imaginary writing, if they wanted; the assignment was not compulsory. Generally they all tried just for the fun of it.

Miscellaneous

1. There was *much* class discussion. Today's able student wants to talk. Fine—but the discussion should be guided. A discussion leader might be selected from the class several days in advance so that he could prepare a definite plan to keep the discussion going. Always of course the discussion should be organized around a specific piece of reading. This is where we at Walnut Hills worked in our reading of essays, usually taking those of content significant enough to arouse opinion and reflection.

2. The teacher did considerably more lecturing than is common in high school classes. College-bound students must learn to take notes. Nothing is more practical for them in the way of college preparation than knowing how to take down salient points of a teacher's comment.

3. The class had general cultural and social contacts outside the classroom. The group attended a play occasionally or a lecture or a concert or an art exhibit. They gathered at one another's homes once in a while to discuss books or hear recordings of a poet reading his works or to meet a person of interest visiting in the community. In other words, their instruction had ceased to be a limited and school-time thing and had become the serious and all-consuming business of self-improvement.

CHAPTER FIFTEEN

The Profession
and the Future

THE IMMEDIATE PRACTICAL NEEDS in the teaching of secondary school English can easily be specified and have often been discussed. Nearly every public high school teacher in America meets too many students each day. The standard teaching load is five classes of approximately one hour each (in places where the class period is shorter, the teacher would have an additional class or two), and there are very few school systems where the number of students to a class is fewer than thirty. In many, the number is forty or more. In other words, most English teachers in public high schools now meet from one hundred fifty to two hundred students each school day—in English classes alone. In addition, these teachers usually have homeroom responsibilities—for approximately thirty-five or forty (or even more) students—occasional (often daily) study-hall obligations, extracurricular duties, and assorted kinds of supervision, many of which bring the teachers back to the school after teaching hours. For the most part, the teaching schedules of private-school teachers are lighter, but they have round-the-clock responsibilities in supervision and nonacademic activities. Teachers of other subjects find their schedules equally severe, but there are significant differences in the amount of paper work and preparation which the English teacher must do. The kind of teaching which has been recommended in the chapters of this book requires much thought, reflection, and after-hours energy and is scarcely possible with the teacher-pupil ratio which exists almost universally today.

Various recommendations have been made in an effort to adjust the figure. That of Dr. James B. Conant seems reasonable and just. In "Recommendation 6: English Composition" of *The American High School Today*, Dr. Conant says that "no English teacher should be responsible for more than one hundred pupils." Presumably, this would mean four classes, of approximately twenty-five students per class. Even this arrangement, however, with the added tasks of homeroom, study hall, and extracurricular supervision, seems heavy; but certainly it would be a great improvement over the situation which exists in most places at present. Fewer classes and fewer students per class are essential if the teaching of English is to be done well.

Far too many extracurricular activities are under the management of English teachers. Undoubtedly this results from the nature of the activities themselves, since many involve expression of one kind or another. These activities would include all school publications (in large high schools the publication of the yearbook is almost a business, involving several thousands of dollars), dramatics, debating, literary clubs, and assemblies. In schools with a staff of twenty or more English teachers, these responsibilities can be equally divided, and in many systems no teacher is asked to handle more than one. But in small schools, no less eager than the large ones to offer all of these opportunities to students, the teachers (or teacher) of high school English is likely to be overwhelmed. I have known teachers to direct two school plays a year, supervise the school paper and the yearbook, and teach a full schedule of six classes with approximately forty students per class every day. A situation of this kind is probably rarer now than it used to be, but in some areas it still exists. Under such circumstances, effective teaching of English is impossible. If more equitable distribution of supervision cannot be made, then the number of extracurricular activities should be curtailed.

But when teachers today are asked which of their duties are especially burdensome, they seldom mention academic or extracurricular work. Far more troublesome, and even time-consuming, are the constant clerical chores which they must perform—the endless bookkeeping. Teachers of all subjects now are deluged with forms to be filled out and records to be kept; the paper work increases every year. The forms become more and more intricate, the reports more and more complex. Bureaucratically, the school has picked up where the government leaves off, and the file cabinets are bulging. At certain fixed times of the year teachers are required to put in long hours on attendance records, guidance charts, and academic progress sheets; and their daily lives are a long succession of absence notes and tardy slips and lunch-room tickets and money collected for the yearbook, the school play, the Student Council dance, and the athletic club banquet. It would not be a bad idea for every high school teacher to be certified as a public accountant.

Requiring teachers to do this kind of work is uneconomical in a number of ways. Obviously it is wasteful of a teacher's energy and takes from the teaching performance what might be spent in creative preparation. It is even more uneconomical in the very practical sense that it requires people of professional status and salary to do work which could be done by a few full—or part-time clerks. Every school system should do a careful analysis of the amount and kind of paper work it requires. Many of the forms now in use could be either simplified or eliminated; often, superintendents and principals are not fully cognizant of how much wasteful duplication exists in the recording processes which they take for granted. It seems unfortunate at times that America does not operate under a constant paper shortage. If we did, we would soon learn, as the Army did in World War II, how many of the forms we now insist upon we could really get along without; and the clerical pressures on our teachers would greatly diminish. It is time for teachers to resist the mounting paper work; they are teachers, not file clerks.

School buildings have vastly improved in most areas since World War II, partly because of the large increases in school population. For the most part the American public has been quite generous in passing bond issues; people of the community have given willingly of their time and effort to support enthusiastically public drives to get more and better space. Much, of course, remains to be done. So rapid is our growth that a building is scarcely up before it is already too small; we accept crowding as something inevitable.

Unfortunately in the planning of new buildings on the secondary level, teachers of academic subjects seem to get a little less than their share. Communities are understandably more impressed with the spectacular side of school activitiy, so the auditoriums and the gymnasiums and the locker rooms and the swimming pools and the cafeterias become more and more impressive, while the classrooms—and the library—manage only to hold their own. School planners often feel that they have fulfilled their responsibility to the cause of revolutionary new classroom arrangement when they have provided the room with movable chairs and green- instead of black-boards. Teachers of English would like more than movable chairs and fluorescent lights. They want book shelves and tables for *many* books; no room in which English is taught should be without a room library, well-stocked. They want long tables—for all sorts of things: for periodicals and newspapers, for conferences with students, for illustrative materials and teaching aids. Teachers of English need motion-picture machines, opaque projectors, phonographs, and recordings. But, above everything else, they need books. In his English class, the secondary school student should be surrounded by books; he should see books everywhere he looks. The axiom is a simple one: if we want students to read, we must make books available to them. To be sure, the school library must share the task, and there must be constant cooperation between librarian and English teacher. Library books must be constantly in motion. A library, school or otherwise, which does not increase its circulation monthly is not operating well. To this end, teachers of English should be aware of what their school libraries contain, should be making constant requisitions of the librarian, should be alert to what publishers are bringing out so that the library can keep up to date, should be aware of their students' special interests so that the library will serve them. One of our most forward moves in the public school has been to bring in trained librarians. Their assistance, to teachers of English particularly, has been immeasurable, but obviously, they have to count on a reciprocal interest in teachers. Teachers of English must know, and be constantly working for, the improvement of their school libraries.

These are a few of the needs on the immediately practical level. There are others of more cultural magnitude. First of all, there must be permanently dispelled, wherever it might possibly remain, the notion that *anybody* can teach English. For far too long in American education it was assumed, usually by harassed administrators, that the teaching of English could be handled by just about anyone, and it was not uncommon in small high schools twenty years ago to see English being taught as a sort of side line by teachers of mathematics, social studies, and commercial subjects, and by coaches. The assumption was, apparently, that anyone who speaks English must surely know something about teaching it, if he is a teacher of anything else, and we had, as a result, some very strange manipulations of language. Probably this feeling that anyone can teach English has disappeared completely, but it survives in different form in the practice of joining English with social studies, usually on the junior high school level. This arrangement has various names, and the underlying assumptions have been commendable, but I have seen none of these programs operate to the advantage of English. In every case the teaching of English has suffered in favor of heavy concentration on social studies. (Obviously I am not speaking here of integrated programs handled by several teachers of different subject matter preparation.) This, it seems to me, is particularly unfortunate in the junior high school, where rigorous training in language makes possible the academic success of the senior high school years. When any two subjects are combined in the curriculum, no matter how close the relationship between them seems, there is bound to be a certain amount of uneasiness in the union. There will be jealousies both ways—some teachers trying to protect English and others trying to protect social studies—and no one coming to agreement on what truly serves both. The course of study in English is full and rich—there is too much in it already—and it does not have to rely on supplementary materials which will keep it socially productive.

Teachers of English, then, are exactly that; they are not biologists or typing instructors or physical education trainers or teachers of French. They have their own subject—in all states now, the *first* subject of the curriculum—and they must give no quarter. So firm a position naturally makes demands of them, the principal one of these being ever higher standards in knowledge of subject. We would seem now to be past the time of subject-matter de-emphasis; we know now that a teacher does not simply *teach children*, as the cliché once had it. A teacher teaches children *something*, a specific body of subject matter, and out of the record of human experience which is his subject, be it chemistry or algebra or economics or poetry, he leads the pupil toward *the pupil's* decisions in matters of personality and social judgment. The amount of subject matter which a teacher of English must master is immense, but master it he must, from the principal parts of irregular verbs to problems of syntax in *Paradise Lost*. The kind of public respect he wants for his job is impossible otherwise.

Thus the task of preparing to teach English is never finished. Successful teachers of English go on learning all the time, through activities within the profession, through additional course work during the summer or in the evenings or on Saturday mornings, through reading, through attending plays, lectures, concerts, museums, and art galleries, through travel, through membership in discussion groups, through stimulating friendships, through the fun and relaxation of modern American living. Good teachers know what is happening—in the world, in education generally, in their own field. Teachers of English should know current literary activity; they should read much periodical literature—not just *The Saturday Review, Reader's Digest,* and *The New Yorker*—but some of the quarterlies and little magazines: *The Kenyon Review, The Hudson Review, Partisan Review, Accent, Poetry;* as well as the journals of thought and opinion: *The Reporter, The Nation, The New Republic, Commentary.* This is part of pride in the profession and of making oneself ever more effective. The best teacher I have ever known once put it this way: "I try to teach in such a way that I can always say of each of my students that I taught him English better than I was ever taught it."

"In dreams begin responsibilities," wrote William Butler Yeats, and our dreams for the future of the profession make imperative our constant effort to recruit for it. If we believe in teaching we will always be on the alert to make teachers of the best young people with whom we come into contact. We must help them to see the magnificent rewards of the profession; to overcome the feeling they may have picked up from inept advisers that teaching is an inferior profession and that the public's lack of respect for it is demonstrated by the inadequate salaries. There has been far too much talk about teachers' salaries in recent years. Certainly they are too low and certainly they must be improved, and are being improved to the point at which no other profession now offers to young women so prosperous and comfortable a life as teaching. Let us put the cart before the horse. Let us demonstrate, in true American fashion, that we have made teaching so much better that we now deserve better salaries. Every teacher who honors his profession proselytizes for it. Because he believes in the contribution which it makes to the good society, he wants others to have the joy of that contribution. The contribution of the *English* teacher is especially large.

The good teacher never for a minute stops being a teacher. He is alert to the teaching potential of everything he encounters; he has extra sensitivity to the fact that all life is a reservoir of teaching materials, that every human experience is a means of refining and redefining the position of teacher, an occasion to grow as an educator. Thus he needs repeatedly to share his experience, to tell others about something he did in the class which had especially good results. Partly, this is made possible by membership in various professional organizations which hold annual national meetings and possibly more frequent regional, state, or local conferences. For teachers of English, the organization is the National Council of Teachers of English, with headquarters at 704 South Sixth Street, Champaign, Illinois. For secondary school teachers the publication of this organization is *The English Journal*, very ably edited by Dwight L. Burton. Every issue is filled with articles offering suggestions for imaginative teaching and with news of English teachers everywhere. Annually the National Council meets at Thanksgiving time, and the general and special sessions are addressed by experts in all the fields of the English teacher's work. Membership in the National Council and attendance at its meetings is virtually a professional obligation. In addition, teachers will profit from membership in local chapters of the National Council, wherever these exist, and in such other organizations as the National Education Association and state associations. *The NEA Journal* is a very readable professional magazine, aggressively alert to the needs of educators throughout America.

If these and other organizations which serve the secondary school teacher (and the elementary teacher as well) have a single serious deficiency, it is, I think, that they do not have sufficient contact with the world of higher education, with the college and university. In spite of recent attempts to bring them closer together, the high school teacher and the college teacher are still, for the most part, far apart, with neither having a really informed notion of the problems of the other. Efforts at articulation are being made, more intelligently now than ever before, perhaps, and through the efforts of the Advanced Placement program, for example, college and high school teachers are sitting down together at conferences, at examination planning sessions, and at examination grading sessions where they work together with only one objective in mind: to improve the quality of their work through an exchange of their beliefs and standards. Under the two-year leadership of Professor Charles R. Keller, former chairman of the Department of History at Williams College, the Advanced Placement program made tremendous strides in bringing the secondary schools and colleges to an awareness of one another and of the possibilities of mutual service. Advanced Placement continues its progress in this direction, and Professor Keller is now in charge of an equally salutary experiment: the John Hay Fellows Program, sponsored by the Greenwood Fund of the John Hay Whitney

Foundation and the Fund for the Advancement of Learning. This program brings to six universities each year (Harvard, Yale, Columbia, Northwestern, the University of Chicago, and the University of California at Berkeley) a number of secondary school teachers in the humanities (90 in the academic year 1960–1961). These people get a year's leave of absence from their schools, the John Hay program matches their salaries, pays traveling expenses for both the Fellow and his family to the university, pays tuition and fees at the university, and under the guidance of an adviser on the faculty there sets up a year's program of study which permits the teacher to take whatever courses he wishes. An important requirement is that the Fellow return to the school from which he came, for at least one year, where he is expected to put into operation some activities resulting from his year's study. In addition, a Summer Institute for approximately fifty other secondary teachers in the humanities is held at Williams College. The objective of the Program is clearly stated: improvement in the quality of public school instruction in the humanities. Interested teachers of English should write to Mr. Charles R. Keller, Director, John Hay Fellows Program, 9 Rockefeller Plaza, New York 20, New York. There are, of course, other programs for teachers of science and mathematics, for example, the Academic Year Institute.

Contact between colleges and high schools *must* be strengthened. One way of doing this is to try to put forever to rest the long hostility of the liberal arts college and the school of education. To the men and women who have been working together constructively on articulation, the constant jabs and thrusts back and forth between the liberal arts people and the teachers' college people seem tiresome and dated, in virtually every case the result of confusions and misunderstandings which would vanish in an instant if both groups were willing to make a few concessions. With good cause students in schools of education find liberal arts snobbishness offensive. Wanting to be a good high school teacher should not be a cause for having to feel apologetic in humanities courses where one is in contact with liberal arts students. I have known college professors, and I regret to say that nearly all of them were professors of English, who lost no opportunity in the classroom to disparage schools of education and the men and women enrolled in them. The contention of nearly all the liberal arts people is that teachers do not need special training in teaching; that professional courses are a waste of time, and that anyone with a B.A. degree, and certainly with an M.A. degree, is more than qualified to teach on a secondary level. This is one of the most unfortunate legacies of the romantic movement—the notion that teaching is an *art*, which one either has or has not, and that any discussion of the craft of teaching, or of any set of rules, practices, or principles governing activity in the field is both capricious and wasteful. The ability to teach, therefore, is nothing more than mastery of subject; consequently schools of education are absurd.

The responsible college professor today, whether in liberal arts or elsewhere, is too wise a humanist and too careful an observer of the actuality of overcrowded schools and too few teachers to subscribe to such romanticism, but it is time that more professors in the humanities spoke out against the notion that teaching is something which cannot be trained and developed. Teaching *is* very often an art, and one can take real esthetic delight in watching a successful teaching performance; but sober consideration will usually lead one to conclude that the success was due to careful hours of planning the lesson and not to some unforeseen and unexpected descent of either Muse or Paraclete. There was never a plethora of artists in any medium, and there are too many schools bursting at the seams to justify our waiting for such a descent. Quite a number of teachers who think of themselves only as artists have brought about a considerable amount of bad learning. The freshman English course in most of our liberal arts colleges will offer sufficient evidence that a liberal arts degree is, in itself, insufficient preparation for teaching. In my considered judgment, the worst teaching being done anywhere in America today takes place in freshman composition courses in liberal arts colleges. The director of the very best of these courses once confessed as much to me. "Many of our students," he said, "come to college from first-rate high schools and prep schools where they have had distinguished and informed teachers, and we then put them up against graduate students and instructors of very limited experience. The result is wholesale disaffection and disillusion."

Neither liberal arts college nor school of education has anything to gain by this eternal sniping; both have a great deal to lose. There are healthy and exciting signs that the animosity is over; it seems outrageously dated now. The new spirit is best represented for me by an experience I had last spring at the University of California at Davis, where a group of young men, all of them professors in the humanities, all of them trained in first-rate liberal arts colleges, and all of them fathers of youngsters in the public school, got together with officers of the University and with professional educators to work out together a plan for the most effective possible training of teachers in that area. The dedication of these men was beautiful to watch; they *cared* about American education all along the line —from kindergarten to the Ph.D. Professor Donald M. Reynolds, a young bacteriologist, Ivy-League trained, led the effort; and his healthy enthusiasm was indicative that he wanted to do sensible traffic with the future. His ardency said, There is a world to be saved; I know that education is essential to the task, and the educator who does not serve the *whole* cause of American education *serves none of it.*

Unfortunately it is true that by the excesses to which they have gone the schools of education have often merited satirical treatment. All of us have joked about what goes on in some of the professional courses, about page after dismal page of jargon in the textbooks, about the self-assurance of the new educational psychology, and about the subjects of masters' and doctors' theses. Teachers' colleges have gone all out for the behavioral sciences, and, as with any new movement, there have been extravagant claims and unwise predictions, which all too often have had much more publicity than they deserved. The result was that they soon became the butt of vocal critics, highly literate men like Arthur Bestor, Mortimer Smith, Alfred Jay Nock, John Hersey, John Keats, and others, men whose motives were scarcely to be questioned. They had a made-to-order target and they had plenty of ammunition. When the Soviet Union came along to do in science what the United States was unable to do, suddenly everyone began attacking the schools. As Professor Howard Mumford Jones put it in *Reflection on Learning,* we jumped to the conclusion that "American science is a failure, American education is a fraud, American defense leaders incompetent, and an invasion from Mars or Siberia imminent."

The hysteria seems spent, and the attacks on the schools have diminished. The order of the day is quiet constructiveness, with all sides working together. There are severe and deserved criticisms of the schools, but these are coming, importantly, from friends, who ask only that we guard against the anti-intellectualism of which some of our professional educators and teachers have been guilty. Professor Lionel Trilling sounded a note of warning several years ago.

We carefully dissociate ourselves from the reactionary elements that attack modern modes of education, and still we come more and more to believe that the elaborate ideology of "integration with the group," of "cooperation," of "whole development," of "social studies" and "communication arts" is in effect the highly intellectualized rationalization of some deep-seated anti-intellectualism. We know that the conscious intention of this pedagogy is to foster equality and democracy and good will, but we begin to perceive that it is hostile to distinction, and to mind, and to accuracy of thought, and at a moment in our history when distinction, and mind, and accuracy of thought were never more needed. Devoted as this pedagogy is to the ideal of integrating the self with society and culture, we come increasingly to believe that the self it conceives is far from being what we hope the self may be.

This is scarcely the place to do battle with the social sciences, and I would resist the impulse even if it were. The extreme humanistic position was taken in *The New Republic* by Karl Shapiro in June, 1958, in an article titled "Why Out-Russia Russia?"

Sociology is, of course, the mastermind of all the social sciences. Writers and teachers should never miss an opportunity to expose this form of quack literature. The latest sociological document I read was by the famous Mr. Reisman and was concerned with "Car Culture." Here is one sentence: "The Mennonites of Northeast Indiana drive 1929 black Plymouth sedans." This was not meant as a surrealist poem but as a sober scientific truth, with Lord knows what profound overtones. That quotation may not be the sum total of sociological knowledge, but it is close.

All of this middle ground between science and art, this no-man's-land called so cleverly social science, is ground that has to be cleared before the humanities can get on the march. The humanities must, in fact, rescue science from its uncomfortable position of authority, a position the true scientist will gladly abdicate. The social scientist will not abdicate, and will have to be heaved out with all his artificial and obscurantist jargons—the language of the teachers' college, of the psychological questionnaire, the language of bureaucracy, and the language of Car Culture. The humanities and the natural sciences can join forces to drive these pseudo-sciences and pseudo-arts into the limbo where we keep works of phrenology and numerology and the Baconian theory of Shakespeare.

It must be said with regret that Mr. Shapiro's impatience is all-too-understandable; much too often our sociologists, and our educational sociologists particularly, have seemed merely to be stating the obvious or conducting elaborate statistical investigations to prove an only too evident distress. Certainly the jargon is distasteful, because it is affectation, and the mumbo-jumbo of easy sociological and psychological generalization dismays the person who resists any narrowing of the dimensions of the individual man. But this is scarcely the moment of our history to talk about heaving *anyone* out of the educational effort, provided he is a man of good will, as I take the social scientist to be. To resist his excesses and to demand a refinement of his language is not to drive him into limbo or any other exile. If he had given us nothing more than a strengthened sense of community, a greater awareness of the dynamics of the individual's relation to culture and reality, the social scientist would be worthy of much of the eminence he has enjoyed. That eminence may be somewhat in decline, but it will not benefit the teacher of English to hurry the social scientist into extinction. In education on the secondary level this is especially the time when the insights of all who struggle in any capacity with problems of learning should be heeded. Some of our most distinguished scholars of humane learning have already set the example. The spirit with which they serve the future of American education is that of the old rationalism, the good temper and sweet reasonableness which gets things done.

To this task of the constant improvement of American education, the teacher of secondary school English has much to bring, perhaps the most of all, since he is the guardian of the medium in which alone it can be accomplished, namely, language. The knowledge which he brings to the teaching of the science of communication and the love which he brings to the teaching of the art of literature are both essential to the kind of development in his students which humane learning attempts to achieve. By promoting exactness of thinking through heavy stress on composition, by encouraging esthetic responsiveness through study of literature, by stimulating through meticulous examination of language a sense of its apparently inexhaustible power to civilize, and, if abused, of its equally formidable power to corrupt, the teacher of secondary school English can bring to his work the delights of reverence, strength, and order. The guardian of our language guards our souls.

Selected Reading List for High School English Classes

THIS LIST IS AN ATTEMPT to construct for the secondary school a reading list exclusively of adult books. Some of the books, to be sure, should be used only with advanced classes. The appearance of an author's name does not mean approval of everything be has written; works listed have been selected carefully. Thus *The Glass Menagerie* by Tennessee Williams is included but his other plays are not. Obviously the list is neither exhaustive nor complete.

Following this list is a selected list of American literature written since 1920.

Fiction

Anderson, Sherwood: *Winesburg, Ohio*

Austen, Jane: *Emma   Mansfield Park   Northanger Abbey   Persuasion   Pride and Prejudice   Sense and Sensibility*

Baker, Dorothy: *Young Man with a Horn*

Balzac, Honoré de: *Cousin Bette   Eugénie Grandet   Père Goriot*

Brontë, Charlotte: *Jane Eyre*

Brontë, Emily: *Wuthering Heights*

Butler, Samuel: *Erewhon   The Way of All Flesh*

Camus, Albert: *The Plague   The Stranger*

Cather, Willa: *Death Comes for the Archbishop   A Lost Lady   My Ántonia   O Pioneers!   Sapphira and the Slavegirl   Shadows on the Rock*

Chase, Mary Ellen: *Mary Peters   Silas Crockett   Windswept*

Clark, Walter Van Tilburg: *The Ox-Bow Incident*
  The Track of the Cat
Clemens, Samuel (Mark Twain): *The Gilded Age*
  Huckleberry Finn   *The Mysterious Stranger*
  Pudd'nhead Wilson
Conrad, Joseph: *Almayer's Folly*   *Heart of Darkness*   *Lord Jim*
  The Nigger of the Narcissus   *Nostromo*   *Youth*
Cozzens, James Gould: *Guard of Honor*   *The Just and the Unjust*
  The Last Adam   *Men and Brethren*
Crane, Stephen: *George's Mother*   *Maggie, A Girl of the Streets*
  The Open Boat   *The Red Badge of Courage*
Defoe, Daniel: *Journal of the Plague Year*   *Moll Flanders*
Dickens, Charles: *Bleak House*   *David Copperfield*
  Great Expectations   *Hard Times*   *Martin Chuzzlewit*
  The Pickwick Papers
Dostoevsky, Feodor: *Crime and Punishment*
Dreiser, Theodore: *An American Tragedy*   *The Financier*
  The Genius   *Jennie Gerhart*   *Sister Carrie*   *The Titan*
Eliot, George: *Adam Bede*   *Felix Holt*   *Middlemarch*
  The Mill on the Floss   *Romola*
Faulkner, William: *Absalom, Absalom!*   *As I Lay Dying*
  Go Down, Moses   *Intruder in the Dust*   *Knight's Gambit*
  Sartoris   *The Unvanquished*
Fielding, Henry: *Joseph Andrews*   *Tom Jones*
Fitzgerald, F. Scott: *The Great Gatsby*   *The Last Tycoon*
Flaubert, Gustave: *Madame Bovary*
Forster, E. M.: *Howard's End*   *A Passage to India*
  A Room with a View   *Where Angels Fear to Tread*
Galsworthy, John: *The Forsyte Saga*
Glasgow, Ellen: *Barren Ground*   *In This Our Life*
  They Stooped to Folly   *Vein of Iron*   *Virginia*
Goodrich, Marcus: *Delilah*
Gordon, Caroline: *Alec Maury, Sportsman*
  The Forest of the South
Greene, Graham: *Brighton Rock*   *The Heart of the Matter*
  The Power and the Glory
Guthrie, A. B., Jr.: *The Big Sky*
Hardy, Thomas: *The Mayor of Casterbridge*
  The Return of the Native   *Tess of the D'Urbervilles*
Hawthorne, Nathaniel: *The Blithedale Romance*
  The House of the Seven Gables   *The Marble Faun*
  The Scarlet Letter

Hemingway, Ernest: *A Farewell to Arms*
   The Old Man and the Sea *The Sun Also Rises*
Hersey, John: *A Bell for Adano* *A Single Pebble* *The Wall*
Huxley, Aldous: *Brave New World*
Jackson, Shirley: *The Lottery*
James, Henry: *The American* *Daisy Miller* *Portrait of a Lady*
   The Spoils of Poynton *The Turn of the Screw*
   Washington Square *What Maisie Knew*
Joyce, James: *Dubliners* *A Portrait of the Artist as a Young Man*
Kafka, Franz: *The Castle* *Selected Short Stories* *The Trial*
Koestler, Arthur: *Darkness at Noon* *Thieves in the Night*
Lawrence, D. H.: *The Rainbow* *Sons and Lovers*
Lewis, Sinclair: *Arrowsmith* *Babbitt* *Dodsworth* *Main Street*
Mann, Thomas: *Buddenbrooks* *The Magic Mountain*
   Joseph and His Brothers
Marquand, J. P.: *H. M. Pulham, Esq.* *The Late George Apley*
   Point of No Return *So Little Time* *Wickford Point*
Maugham, W. Somerset: *Cakes and Ale* *Of Human Bondage*
   The Razor's Edge
Melville, Herman: *Benito Cereno* *Billy Budd* *Moby Dick*
   Omoo *Redburn* *Typee* *White Jacket*
Orwell, George: *Animal Farm* *1984*
Porter, Katherine Anne: *Flowering Judas* *Pale Horse, Pale Rider*
   The Leaning Tower (These are collections of short stories)
Rawlings, Marjorie Kinnan: *The Yearling*
Richardson, Samuel: *Clarissa*
Roberts, Elizabeth Madox: *The Great Meadow*
   The Time of Man
Salinger, J. D.: *The Catcher in the Rye* *Nine Stories*
Scott, Sir Walter: *The Heart of Midlothian*
Silone, Ignazio: *Bread and Wine* *A Handful of Blackberries*
   The Secret of Luca *The Seed beneath the Snow*
Steinbeck, John: *The Grapes of Wrath* *Of Mice and Men*
   Tortilla Flat
Stendhal (Henri Beyle): *The Red and the Black*
Tate, Allen: *The Fathers*
Thackeray, William Makepeace: *Henry Esmond* *Pendennis*
   Vanity Fair
Tolstoi, Leo: *Anna Karenina* *War and Peace*
Trollope, Anthony: *Barchester Towers* *The Warden*
Turgenev, Ivan: *Fathers and Children (Sons)* *On the Eve*
   The Sportsman's Notebooks

Warren, Robert Penn: *All the King's Men   Band of Angels*
 Night Riders   World Enough and Time
Waugh, Evelyn: *Brideshead Revisited   Decline and Fall*
 A Handful of Dust   The Loved One   Put Out More Flags
 Scoop   Vile Bodies
Welty, Eudora: *Delta Wedding   The Golden Apples*
 The Ponder Heart   (any volume of her short stories)
Wescott, Glenway: *Goodbye, Wisconsin   The Grandmothers*
Wharton, Edith: *The Age of Innocence   The Children*
 The Custom of the Country   Ethan Frome
 The House of Mirth   The Old Maid
Wolfe, Thomas: *Look Homeward, Angel*
Woolf, Virginia: *Between the Acts   Mrs. Dalloway*
 To the Lighthouse   The Years

Miscellaneous Prose

Amory, Cleveland: *The Last Resorts   The Proper Bostonians*
Barzun, Jacques: *God's Country and Mine   Teacher in America*
Daniels, Jonathan: *A Southerner Discovers New England*
 A Southerner Discovers the South
Davis, Elmer: *But We Were Born Free*
 Two Minutes before Midnight
Eastman, Max: *The Enjoyment of Laughter*
Forster, E. M.: *Two Cheers for Democracy*
Frank, Anne: *The Diary of a Young Girl*
Hamilton, Edith: *The Great Age of Greek Literature*
 The Greek Way   Mythology
Hersey, John: *Hiroshima*
Josephson, Matthew: *The President Makers   The Robber Barons*
Mumford, Lewis: *The Brown Decades   The Culture of Cities*
 Sticks and Stones   The Story of Utopias
 Technics and Civilization
Northrup, F. S. C.: *The Meeting of East and West*
Orwell, George: *Dickens, Dali and Others   Shooting an Elephant*
Rourke, Constance: *American Humor*
Saint-Exupéry, Antoine de: *Flight to Arras   Night Flight*
 Wind, Sand, and Stars
Schlesinger, Arthur M., Jr.: *The Age of Jackson*
Thoreau, Henry David: *Walden*
West, Rebecca: *Black Lamb and Gray Falcon*
White, E. B.: *One Man's Meat   The Second Tree from the Corner*
 The Wild Flag

Whitehead, Alfred North: *Adventures of Ideas*
  Science and the Modern World
Willison, George: *The Old Dominion* *Saints and Strangers*
Zinsser, Hans: *Rats, Lice and History*

Biography, Autobiography, and Letters

Benton, Thomas Hart: *An Artist in America*
Bowen, Catherine Drinker: *Yankee from Olympus*
Bowers, Claude G.: *Thomas Jefferson*
Brooks, Van Wyck: *America's Coming of Age*
  The Flowering of New England
  New England: Indian Summer
  The Times of Melville and Whitman
Cather, Willa: *Not Under Forty*
Chesterton, G. K.: *Charles Dickens* *Chaucer*
Clemens, Samuel (Mark Twain): *Innocents Abroad*
  Life on the Mississippi
Curie, Eve: *Madame Curie*
Drinkwater, John: *Oliver Cromwell*
Edman, Irwin: *Philosopher's Holiday* *Philosopher's Quest*
Einstein, Alfred: *Beethoven*
  Mozart, His Character and His Work
Fischer, Louis: *Gandhi and Stalin*
Freeman, Douglas S.: *Robert E. Lee* *Lee's Lieutenants*
Josephson, Matthew: *Stendhal*
Mencken, H. L.: *Happy Days*
Mumford, Lewis: *Green Memories*
Pearson, Hesketh: *G. B. S., A Full Length Portrait*
Repplier, Agnes: *Père Marquette*
Rolland, Romain: *Goethe and Beethoven*
Rourke, Constance: *Audubon*
Sheehan, Vincent: *Personal History*
Stowe, Lyman B.: *Saints, Sinners and Beechers*
Strachey, Lytton: *Elizabeth and Essex* *Queen Victoria*
Wharton, Edith: *A Backward Glance*
Wright, Richard: *Black Boy*
Zinsser, Hans: *As I Remember Him*

Plays

Aeschylus: *Agamemnon* *Prometheus Bound*
Anderson, Maxwell: *Both Your Houses* *High Tor* *Winterset*

Anouilh, Jean: *Antigone*
Aristophanes: *Birds   Clouds   Frogs*
Barry, Philip: *Here Come the Clowns   Holiday*
　　The Philadelphia Story
Behrman, S. N.: *Biography*
Carroll, Paul Vincent: *Shadow and Substance   The White Steed*
Chekhov, Anton: *The Cherry Orchard   The Sea Gull*
　　The Three Sisters   Uncle Vanya
Congreve, William: *The Way of the World*
Eliot, T. S.: *The Cocktail Party   Murder in the Cathedral*
Euripides: *Electra   Medea*
Farquhar, George: *The Beaux' Stratagem*
Green, Paul: *The House of Connelly   In Abraham's Bosom*
　　Johnny Johnson
Greene, Graham: *The Living Room   The Potting Shed*
Giraudoux, Jean: *Tiger at the Gates*
Hellman, Lillian: *Another Part of the Forest   The Little Foxes*
　　Watch on the Rhine
Howard, Sidney: *Dodsworth   The Silver Cord*
　　Yellow Jack
Ibsen, Henrik: *A Doll's House   An Enemy of the People*
　　The Wild Duck
Kanin, Garson: *Born Yesterday*
Kaufman, George, and Hart, Moss:
　　The Man Who Came to Dinner   You Can't Take It with You
Kelly, George: *Craig's Wife   The Show-Off*
　　The Torch-Bearers
Kingsley, Sidney: *Men in White*
Lindsay, Howard, and Crouse, Russell: *Life with Father*
　　State of the Nation
Miller, Arthur: *All My Sons   The Crucible   Death of a Salesman*
　　View from the Bridge
Molière: *The Misanthrope   Tartuffe*
　　The Would-be Gentleman
O'Casey, Sean: *Juno and the Paycock*
　　The Plough and the Stars
Odets, Clifford: *Awake and Sing   Golden Boy*
O'Neill, Eugene: *Ah, Wilderness   Beyond the Horizon*
　　Emperor Jones   The Great God Brown   The Hairy Ape
　　Long Day's Journey into Night   "Marco Millions"
　　Mourning Becomes Electra   Strange Interlude
Pinero, Sir Arthur Wing: *The Second Mrs. Tanqueray*

Pirandello, Luigi: *As You Desire Me*
    Right You Are if You Think You Are
Rice, Elmer: *The Adding Machine   Counselor-at-Law*
    Street Scene
Saroyan, William: *The Time of Your Life*
Shaw, George Bernard: *Androcles and the Lion*
    Arms and the Man   Back to Methuselah
    Caesar and Cleopatra   Candida   The Doctor's Dilemma
    Heartbreak House   Man and Superman   Pygmalion
    Saint Joan   The Simpleton of the Unexpected Isles
Shaw, Irwin: *The Gentle People*
Sherwood, Robert: *Abe Lincoln in Illinois   Idiot's Delight*
    The Petrified Forest   There Shall Be No Night
Sophocles: *Antigone   Oedipus at Colonus   Oedipus Rex*
Strindberg, August: *The Father*
Synge, John Millington: *The Playboy of the Western World*
    Riders to the Sea
Wilde, Oscar: *The Importance of Being Earnest*
    Lady Windermere's Fan   A Woman of No Importance
Wilder, Thornton: *The Matchmaker   Our Town*
    The Skin of Our Teeth
Williams, Tennessee: *The Glass Menagerie*

SELECTIONS FROM AMERICAN LITERATURE
SINCE 1920

The list which follows is the result of a search for pieces of
fiction written in America since 1920 which can be used successfully in the secondary school classroom. The stories are of two
kinds: (1) those by authors who have not previously been thought
suitable for secondary school use, and (2) some little-known
pieces which seem especially appropriate to high school instruction. For various reasons, some of the major figures of twentieth-
century American literature, including several Nobel Prize win-
ners, have been ignored by the secondary school, and this list
represents an attempt to select from their work novels and short
stories which high school teachers can use without embarrassment
or fear of community disapproval. Generally the selections of this
list avoid what would be thought of as themes too "mature" or
"sensational" for teenage youngsters, as they avoid persistent profanity or obscenity. Some stories with a higher degree of sophisti-

cation than others have been indicated with an asterisk; probably they will be better suited to advanced classes.

Some authors especially productive since 1920 have been omitted for the obvious reason that their stories are already part of the secondary school curriculum, and little if any objection to any of their works can be anticipated: I think in this connection of such writers as Willa Cather, Ellen Glasgow, Mary Ellen Chase, William Saroyan, and even Sinclair Lewis. Thus the omission of an author is significant for either of two reasons: (1) he is already regarded as entirely "safe," or (2) none of his stories seem to lend themselves to secondary school teaching. Authors of the latter sort would be James T. Farrell and, probably, John O'Hara. The omission of an author from any one of the following three lists, however, is definitely not to be regarded as critical evaluation of his work.

No claim is made that this list is, in any sense, complete. Every teacher who uses it will undoubtedly have a number of favorite selections not included here.

Fiction

Titles of novels are in italics; of short stories, in quotation marks.

Agee, James: *A Death in the Family*
Anderson, Sherwood: "I'm a Fool"   *"I Want to Know Why"
   Winesburg, Ohio
Baker, Dorothy: *Young Man with a Horn*
Baldwin, James: *Go Tell It on The Mountain*   *"Sonny's Blues"
Bellow, Saul: *The Adventures of Augie March*
Boyle, Kay: "Defeat"   "They Weren't Going to Die"
   "Winter Night"
Clark, Walter Van Tilburg: *The Ox-Bow Incident*
   The Track of the Cat
Cozzens, James Gould: *Guard of Honor*
   The Just and the Unjust
Deasy, Mary: "The High Hill"
Dos Passos, John: *Adventures of a Young Man*
   Manhattan Transfer   *Number One*   *Three Soldiers*
Faulkner, William: *Absalom, Absalom!*   "Barn Burning"
   "The Bear"   *Go Down, Moses*   *Intruder in the Dust*
   Knight's Gambit   "Race at Morning"   *Sartoris*
   "Spotted Horses"   "Two Soldiers"   *The Unvanquished*

Fitzgerald, F. Scott: "Baby Party" "Babylon Revisited"
  "A Diamond as Big as the Ritz" *The Great Gatsby*
  The Last Tycoon "Rich Boy" "Winter Dreams"
Goodrich, Marcus: *Delilah*
Gordon, Caroline: *Alec Maury, Sportsman* "The Captive"
  The Forest of the South
Hemingway, Ernest: "Big Two-hearted River" "A Day's Wait"
  *A Farewell to Arms "In Another Country"
  "Indian Camp" "The Killers" "My Old Man"
  The Old Man and the Sea
  *"The Short Happy Life of Francis Macomber"
  *The Sun Also Rises "The Undefeated"
Hersey, John: **A Bell for Adano* *A Single Pebble* *The Wall*
Jackson, Shirley: "After You, My Dear Alphonse" *The Lottery*
Lardner, Ring: "Champion" "Golden Honeymoon"
  "Haircut" "There Are Smiles"
Marquand, J. P.: *H. M. Pulham, Esq.* *The Late George Apley*
  Point of No Return *So Little Time* *Wickford Point*
McCullers, Carson: "The Jockey" *Member of the Wedding*
  "Wunderkind"
Miller, Arthur: **Focus*
O'Connor, Edwin: *The Last Hurrah*
Parker, Dorothy: "Big Blonde" "Clothe the Naked"
  "The Standard of Living" "A Study in Black and White"
Porter, Katherine Anne: *Flowering Judas* "The Leaning Tower"
  Noon Wine
Salinger, J. D.: **The Catcher in the Rye*
  (Some teachers may shy away from this, but it is a great favor-
  ite with the students already, especially the boys, and there is
  little question about its fundamental moral seriousness.)
  *"Franny" *"Zooey" *Nine Stories*
Schulberg, Budd: *The Disenchanted*
Shaw, Irwin: "Main Currents of American Thought"
  "The Passion of Lance Corporal Hawkins"
Stafford, Jean: "A Country Love Story" "The Interior Castle"
  The Mountain Lion
Stegner, Wallace: **The Big Rock Candy Mountain*
Steinbeck, John: "The Chrysanthemums" "Flight"
  The Grapes of Wrath "The Leader of the People"
  Of Mice and Men "The Red Pony" *Tortilla Flat*
  "The White Quail"
Tate, Allen: *The Fathers*

Trilling, Lionel: "Of This Time, of That Place"
"The Other Margaret"
Warren, Robert Penn: *All the King's Men* *Band of Angels*
Night Rider *World Enough and Time*
Welty, Eudora: "A Curtain of Green" *Delta Wedding*
Golden Apples "Keela, the Outcast Indian Maiden"
"The Petrified Man" *The Ponder Heart*
"A Visit of Charity" "A Walk Through the Forest"
"The Whistle"
Williams, William Carlos: "The Use of Force"
Wolfe, Thomas: *Look Homeward, Angel*

Poetry

These selections from American poets since 1920 have not, for the most part, been used in the secondary school. Once again, as in the case with fiction, the list is a very limited one; it was obviously impossible to read selectively all American verse of the last four decades. Perhaps the list will be more useful as a selection of poets, and teachers can go on to investigate the collected poems of the poets for further material. I have not included the poets who are already staple fare, for example, Edwin Arlington Robinson, Robert Frost, Carl Sandburg, Stephen Vincent Benét, Edna St. Vincent Millay, and Mark Van Doren. I have gone instead to those poets who have not yet made very conspicuous appearances in the high school classroom.

Agee, James: "A Lullaby" "Rapid Transit"
Bishop, John Peale: "Experience of the West"
Bogan, Louise: "Cassandra" "Medusa" "Statue and Birds"
"Train Tune"
Crane, Hart: "My Grandmother's Love Letters"
"Van Winkle" and "The River" from *The Bridge;* the poem
in its entirety is probably too difficult for high school students.
Cummings, E. E.: "As Freedom Is a Breakfast Food"
"next to of course god america i"
"Poem, or Beauty Hurts Mr. Vinal" "Portrait"
"Sweet Spring Is Your"
"What If a Much of a Which of a Wind"
Eliot, T. S.: "Aunt Helen" "The Hollow Men"
"Journey of the Magi"
"The Love Song of J. Alfred Prufrock"
"Portrait of a Lady" "A Song for Simeon"

Jarrell, Randall: "Burning the Letters"   "Eighth Air Force"
  "Jews at Haifa"
MacLeish, Archibald: "America Was Promises"   "Ars Poetica"
  "Lines for an Interment"
  "Not Marble nor the Gilded Monuments"
  "Speech to the Detractors"   "You, Andrew Marvell"
McGinley, Phyllis: "I Know a Village"
Moore, Marianne: "The Mind Is an Enchanting Thing"   "Poetry"
  "Silence"   "That Harp You Play So Well"
  "To a Steam Roller"
Ransom, John Crowe: "Bells for John Whiteside's Daughter"
  "Blue Girls"   "Here Lies a Lady"   "Janet Waking"
  "Lady Lost"
Rukeyser, Muriel: "Boy with His Hair Cut Short"
  "Four in a Family"
Schwartz, Delmore: "Tired and Unhappy, You Think of Houses"
Shapiro, Karl: "Air Liner"   "Auto Wreck"   "Boy-Man"
  "Elegy for a Dead Soldier"   "Hollywood"   "October 1"
  "Travelogue for Exiles"   "Troop Train"
Tate, Allen: "Ode on the Confederate Dead"
  "Sonnets at Christmas"
Viereck, Peter: "Ennui"   "Kilroy"
Wilbur, Richard: "Folk Tune"
Williams, William Carlos: "The Lonely Street"   "Poem"
  "Tract"
Winters, Yvor: "John Sutter"   "A Testament"
  "On the Death of Senator Thomas J. Walsh"
  "To a Military Rifle 1942"

Plays

Many of these plays have been in the secondary school English course for some time now, but they have been listed along with others less familiar. Here the selection is quite thorough, with certain plays of an author deliberately accepted and certain others rejected. The asterisk again means material better suited to advanced classes.

Anderson, Maxwell:
  Virtually all of Anderson can be used in the secondary school, but teachers might investigate the particular effectiveness of *High Tor, Both Your Houses*, and *Winterset*.

Barry, Philip: *Here Come the Clowns   Holiday*
  The Philadelphia Story
Behrman, S. N.:
  Biography. Students would probably find the other Behrman plays either too "talky" or a bit beyond their experience. An exception might be *Rain from Heaven*, though this may seem dated now.
Eliot, T. S.:
  Murder in the Cathedral. A few very able students might enjoy *The Cocktail Party*, but they are likely to get little from *Family Reunion* or *The Confidential Clerk*.
Green, Paul: *The House of Connelly   Johnny Johnson*
  In Abraham's Bosom
Heggen, Thomas: **Mr. Roberts*
Hellman, Lillian: *Another Part of the Forest   The Little Foxes*
  Watch on the Rhine
Howard, Sidney: *Dodsworth   The Silver Cord   Yellow Jack*
Kanin, Garson: **Born Yesterday*
Kelly, George: *Craig's Wife   The Show-Off*
  The Torch-Bearers
Kingsley, Sidney: *Men in White*
Miller, Arthur: *All My Sons   The Crucible*
  *Death of a Salesman   *View from the Bridge
Odets, Clifford: **Awake and Sing   Golden Boy*
O'Neill, Eugene: *Ah, Wilderness   Beyond the Horizon*
  Emperor Jones   The Great God Brown   The Hairy Ape
  *Long Day's Journey into Night   "Marco Millions"
  *Mourning Becomes Electra   *Strange Interlude
Rice, Elmer: **The Adding Machine   Counselor-at-Law*
  *Street Scene
Shaw, Irwin: *The Gentle People*
Sherwood, Robert: *Abe Lincoln in Illinois   *Idiot's Delight*
  The Petrified Forest   There Shall Be No Night
Wilder, Thornton: *The Matchmaker   Our Town*
  The Skin of Our Teeth
Williams, Tennessee: *The Glass Menagerie*

Index

adjective, 59–63
adverb, 63–65
anti-intellectualism, 228–229
argumentation, false, 123–125
Aristotle, 174–175

Baker, Russell, 43–44
Barzun, Jacques, 79, 86–87
Basic Issues in the Teaching of English, The, 5
Baugh, Albert C., 25
biography, 203–204, 206; teaching approach, 204; types, 204–206
book reports, 158

Campbell, George, 31, 32
clauses, dependent, adjective, 62–63; adverbial, 64–65; noun, 57–58; relative, 62–63
cliché, 46
Coleridge, S. T., 175
colleges, approach to teaching, 226–228
composition, 2–3; approach, 81, 86–87, 103–107; for the gifted, 209–210, 217–218; marking, 88; motivation, 86–87, 103–107; neglect, 81–83, 85; program, 84–91, exercises, 10th grade, 112–113, 11th grade, 114–115, 12th grade, 116–117, objectives, 10th grade, 112, 11th grade, 114, 12th grade, 116; skills, 88, 7th grade, 107–109, 8th grade, 109–110, 9th grade, 110–112; and structural linguistics, 76–77; student attitudes, 102–103
Conant, James B., 4, 81, 84, 141, 220
connotation, 122–123
Corbin, Richard K., 17–18
correction of papers, *see* marking

Croce, Benedetto, 175–176
curriculum, English, reforms, 4–5

Davidson, Donald, 128
denotation, 122–123
Devine, Thomas, 126
dialects, 21
Dickinson, Emily, 175
drama, history, 189–191; non-Shakespearean, 198–199; teaching approach, 189–194; theater, 193–194; types and concepts, 192–193; *see also* Shakespeare
Dykema, Karl, 72

Eliot, T. S., 9
Emerson, Ralph Waldo, 19–20
English (language), 14–15; American, 33; history, 12, 21, 22, 24–32, bibliography, 34–35; origins, 21, 22, *see above* history; spelling, 137–138; usage, 17, 36–38; *see also* grammar; linguistics
English (subject), 1, 3; approach, 13–18; classroom needs, 221–222; and composition, 2–3; curriculum reform, 4–5; and higher education, 225–227; language, 3–4; literature, 3, 4; specialization, 222–223; Yale Conference, 51, 72, 87, 112
English Language Arts in the Secondary School, The, 5, 71
errors, grammatical, 47–50
essay, 200–201; book-length, 203; sources, 201, 202; teaching, 201–203
euphemism, 45–46

false argumentation, 123–125
Faulkner, William, analysis, 167–171

243